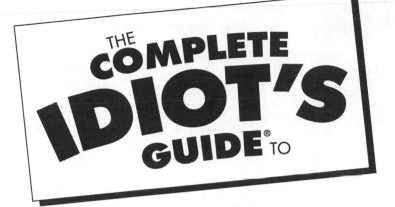

THE
**COMPLETE**
**IDIOT'S**
**GUIDE®** TO

# Latino History and Culture

by D.H. Figueredo

ALPHA

A Pearson Education Company

*To my wife and best friend, Yvone, to my son Daniel, and my daughter Gabriela:*
*the heartbeats of my Latin soul.*

# Copyright © 2002 by D.H. Figueredo

THE COMPLETE IDIOT'S GUIDE TO and Design are registered trademarks of Pearson Education, Inc.

International Standard Book Number: 0-02-8643607
Library of Congress Catalog Card Number: 2002108417

04  03  02      8  7  6  5  4  3  2  1

Interpretation of the printing code: The rightmost number of the first series of numbers is the year of the book's printing; the rightmost number of the second series of numbers is the number of the book's printing. For example, a printing code of 02-1 shows that the first printing occurred in 2002.

*Printed in the United States of America*

Note: This publication contains the opinions and ideas of its author. It is intended to provide helpful and informative material on the subject matter covered. It is sold with the understanding that the author and publisher are not engaged in rendering professional services in the book. If the reader requires personal assistance or advice, a competent professional should be consulted.

The author and publisher specifically disclaim any responsibility for any liability, loss, or risk, personal or otherwise, which is incurred as a consequence, directly or indirectly, of the use and application of any of the contents of this book.

For marketing and publicity, please call: 317-581-3722

The publisher offers discounts on this book when ordered in quantity for bulk purchases and special sales.

For sales within the United States, please contact: Corporate and Government Sales, 1-800-382-3419 or corpsales@pearsontechgroup.com

Outside the United States, please contact: International Sales, 317-581-3793 or international@pearsontechgroup.com

**Publisher:** *Marie Butler-Knight*
**Product Manager:** *Phil Kitchel*
**Managing Editor:** *Jennifer Chisholm*
**Acquisitions Editor:** *Randy Ladenheim-Gil*
**Development Editor:** *Jennifer Moore*
**Production Editor:** *Billy Fields*
**Copy Editor:** *Ross Patty*
**Illustrator:** *Jody Schaeffer*
**Cover/Book Designer:** *Trina Wurst*
**Indexer:** *Amy Lawrence*
**Layout/Proofreading:** *John Etchison, Becky Harmon, Mary Hunt, Vicki Keller*

# Contents at a Glance

# Contents

**Appendixes**

# Foreword

When Dan Figueredo and I first arrived in America as little kids back in the mid-1960s, we lived in Union City, New Jersey. It was a ghost town.

Dozens of shops were closed on Bergenline Avenue, the heart of the shopping district. Doors were padlocked, windows whitewashed, buildings empty. The Italian-Americans who had once owned these stores were moving to the green lawns of suburbia and leaving behind the gritty urban neighborhood that their immigrant parents had settled in a generation earlier.

Union City and nearby West New York, right across the Hudson from Manhattan, first attracted German and Irish immigrants in the nineteenth century. They opened factories and retail shops that catered to their needs, whether it was a German bakery or a newspaper stand.

As the Germans and Irish immigrants achieved the American dream and moved away, it became the Italians' turn. I still remember the aroma of an Italian cheese shop on Bergenline—one of the last holdouts, because by that time it was our turn: the Cubans had come.

By the 1970s Bergenline was a Little Havana. The once-empty stores became lively restaurants where you could grab a shot of strong Cuban espressso, record shops that sold your favorite Beny Moré album, or one of the ubiquitous *bodegas*, the grocery stores where Cuban moms bought rice and black beans for dinner that night.

Most bodegas had a sign that said *"No se fía."* or "No buying on credit." Yet, kindly old bodega owners kept a little notebook under the counter to jot down customers' purchases, payable at the end of the month. *Sí se fía*. It was a reflection of a tightly knit community.

Union City has changed since then. By the late 1980s, Cubans were moving to suburbia after having achieved success, like the Italians, the Irish, and the Germans before them.

But the Hispanic wave in Union City and West New York continues to swell. Now it is the turn of people from throughout the Spanish-speaking world. Take a walk down Bergenline Avenue today and you'll hear Spanish spoken in accents from Argentina, El Salvador, and Ecuador. There are Dominican travel agencies, Mexican restaurants, and Colombian record shops.

And so it is in many places throughout the country. There are some 35 million Hispanics in the United States, about 13 percent of the population and growing. But—and I hope this doesn't sound whiny—we are misunderstood in so many ways.

*The Complete Idiot's Guide to Latino History and Culture* is the best way I know to overcome those misunderstandings. I have covered Hispanic issues for more than a decade as a nationally syndicated newspaper columnist, and let me tell you, Dear Reader, that I have not come across anything as thorough as this book.

Dan recounts the history of the countries we come from. He highlights our traditions, our culture from pop music to high-brow literature. He explains what Hispanics have in common with each other, and how we differ. He goes over the controversy about our very name: Latino or Hispanic? (Me? I prefer the latter.) He clears up misconceptions, particularly my pet peeve, the erroneous and widespread belief that Hispanics form a race. No, Dan correctly says, we come from all races. Dan also writes about our struggles, our successes, our dreams. And he tells why we came here, and where we might be going. All of it with wit and savvy, in a reader-friendly style. The guy knows his stuff, and knows how to write about it.

America's Hispanics are changing our new country and being changed by it. If you want to know how, and have a little fun learning, read on!

—Roger E. Hernández

**Roger E. Hernández** is the author of *Cubans in America*, an illustrated history of the Cuban presence in the United States. His nationally syndicated column is distributed by King Features Syndicate to some 40 daily newspapers, including the *Washington Post, Los Angeles Daily News,* and *Dallas Morning News.*

# Introduction

There was a time, not so long ago, when the word Hispanic or Latino meant one of three possibilities: 1) A person who came from Cuba, 2) A Mexican-American, 3) Someone who was born in Puerto Rico or his parents were Puerto Rican. The particular stereotype was determined by geography: to folks living on the West coast, all Latinos looked like Mexicans. In the Northeast, all Latinos looked like Puerto Ricans. To Floridians, Latinos were Cubans. And what did the stereotypical Hispanic or Latino look like? A short, dark man with a mustache, eating jalapenos and listening to mariachi music.

Fortunately, Americans today are by far too sophisticated and humane to accept such simple stereotypes. We know that Latinos originate from all over Latin America and that they come in all shapes, colors, and sizes. Some have money, others don't. Some are educated, others aren't. Some plan to stay here, others long to go back. Basically, what we call Latino represents a range of diversity, experience, and racial background that can't be easily categorized.

That's where this book comes in. It deals with the whole of the Latino experience in the United States, from family to religion, economics to politics, education to entertainment. Along the way, we'll visit ancient civilizations, talk about Cabeza de Vaca and Cortés, Pelé and Perón, Desi Arnaz and Anthony Quinn, as well as international developments such as the war against Mexico, the building of the Panama Canal, and the Cuban missile crisis. Throughout, you'll find out about the rich culture of the Latino experience—their food, their music, their love of sport.

## The Name Game

You might be wondering why this book called a *Latino* guide rather than a *Hispanic* guide. It's a complicated issue, one that is addressed in detail in Chapter 4, but for now let's work out some simple concepts. Hispanic is a term that has been used pretty much since the start of the twentieth century. Referring to Spain and connecting individuals to Spain and the Spanish language, *Hispanic* is an English word that was conceived by English-speakers.

*Latino* became popular in the 1980s. It's a Spanish word, and it has gender: a man is a Latino; a woman is a Latina. For many, it refers to people from Latin America, thus reaffirming connections with the New World rather than Spain. Latino was coined by Latinos living in the United States; it was a choice that came from within the community. Those who prefer the term Latino believe that Hispanic was a term assigned to the community by the powers-that-be, such as the U.S. Census.

We use Latino in this guide because it allows for the use of gender, and therefore some variety in writing, as well as reflecting the preference of more and more people.

## A Preview of Coming Attractions

This book is divided into five parts. In **Part 1, "Speak in Spanish, You're in America,"** we look at the growing numbers of Latinos in the United States: where they come from, how they got here, and whether they're planning to stay.

In **Part 2, "We're the World: the Latino Universe,"** we take a journey to find out about the history of Latin America, including Mexico and Central and South America.

Everything from family to food, music to movies, sports to spirituality, and literature to lifestyle are covered in **Parts 3, "Body and Soul, Latin Style"** and **4, "From Mambo to Tango, Songs to Sonnets, Soccer to Baseball."**

Finally, in **Part 5, "Living-on-the-Hyphen,"** we'll consider what it's like to be a Latino living in the United States today: how Latinos vote, the kinds of business they run, and their educational goals.

## Along the Way ...

You'll find the following boxes throughout this book:

### Cuidado!

Warning! Tips to help you to avoid stereotypes or draw erroneous conclusions.

### Living La Vida Literaria

Let's see what some Latin American literary greats have to say.

### Para Tu Información

FYI, mi amigos and amigas.

### Hablas Español

You'll be speaking Spanish in no time if you learn the words and terms defined in these boxes.

## Acknowledgments

Mil gracias—a thousand thanks—to my friend and colleague Louis González for bringing to my attention the idea of this project and to my agent Gene Bressie for his support; muchisimas gracia to Randy Ladenheim-Gil for pointing me in the right direction and Jennifer Moore for guiding me along the way. Special thanks to Armando H. Portela, geographer par excellence, who designed the maps for this volume. And thanks also to Dr. Erica Polakoff, Bloomfield College, for the use of her photographs, and Dr. William Luis, Vanderbilt University, and the Samuels Family of New Jersey, for their snapshots.

And, once more, special thanks to my family: Their faith in my writing inspired me.

## Special Thanks to the Technical Reviewer

*The Complete Idiot's Guide to Latin American History and Culture* was reviewed by an expert who double-checked the accuracy of what you'll learn here, to help us ensure that this book gives you everything you need to know about Latin American history and culture. Special thanks are extended to Luis Martínez Fernández, Ph.D.

## Trademarks

All terms mentioned in this book that are known to be or are suspected of being trademarks or service marks have been appropriately capitalized. Alpha Books and Pearson Education, Inc., cannot attest to the accuracy of this information. Use of a term in this book should not be regarded as affecting the validity of any trademark or service mark.

# Part 1

# Speak in Spanish, You're in America

There are three things you can say about Latinos: 1) There are a lot of them, 2) They tend to speak Spanish, 3) They don't seem to be able to agree on how to refer to themselves. It can all be quite confusing. In this part, we'll try to clear up matters by first talking about how Latinos are setting up homes all over the United States, why and how Latinos are here, and the reasons why Latinos keep talking in Spanish, even after learning English. And yes, we'll tackle the Hispanic vs. Latino conundrum, too.

# The Latino Lesson

## In This Chapter

- ◆ The astronomical growth of the Latino population
- ◆ Where Latinos live
- ◆ Journeying from peddlers to plumbers to professionals
- ◆ How Latinos are changing life in America
- ◆ The real Latin look

At the Port-au-Prince airport, a would-be Haitian emigrant handed his satchel to a security guard, who noticed a paperback inside the canvas bag. Examining it, the guard asked in his native French, "This is a Spanish-French dictionary. Aren't you going to Miami?"

"Precisely," the traveler responded with a smile.

Miami, like other metropolitan and rural areas across the United States, is home to increasing numbers of Spanish speakers, the result of Latino growth across the nation. As you'll discover as you read this chapter, Latinos, who in this volume refers to the children of the marriage between Latin America and Spain, are everywhere in the United States.

So, *amigo*, put on your *sombrero* and let's head out to the *barrio* to find out more about Americans' new *compadres*—about their culture and traditions, where they live and why, their social and economic realities, and even what they really look like.

### Hablas Español

A **compadre** is a child's godfather, someone who is expected to take responsibility for the rearing of the child should the parents perish or are unable to provide for the child. The term also refers to a good friend or someone who shares something in common with you. It connotes cordiality and friendship. **Comadre** is the female version of this noun.

### Para Tu Información

Originally sung for pleasure by Mexican ranch workers, **rancheras** are love songs, and they can also be dancing tunes. Though the lyrics are simple, the songs are meant to be delivered with a great deal of emotion and drama. Many Mexican movie stars began their careers as ranchera singers.

# Bienvenido a America

"Mi Casa Blanca es tu Casa Blanca."

Broadcast over CNN News and other networks on an October afternoon, this pronouncement reached millions across the nation. The words, uttered with a slight southern twang and accompanied by a shy smile, came neither from a Latino personality nor a Latino politico; the words came from an unlikely speaker at an unlikely spot: the President of the United States, George W. Bush, speaking from the White House.

That the sounds of Spanish resounded throughout the corridors of the most powerful English-speaking nation in history was a political and cultural acknowledgment of a linguistic reality: Spanish is spoken regularly in the land of Melville and Hemingway. The land that inherited its language from Chaucer and Shakespeare has adopted Cervantes' mother tongue.

You can hear Spanish in a *ranchera* song a Mexican worker is humming in High Point, North Carolina. You can hear it in a conversation between a Venezuelan cashier and an Argentine customer at a supermarket in Princeton, New Jersey. You can hear it in the words of a Peruvian preacher addressing his Central American flock in a church in San Diego, California.

# Do You Hear What I Hear?

If you keep your ears and eyes open to it, you'll start to hear and see Spanish everywhere. On the radio and television, in government and other official documents, and on the ubiquitous billboards and advertising posters that line our highways and clutter our bus stops.

It's not just the language that you'll see and hear more of, but also the Spanish speakers themselves. Increasingly, Latinos are becoming an influential presence in U.S. society, numbering—as Gloria Estefan told President George W. Bush during a recent visit to the *Casa Blanca*—in the millions: 35.3 million, to be precise.

That's the official figure from the U.S. Census. But if you skip the census and speak with community leaders and educators, they will tell you that the actual number is much higher, anywhere from 40 to 50 million. Whichever figure is accurate, the reality is that the Latino presence in the United States is growing and will continue to grow for at least the next 20 years. As *Time* magazine put it on the cover of its June 11, 2001, issue: Welcome to Amexica.

# Do the Math

The number of Latinos living in the U.S. has been increasing significantly in the last few decades, jumping approximately 53 percent from 1980 to 1990, and another 58 percent during the next decade.

## U.S. Latino Population as Recorded by the U.S. Census

| Year | Population |
| --- | --- |
| 1980 | 14,608,673 |
| 1990 | 22,354,059 |
| 2000 | 35,300,000 |

**Para Tu Información**

People usually think of **documented** immigrants as immigrants who are in the country legally, but it also refers to illegal immigrants who have been counted by the census. A documented immigrant is an individual whose name and address appears in some type of legal and official document, as opposed to those immigrants who use fake IDs or simply do not share any personal information with anyone or any type of institution.

The nearly 60 percent increase from 1990 to 2000 surprised many people, including politicians, business leaders, and Latinos themselves. Even population experts—called demographers—and Latino-studies scholars were shocked by the data.

That's a lot of *gente,* or people. These gentle gente generally gravitate towards the coasts—both East and West. However, there are also large clusters of Latinos in the Southeast, predominantly in Florida, and in the Midwest, mostly in Illinois.

**Hablas Español**

**Gente** means people. When someone says "Mi gente," or my people, he or she is showing solidarity with a given group.

*Latino population by region, according to the 2000 U.S. Census.*

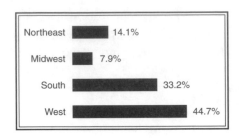

| Northeast | 14.1% |
| Midwest | 7.9% |
| South | 33.2% |
| West | 44.7% |

But what do all these numbers really mean? Maybe the following comparison will help put things in perspective:

- There are more Spanish speakers in the U.S. than in Cuba (11,141,997), The Dominican Republic (8,442,553), Nicaragua (4,812,569), Paraguay (5,585,828), and Puerto Rico (3,889,507) combined (total: 32,872,444).

- There are more Latinos living in the United States than Canadians in Canada, where the population is 31,278,097 million.

- There are as many Latinos in the U.S. as African-Americans, and Latinos outnumber African-Americans in Houston, Los Angeles, New York, Phoenix, San Antonio, and San Diego.

- The Latino population has grown nearly 58 percent since 1990, compared to an overall population increase of 9 percent.

- Mexican-Americans—and Mexicans in Mexico—call Los Angeles Mexico's second largest city.

- There are as many Puerto Ricans in New York as in San Juan—about half a million.

# City-Lovers

Cities have always attracted waves of new immigrants, but for Latinos, especially, it makes sense that they would move to cities. Latinos have a long history of establishing and living in cities. Whereas in colonial America, British subjects established villages and small settlements, Spanish subjects in colonial Latin America founded cities. Writer Carlos Fuentes points out in *The Buried Mirror* that colonial Spain rushed to found cities in the New World:

"… to dominate both distance and wealth, [Spain] had to found cities. Literally hundreds of cities, all the way from San Francisco and Los Angeles to Buenos Aires and Santiago de Chile, sprang up. These were not mere settlements but urban centers of great nobility and permanence …"

**Para Tu Información**

The Spanish-speaking countries of Latin America are: Argentina, Bolivia, Chile, Colombia, Costa Rica, Cuba, Dominican Republic, Ecuador, El Salvador, Guatemala, Honduras, Mexico, Nicaragua, Panama, Paraguay, Peru, Uruguay, and Venezuela.

Even before the arrival of the *conquistadores*, the land that became Latin America was teeming with cities. The capital of ancient Mexico, Tenochtitlan—which already had a borough, called Tlatelolco, 500 years before New York City had boroughs—was home to about 250,000 residents. Cuzco, the capital of the Inca Empire in ancient Peru, had a population of about 200,000 inhabitants. And there were other cities with names that evoke magic and fantasy:

- **Tikal,** a center of Mayan culture
- **Monte Alban,** of the lost Zapotec culture
- **Cempoala,** a city of the Toltecs
- **Tomebamba,** the Inca urban center

**Para Tu Información**

Conquistadores were Spanish soldiers who conquered the Aztec and Inca empires. A presence in Latin America from 1492 to the 1540s, the *conquistadores* were replaced by administrators and tradesmen once the region was colonized.

and dozens of sites for which there are no recorded population estimates, but whose pyramids, temples, and road systems attest to the presence of large populations.

Today, millions of squatters in Latin America have left their villages to move to the capital cities, settling on the outskirts and creating artificial boroughs—in places such as Quito, Peru, and Mexico City, Mexico—that extend the cities miles beyond their political and geographic borders.

Many of these squatters—if not they themselves, then their relatives and friends—have made the journey to American cities. In these cities, they find opportunities, a cosmopolitan ambiance, and a welcome diversity. And in these cities, they can maintain their language and use it while learning another language—maybe.

## Top Latino Cities in the United States

Almost half the people who live in Los Angeles are Latinos. In Chicago, one of every eight people is Latino, and two of every eight people are Latinos in New York City. And in Miami, where the total population is 2,181,400, every other person you meet is a Latino.

## Latino Populations of Major U.S. Cities, as of 2000

| City | Population |
| --- | --- |
| Los Angeles | 4,401,833 |
| New York | 2,258,870 |
| Miami | 1,268,820 |

*continues*

### Latino Populations of Major U.S. Cities, as of 2000 (continued)

| City | Population |
| --- | --- |
| Chicago | 1,195,991 |
| Houston | 1,047,703 |
| San Antonio | 855,651 |

These figures account only for those who actually live in those cities. When you consider the Latinos from nearby towns and smaller cities, who travel into the metropolises either for work or shopping, the numbers increase significantly. For example, 231,549 Latinos live in Jersey City, just across the Hudson River from New York. In nearby Newark, you'll find 260,876 Latinos. And the counties surrounding New York—Essex, Hudson, Middlesex, and Union—serve as home base for almost 500,000 Latinos. On any given day, the Latino population in Manhattan can swell by the thousands.

*Latino economic enclave in Union City, NJ.*

### Latino Population in and Within Commuting Distance of Major Cities, as Tallied by *Demographics USA 2000*

| City | Population |
| --- | --- |
| Los Angeles | 6,504,331 |
| New York | 3,525,388 |
| Miami | 1,486,257 |
| Chicago | 1,279,683 |
| Houston | 1,209,459 |
| San Antonio | 1,079,712 |

That's a lot of gente. It means that if you venture to Fourteenth Street in Manhattan, you will bump into the proverbial "Latin from Manhattan," as well as Latinos from New Jersey, Connecticut, and even Pennsylvania, all speaking Spanish. So, if you are advertising a product that targets the Latino community, placing a billboard somewhere along Fourteenth Street is a smart business move. And, if you want to learn Spanish by immersion but can't afford to travel outside the United States, hanging out in Manhattan— or Miami or Chicago—might just give you the education you're looking for.

**Para Tu Información**

It is possible to live in Miami without uttering a word of English. You can shop at a supermarket owned by Cubans, visit a Uruguayan doctor, buy medicine from a pharmacy managed by a Chilean, and socialize at restaurants with folks from the Dominican Republic. You can vote for a Spanish-speaking official and listen to the news in Spanish. You can go for days without hearing English spoken.

# Away from the Bright Lights

Not all Latinos are content with the bright lights, big city environ, though. Increasingly, Latinos are moving to medium- and small-sized cities that are relatively unknown outside the United States., places such as Albuquerque, New Mexico; Atlanta, Georgia; Grand Rapids, Michigan; and Rogers, Arkansas.

**Para Tu Información**

The small and scenic town of Rogers, Arkansas, is home to 7,000 Latinos, a novelty considering there were hardly any Latinos, or anyone with a Spanish surname, in the area a decade ago. In Grand Rapids, Michigan, Latinos account for almost 5 percent of the nearly 200,000 residents. One hundred sixty thousand Latinos hang their sombreros in the Atlanta area. And Albuquerque, boasts 270,555 Latinos, which is 35 percent of its general population.

Latinos also live in farming communities. In California, it is estimated that about five million Latinos reside in or near farming areas, usually in the San Joaquin and Imperial valleys and in the heartland of the state. Immigrants from Mexico and Central America have moved to the rural Carolinas to work in the fields there. And according to the Christian Science Monitor, Latinos who have moved to the rural state of Iowa have actually reversed the population decline in certain Iowa counties.

# Next Stop: Suburbia

Like immigrant populations before them, Latino immigrant population trends can be divided into distinct phases, dubbed by one newspaper reporter as the path from peddler to plumber to professional. The stages in the immigration cycle can be described as follows:

1. **The Peddler Stage.** The first generation immigrants, the new arrivals, generally settle in cities, live in apartment buildings, use public transportation, and work at entry-level jobs, usually in the service industry or as manual laborers.

2. **The Plumber Stage.** The second generation, the immigrant's children, work in offices or at a trade such as plumbing, drive cars, and move to a modest house outside the city.

3. **The Professional Stage.** The grandchildren of the immigrant become professionals, spend a lot of time driving, and live comfortably in the suburbs.

This happened at the turn of the twentieth century as immigrants from Italy came to the United States, again 50 years ago with the arrival of immigrants from Germany, Hungary, Poland, and Russia, and is happening again right now.

## Para Tu Información

Immigrants are moving out of cities and into the suburbs faster than they did in the past. More and more Latinos are skipping the peddler-plumber-professional phase and heading right for the suburbs. Sometimes several families pool resources to rent or buy a suburban home, each family occupying a single room in the house. The immigrants often work in landscaping or other labor-intensive jobs, and walk, bike, or ride with their employers to the job site.

## Reaching for the American Dream

The move to the suburb is usually seen as a break away from the ethnic enclave—the *barrio*—and is motivated by the same reasons that other people leave the cities for the suburbs: better, or at least not as crowded, schools, nicer-looking neighborhoods, lower crime rates, and a sense of prestige. The suburban dweller fits the image of success in America, of someone who has "made it," who has realized the American Dream.

## Hablas Español

*Barrio* refers to a block or an area of several blocks. It also means neighborhood.

As a Puerto Rican attorney living in a Fairfax County (Virginia) suburb recently told a reporter, moving to the suburbs is "indicative of people achieving certain things in their lives."

Many Latinos won't admit it, but they also often move to the suburbs because of the stigma associated with being an urban Latino. A Latino who lives in an urban barrio is regarded as poor, under-educated, and unprepared to fare well in society. But a Latino from the middle-class suburb of Princeton, New Jersey, for example, is usually seen as well-educated, having broken loose from the cycle of poverty. The stereotypes aren't always true, but they are powerful nonetheless.

## You Can Take the Latino Out of the Barrio, but ...

Although half the Latinos living in metropolitan areas make the suburbs their home (according to an Associated Press release dated June 25, 2001), usually the move is neither a complete break from the barrio nor a complete assimilation or "Americanization." Syndicated columnist Roger Hernandez writes about a judge who lives in a colonial-style house in an affluent town in northern New Jersey—how much closer can you get to a Norman Rockwell painting? Yet, the interior of the house is filled by souvenirs from Cuba, especially a large picture of Havana, the judge's birthplace. The same is true for Ecuadorians, who display their country's flag in family rooms, and Mexicans, who display paintings of the Virgin of Guadalupe in their bedrooms.

> **Para Tu Información**
>
> **Acculturation** is the process through which a person accepts another culture while holding on to his or her original culture. **Assimilation** is the process through which one adopts another culture, leaving behind the original culture. **Americanization** is the process of becoming an American or of espousing American ideals and behavior.

## ... You Can't Take the Barrio Out of the Latino

Surburban dwellers often feel an urge to return to the barrio. Hernandez himself likes to drive the 12 miles from his home in the suburb of Upper Montclair, New Jersey to Union City, where Cubans reigned supreme in the 1960s and 1970s, to sip a cup of *cafecito*, strong Cuban espresso, and hear Spanish being spoken at the *bodegas* and butcher shops. A compatriot of his, the scholar Gustavo Perez Firmat, often travels from the Northeast to Miami just to be around other Cubans. It scratches what Hernandez calls "a cultural itch."

> **Hablas Español**
>
> A **bodega** is a small grocery store that specializes in Spanish products. Literally, **cafecito** means little coffee, but it refers to a demitasse, or the strong Cuban coffee served in a small porcelain cup and sweetened with white sugar.

# More to Come

Even if new immigration barriers imposed after the terrorist attacks of September 11, 2001, slow down the flow into the United States from south of the border, the Latino population that is already here will continue to grow from its own ranks, and not as the result of immigration. It is, after all, a young population—the median age is 26—who favors family life and having children. Mexicans, for example, are accustomed to large families, and the fertility rate for Mexican women in Mexico is twice that of Anglo women. This pattern has been largely transplanted to the United States.

It is estimated that there will be 45 million Latinos in the United States by 2010. By, 2020, there might be 55 million. And at the halfway point of the century, the numbers might be as high as 75 million.

*(Map by Armando H. Portelo)*

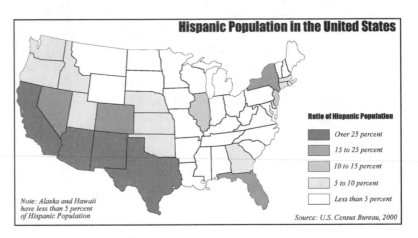

**Hispanic Population in the United States**

**Ratio of Hispanic Population**

- Over 25 percent
- 15 to 25 percent
- 10 to 15 percent
- 5 to 10 percent
- Less than 5 percent

Note: Alaska and Hawaii
have less than 5 percent
of Hispanic Population

Source: U.S. Census Bureau, 2000

# How Latinos Spend Their Money

That's a lot of gente working hard. And that means cash. The *"mucho trabajo y poco dinero"* truism is not true here. Though there is poverty in the Latino community, and there are many poor Latino families, the assumption that as a group Latinos do not have buying power simply isn't true. Heinz Corporation certainly didn't see it that way when it started to manufacture salsa, tapping on an industry which brings in about $500 million a year.

The Latino consumer market is worth over $380 billion. It is estimated that on any given year Latinos generate $28.9 billion in sales in Los Angeles, nearly $20 billion in New York, $9 billion in Miami, $6 billion in Chicago,

**Hablas Español**

The expression "mucho trabajo y poco dinero" is commonly heard throughout Latin America and in the Latino community. It means working hard but making little money.

and just as much in San Francisco. According to *Hispanic Market Report*, published in the winter of 1996, Latinos spend the same or more than African-Americans and Anglos in these categories:

◆ Food consumed at home

◆ Apparel

◆ Telephone services

◆ Rental housing

◆ TV/radio and other equipment

◆ Personal care products

◆ Public transportation

◆ Cleaning supplies

This same report states that Latinos spend 75 percent of their income on housing, food, transportation, and clothing. Thirteen percent goes to insurance, pensions, health, and personal care. Eleven percent is spent on entertainment, including alcoholic beverages, tobacco, and reading and educational materials.

Latinos prize home-ownership—over 46 percent are homeowners—and several families, or a couple of generations within a family, might live together to combine their income and pay the mortgage. These large families, or groups of families, generate large purchases of food and clothing and household items.

# The New Flavor of Life

Latinos aren't just changing the language of the United States and pumping their hard-earned money into its economy, they are changing the flavor of daily life for everyone living in the United States:

◆ Schools and school boards are initiating bilingual classes or increasing the number of English-as-a-second language courses they offer to accommodate growing numbers of Spanish speakers. Night school divisions are scheduling classes to teach English to newcomers, and school administrators are recruiting bilingual teachers and staff.

◆ Publishers, television producers, and filmmakers are recognizing the growing Latino population and are creating products with Spanish-language content or with a decidedly Latino focus.

◆ Increasing numbers of Latino officials are being elected to public office. Many of these officials will have triple agendas: local, national, and the old country. This is so with Congressman Bob Menéndez, from New Jersey, who advocates for peaceful political change in Cuba as much as he sponsors legislation favorable to his home state.

- Latino immigrants are reinvigorating Main Streets across the country, replacing hot-dog stands with taco stands and grocery stores with bodegas. Similarly, supermarkets are beginning to designate an aisle for the sale of products from Latin America, and local newsstands are carrying Spanish-language publications.

- Because the majority of Latinos are christened Catholics, Catholic churches are seeing increases in Latino membership, and some are even holding Spanish-language masses. Similarly, some protestant denominations , particularly Pentecostal churches, are increasingly attracting a Latino presence.

Unfortunately, not everything is rosy in the Latino world; there is some bad news. As with any new immigrant population, Latinos face many challenges, including:

- Poor academic achievement, low school attendance, and a high drop-out rate, often due to lack of English-language skills.

- Latino youth, particularly in poverty-stricken areas, are involved in drug abuse and trafficking, gangs, and other criminal activity.

- Lack of acceptance by mainstream society due to cultural, political, and religious differences.

A look to history tells us that this inventory of problems is not new; actually, it is a list of items that is resurrected over and over again as newcomers populate U.S. towns. Italians were accused of the same sins at the beginning of the twentieth century, as were Irish immigrants during the nineteenth century. And so were Chinese immigrants during the 1870s and '80s.

# Tall, Dark, and Handsome?

During Hollywood's golden years, three actors—César Romero, a Cuban-American; Ricardo Montalbán, a Mexican-American; and Fernando Lamas, an Argentine—established what became known as the "Latin look." Tall, dark-complected, graceful, and, of course, very handsome, this look became the accepted and expected image for all Latinos.

But another "Latin look" started forming in people's minds based on the part of the country they lived in. For people living on the West coast, all Latinos looked like Mexican Indians: short and square and brown with sleek hair and dripping mustaches. To those living on the East coast, all Latinos resembled Puerto Ricans: short and dark-skinned with thin mustaches.

These images persisted throughout the 1960s, '70s, and '80s, and even newspapers like *The New York Times* used the terms Latino and Hispanic as short hand for a certain physique: short and dark with curly hair and a mustache.

There is no single Latino look:

### Para Tu Información

What do Latinos look like to each other and to themselves? It varies, depending on where you come from. Half of the Mexican-Americans in the United States think of themselves as white and about 40 percent describe themselves as mixed. Less than half of the Puerto Ricans in the states regard themselves as white, whereas over 80 percent of Cuban-Americans view themselves as white.

- Latinos look white, like Andy García, Vickie Carr, and Ricky Martin.
- They're tan, like Erik Estrada, Jennifer López, and Paul Rodriguez.
- And they're black, like Celia Cruz, El Duque, and Rosie Perez.

What do Latinos look like? Like you. Like me.

## The Least You Need to Know

- The word Latino refers to culture and not race.
- More than 35 million Latinos make the United States their home.
- There are as many Latinos in the United States as there are African-Americans.
- Latinos live all over the United States but prefer big cities on the West, the East, and the Southeast.
- There is no single Latin look—some Latinos look white, others are tan, and others are dark-complected.

# Two Paths, One Destination: Immigrating to America

## In This Chapter

- ◆ The ins and outs of legal and illegal immigration
- ◆ The difference between political and economic immigrants
- ◆ Getting a Green Card
- ◆ Becoming an American

Now that you know how many Latinos live in the United States, you're probably wondering how they all got here. Many of them, of course, were born in the United States—the children of first, second, and third generation immigrants. But many other Latinos living in the United States are immigrants themselves, having entered the country through legal or illegal channels.

Even as you read this book, it's likely that a poor Mexican farmer is crouching behind a pile of debris, rocks, and shrubs, holding his breath, preparing to sprint across a dry riverbed of the Rio Grande, hoping to make it undetected to the American side of the Mexican-American border. Chances are, though, the border patrol will catch him—by some estimates, three out of ten of those crossings will be caught—especially with the increased surveillance and monitoring instituted after September 11, 2001. Even if he doesn't get caught, he might suffer a worse fate, such as being robbed and beaten by bandits or getting lost and meeting a lonely and thirsty death on a stretch of sand in the Colorado desert.

Still, they cross over, more than 200,000 a year.

As the Mexican farmer waits to cross the border, somewhere in Latin America another would-be immigrant stands in line at an American consulate, waiting for an official to call out his or her name and kick off the process that might deliver him or her to the Promised Land. Chances are it will take this immigrant a long time to realize his or her dream—a long time and a lot of money.

## The Roads to El Norte

> **Hablas Español**
>
> **El Norte** literally means the north, but the word refers specifically to the United States.

These two people are following two different paths that lead to the same destination: the United States. One of these paths is legal, and the other isn't. Thousands of Latinos start down both paths every year.

# Walking Through the Front Door: Legal Entry

To enter the United States legally from Latin America, you usually need a visa. The United States grants two types of visas: immigrant visas and non-immigrant visas. The first allows for permanent stay. Non-immigrant visas are for tourists, patients seeking medical treatment, businessmen on a business trip, students, and highly skilled workers contracted for a specific temporary job.

> **Para Tu Información**
>
> A visa is a permission, allowing an individual the right to visit a country. The visa is stamped or placed on a person's passport, and its presence means that the would-be traveler has been investigated. Upon reaching the country, the traveler presents his or her passport to the immigration official at the airport, who then decides whether or not the person is allowed into the country.

The State Department classifies immigrants as either "unlimited immigrants" or "limited immigrants." In the first category are individuals with no restrictions for entry into the United States. Unlimited immigrants are:

- American citizens
- People married to American citizens
- Widows or widowers of American citizens
- Parents of American citizens
- Legal U.S. residents (Green Card holders)

Limited immigrants must be sponsored by legal residents of the United States or have a job offer in order to be considered for entry.

The State Department assigns preferences, or priorities, based on family relations or employment. Top preference is given to would-be immigrants who are the offspring of American citizens. Second preference goes to the spouses and unmarried children of a permanent resident alien. Next, come the spouses of the children of U.S. citizens. Last are the siblings of U.S. citizens.

## Working for the Yankee Dollar

People can obtain visas to enter the United States based on the promise of employment or the demonstrated ability to carry out a unique job in the United States Not everyone qualifies for such a visa; the categories include the following:

◆ Internationally recognized artists, athletes, business people, professors, and scientists

◆ Executives and managers of American companies

◆ Professionals holding advanced degrees

◆ Highly skilled workers of jobs and professions requiring at least two years of experience and training

◆ Seasonal workers who come and go each year

## Immigrations Specials

The State Department may also grant visas to "special immigrants," which may include religious workers, employers of selective international organizations, and investors. An investor is a person who has the means to create a commercial enterprise in the United States and provide employment to more than 10 workers who are not related to him or her. Political dissidents may also receive special visas.

**Para Tu Información**

The Employment Creation Investors Visa—the investor's visa, for short—was created in 1990. It allows wealthy foreigners to obtain a visa if they promise to invest between $500,000 and $1 million in the United States. This type of visa is highly controversial, with critics dubbing it the "America For Sale" visa.

## Tick, Tock, Tick, Tock ...

How long does it take to get to the United States legally? Once the visa is in your hands, you have up to six months to make your traveling arrangements. That's the easy part—getting an appointment at the consulate to start the application process is usually the tough part. There are countries—Colombia, for example—where the waiting list is as long as three years.

## There's No Free Ride

The fee to set up the appointment at the consulate is $65. The visa application is $260. Immigrants also need to have enough money to cover the plane fare and the moving costs once they arrive in the United States. This can be quite a formidable task when you consider that in some Latin American nations—especially in the Central American region—the average monthly salary is about a $100.

> **Cuidado!**
>
> Only the department of Immigration and Naturalization Services (INS) has the power to let an immigrant enter the United States and stay here. Some crooks offer to help immigrants obtain visas by pretending to be officially connected with the INS. They call themselves representatives of something like the Immigration and Naturalization Agency or Department of Immigration and Naturalization and trick immigrants into paying for fraudulent services.

# Sneaking Through the Back Door: Illegal Entry

The illegal route to the United States is just as long, and usually a lot more costly than the legal route. It usually begins at the American-Mexican border, a 2,000-mile long invisible barrier of arid soil, cacti, and muddy river waters. Near San Diego, metal fences, barbed wire, and concrete walls, lit by hundreds of powerful lights, separate the Mexican side from American terrain.

Most of those making the trip across the southern border are Mexicans, but about 19 percent come from Central America and the Caribbean, and another 6 percent journey from South America.

> **Para Tu Información**
>
> On the highway along the American side of the Mexican-American border, there are signs that depict a silhouette of a man, woman, and child dashing across the highway. The signs are similar to the deer crossing signs on roads in areas with heavy concentrations of deer.

The first step is taken at home, where the would-be traveler decides to leave family and friends behind (or take them with him or her, depending on the situation) and head to El Norte. It is a process of self-exploration. It could happen over night—as it did to thousands of Chileans who, after President Salvador Allende was overthrown, realized they had to flee Chile. Or it could take months, as is the case with hundreds of Venezuelans who, fearing the establishment of a dictatorial regime by President Omar Chavez, are fleeing to the United States.

Once the decision is made, the next step for many is to borrow funds from a loan shark, who will then collect the money from the borrower's family sometime after the person has entered the United States safely. Reaching a border town, in places such as Tijuana, the would-be traveler finds a smuggler who can smuggle him or her across. A transformation takes place here: the would-be traveler becomes a *pollo*, a chick, and the smuggler, a *coyote*. The coyote charges more than $1,000 to guide the chick across the border and into the United States and to protect him from bandits.

If the coyote is honorable, he or she—for there are many women who earn their living as coyotes—will lead the chick to the Promised Land, making arrangements for someone to pick a group of them up and drive them to Los Angeles or other points on the West coast. But if the coyote is crooked, he or she might take the money and run, deserting his or her "cargo" in the desert, or worse, being so reckless with the pollos as to cause their deaths. In the mid-1980s, a coyote locked up his charge inside a truck and left them to die of heat exhaustion and thirst. In the mid-1990s, a smuggler was driving so recklessly that he flipped over his van, crushing to death eight illegal aliens he was sneaking across the border.

---

### Living La Vida Literaria

"At dark a man in a shiny warmup jacket, his wife, and three children started down the narrow path into the deepest part of the canyon. The woman carried a baby slung across her back … Up on the hill the coyotes nodded to their little herds of chickens to get ready. The emigrants went quietly, moving like animals through the night, atavistic shapes, bent low to the ground, Neolithic runners in post-modern shoes."

—Earl Shorris, from *Latinos, A Biography of the People*

---

Once the pollos reach their American destination, another transformation takes place. They become someone else. They obtain fake papers and IDs. Or they become nameless, trying not to give anyone their true names, trying to carry on some semblance of a life in silence and obscurity. Writer Sandra Cisneros calls them Geraldos with no last names. She writes in *House on Mango Street*: "His name was Geraldo. And his home is in another country. The ones he left behind are far away, will wonder, shrug, remember. Geraldo—he went north … we never heard from him again."

## Other Points of Entry

The blue waters of the Caribbean Sea border another popular point of entry for Latinos who want come to the United States: Key West, Florida. Since 1959, thousands of Cubans have braved the shark-infested waters of the Caribbean to escape Castro's dictatorship.

In the 1960s and '70s, they embarked on yachts and sailboats. Since the 1980s, these travelers have taken to the sea on homemade vessels dubbed *balsas*, which is why the travelers are called *balseros*. Most balseros who make it to American shore are allowed to stay (more about Cubans in Chapter 3), settling predominantly in Florida.

Thousands of Dominicans have attempted the crossing as well. In the mid-1990s, the American Coast Guard detained 4,000 Dominicans a year on the high seas. These would-be immigrants were shipped back to the Dominican Republic since the current policy is to return home anyone caught in American waters.

Other Dominicans take a different, but still illegal, route: an 18-hour sea-journey from the Dominican Republic to Puerto Rico, a U.S. Territory. Once they arrive on that island, they linger for a few months, working at odd jobs and saving some money. Then they book passage on a flight from San Juan, Puerto Rico, to New York. By pretending to be Puerto Ricans, who are American citizens, they don't have to go through U.S. Customs and don't have to meet an Immigration agent, and so have an easier time entering the country illegally. Most Dominicans move to Manhattan, where they join the Dominican-American community, numbered at about one million.

### Hablas Español

A **balsa** is a small homemade raft; for Cuban immigrants, it refers to anything that floats on water. Cubans have taken to sea on balsas that consist mainly of a plank and two rubber tires. A **balsero** is someone who travels on a balsa.

### Para Tu Información

Puerto Ricans have been American citizens since 1917. They can travel back and forth to the mainland without restrictions. Thus, a Dominican who migrates illegally to Puerto Rico can obtain fake IDs and board a jet bound for the United States.

*The routes of illegal immigration.*

*(Map by Armando H. Portelo)*

# No Need for Stinking Papers

Some people—both Latinos and non-Latinos—believe people should be able to cross the border whenever they want to, to be able to come and go without legal restrictions. Many people even go one step further and argue that there shouldn't even be a border between Mexico and the U.S. They base their argument in part on the fact that most of the Southwest was Mexican territory until 1846. At that time the United States, as a result of the Mexican-American War, took possession of Arizona, California, Nevada, Texas, and part of Utah and Washington (see Chapter 11 for more on this history).

# Make Up Your Mind, Uncle Sam!

Immigration legislation is a relatively new development. From colonial times to the mid-nineteenth century, there were no laws regulating entry into the country. Since then, like the weather in New England, immigration laws have changed constantly. The laws are changed based on numerous factors, including global developments, local politics, labor needs, and the mood of the nation.

In 1910, the United States allowed over 700,000 Mexicans, who were escaping the devastation of the Mexican Revolution, to cross the border. During World War II, nearly 220,000 workers trekked north as participants of the *Bracero* program. The program, part of the Emergency Farm Labor Act, was established to allow Mexican laborers to replace the thousands of young American farmers fighting in Europe and in the Pacific. Then, in 1986, the Immigration and Reform Act granted amnesty to nearly three million legal aliens who had been living in the United States since 1982.

Perhaps the most notorious immigration law emerged in 1880. It was the xenophobic Chinese Exclusion Act of 1882, which prohibited Chinese from coming to the United States and set up, for the first time, immigration restrictions based on national origin. Here are some of the laws enacted during the 1900s:

- **Immigration Act of 1917:** The act banned immigration from Asia and required immigrants to take a literacy test before arriving at the United States.

- **Immigration Act of 1924:** This legislation favored immigration from Europe and established quotas that allowed immigration only from those nations already represented in the United States, Central, and South America were lumped together under the quotas assigned to Spain.

**Para Tu Información**

The **Bracero** program was designed specifically to bring to the U.S. Mexican agricultural workers. Later on, the program was expanded to include factory workers and some construction workers. The expression came from the word "brazos," meaning arms, and it referred to manual labor.

### Para Tu Información

To **emigrate** is to leave your country; to **immigrate** is to settle in another country. To **migrate** is to move from one country to another. An **immigrant** is someone who travels to a foreign country and takes residence there.

The counterparts to the above words in Spanish are: **emigrar**, **imigrar**, and **imigrante**.

◆ **Immigration and Nationality Act of 1952:** Assigned quotas to countries recognized by the United Nations, but continued to exclude immigration from Asia.

◆ **Immigration and Nationality Act of 1965:** Ended the national origin quotas, opening the doors of immigration to the people from Asia and Latin America.

◆ **Immigration Act of 1990:** Established preferred status for family-sponsored aliens and for professionals and individuals with unique talents and skills, such as athletes and performers.

## Brother, Can You Spare a Quota

Just because national quotas were eliminated in 1965, it doesn't mean that there are no longer any quotas. There are, but now they're called "worldwide limitations." This is the annual breakdown: 1) 366,000 family-sponsored immigrants; 2) 123,291 employment-based immigrants. The limitations apply to countries as well: only 7 percent of the immigrants may come from each nation per year.

The Diversity Lottery, also called the Green Card Lottery, grants visas to 55,000 would-be immigrants, selected randomly. The system allows an individual with no family and employment preference the opportunity to come to the United States. It also attracts immigrants from countries with a low immigration rate. What this means is that most people in Latin America can try to get a winning lottery ticket—except for those from Colombia, the Dominican Republic, El Salvador, and Mexico—countries that already furnish the United States with lots of immigrants.

### Para Tu Información

The address for the Latin American section of the Green Card Lottery is:

DV-2003 Program
Kentucky Consular Center
4004 Visa Crest
Migrate, KY 41904-4000
USA

There are no fees to enter the lottery.

Lottery participants must be high school graduates, have two years of work experience in a profession that requires some type of training, and meet all the requirements to get a visa through regular channels. Entrants simply write their name and birth date on a sheet of paper, include a photograph, and mail it to the National Visa Center in Kentucky. Nothing more is needed.

# Money or Politics?

The U.S. government distinguishes between economic and political immigrants.

**Cuidado!**

Don't be surprised if you hear people dismissing the idea of political immigration. Some people argue that all immigration is economic immigration, and is based on the desire to make money and live comfortably. Others counter this argument by saying that making money and living comfortably is all about freedom of choice, which is denied to people in some countries.

- ◆ **Economic immigrants** are considered to be voluntary participants in the immigration process, choosing to leave their country in order to live in the United States and lead a better life.
- ◆ **Political immigrants** seek safe harbor in the United States from political persecution in their own country.

The distinctions are often lost on the immigrants themselves, as it is usually the political conditions in their home countries that create both the poverty and the political situation that lead them to emigrate in the first place.

## Land of Opportunity: Economic Immigrants

Like their European counterparts of the nineteenth century, economic migrants are dreamers of the American dream: they come here to make it.

These immigrants often have little formal education and no skills. Poverty back home, or social circumstances favoring an elite minority, propelled these dreamers out of their country. They come to the United States to work hard, provide for their families, and/or send money to the folks in the old country. As soon as possible, they journey home to bring goods and show how well they've fared in the land of gold.

Economic immigrants can be generalized into two different categories: those who dream of retiring back home, refusing to see his or her stay in the United States as a permanent condition; and those who are here to stay.

# Home of the Free: Political Immigration

Political immigrants seek safe harbor in the United States from political persecution in their own country. Two designations are used to describe them: asylum-seekers or asylees, and political refugees.

**Para Tu Información**

The United States didn't have a refugee policy until the end of World War II when the need to help displaced European refugees arose. In the 1950s and '60s, dissidents escaping from communist regimes were allowed entry to the United States, under the category of political refugees, and were granted special visas.

Asylum-seekers are often portrayed in a dramatic light. At the end of the movie, *House of Spirits*, dissident Antonio Banderas is hidden under a car seat, smuggled past the heavily armed guards who are looking for him, and delivered into the safe haven of an embassy. That was indeed one way to obtain political asylum, a way employed by hundreds of Cubans during 1959 and 1960 when they ran into the American embassy in Havana and asked for protection. But this particular method is no longer in style. Embassies are now heavily protected—even more so after the September 11 attacks—and it is virtually impossible to dash unexpectedly into the compound. The way to seek asylum now is to get a visa and, upon reaching the United States, request political asylum from the INS.

There is very little difference between an asylee and a political refugee. Both refer to an individual facing persecution and oppression at home. Today, though, an asylee is someone who asks for asylum while in the United States and a refugee is someone who requests political protection outside the United States.

Political immigrants regard themselves as quite different from economic immigrants. The latter come to the United States for a materialistic purpose: the making of a better life. The former feel that in coming to the United States they left behind the better life.

That might well be the case. Political immigrants tend to be either wealthy or professionals who had property and social status in the old country. Suffering immigration because of an ideal, they consider themselves patriots who gave up their own private good for the good of the country. Economic immigrants, on the other hand, are depicted as members of the lower classes, people who failed to make it at home and are trying to make it here. Seen as outsiders by mainstream Anglos, these immigrants are sometimes shunned by the more educated political asylees or refugees.

# Sticking Around

No matter the reason—economic or political—for entering the country, once an immigrant is here, there are two ways he or she can remain in the United States:

- ◆ Become a permanent resident by obtaining a Green Card
- ◆ Become a naturalized citizen

## The Ticket to Freedom Is Green

Permanent residency comes in the shape of a card, the so-called Green Card, which is actually no longer green. The official name of this small document is the Alien Registration Green Card, and Green Card holders are supposed to carry their card all of the time. Green Card holders must pay taxes like everyone else and can be drafted by the armed forces.

Permanent residents are allowed to stay in the United States for as long as they want, and they can get any type of work, go to school, move around the country, and even go abroad—as long as they come back within the year. In essence, permanent residents have the same rights as citizens, except for the right to vote.

Immigrants can apply for a Green Card after they have been in the United States for at least three years.

## Yankee Doodle Dandy

Immigrants can apply for citizenship two years after receiving their Green Card. Applicants must meet the following requirements:

- Be at least 18 years of age
- Demonstrate that you have lived in the United States for five years or more
- Have no criminal record
- Speak English
- Show knowledge of American institutions, history, and culture

Applicants are interviewed by a judge, who recommends whether they can become naturalized citizens. If the decision is positive, the immigrant participates in a public ceremony during which he or she swears allegiance to the United States. As an American citizen, the immigrant has the right to vote, and no one can ever revoke his or her citizenship.

## The Least You Need to Know

- Latino immigrants enter the country legally and illegally.
- Immigrant visas allow immigrants to stay in the United States for a long period of time.
- The Green Card affords permanent residency in the United States.
- It is possible to become a naturalized citizen after living legally in the United States for five or more years.

# The Reconquest of America

## In This Chapter

- ◆ The first Europeans in America
- ◆ John Smith and Pocahontas, Spanish style
- ◆ The United States annexes Mexican territory
- ◆ The long history of Latino immigration to the United States

In a classroom, a teacher asked, "Aside from the Native American languages, what was the first language spoken in America?" Raising his hand, an eager student volunteered, "Spanish." Smiling, the teacher said, "Good try, but wrong answer." In this chapter, you will find out who was right and who was wrong in that class. We'll clarify how the Spanish explorers and colonizers were the first to settle the territory that would become the United States and how Latinos had as much a role in the formation of this country as any other group. In fact, you will discover that Latinos are not newcomers at all.

## History of Latinos in the United States

Let's take a quiz. Now, this is tricky:

1. What book can be regarded as the first American book, and in what language was it written?

2. What two armies were involved in the first major conflict in what today is the United States?

3. Name the explorer saved from death by a Native American woman.

4. Name the first European settlement in the United States.

If you were paying attention in grade school, you'll probably say John Smith's English-language *History of Virginia* for the first answer. For question number two, the likely choice is the British colonists against the Huron Indians. John Smith will of course be your response for query number three (who doesn't know the story of Pocahontas?). And for the final question, your answer will be the British colonial settlement of Jamestown.

If these were your answers, you'd probably get an A in history class, but your answers are wrong.

It's not your fault. Elementary and secondary schools don't teach about the Latino presence in United States, and even universities—with some exceptions, such as the University of Texas and Florida International University—shy away from documenting Latino history. So we'll tackle the subject ourselves, providing the quiz-busting answers as we go along.

# La Primera Palabra

In 1528, Alvar Nuñez Cabeza de Vaca, after exploring Florida, was shipwrecked off the coast of present-day Texas. He managed to make it ashore, where he was captured and enslaved by nomadic Native Americans. Befriending his captors, Cabeza de Vaca became a medicine man. So gifted a physician was he that he revived a man taken for dead. As his reputation grew throughout the Native American nations of the Southwest, so did his affection for his newfound brethren. Traveling from tribe to tribe, Cabeza de Vaca walked the Southwest, reaching the north of Mexico in 1536, where he rejoined his compatriots.

**Hablas Español**

Palabra means word. Primera means first.

Let's flash forward: In 1542, Cabeza de Vaca chronicled his epic journey in a volume titled *La relación*. Pure novelty, the book depicted the lay of the land that would become the United States, its flora and fauna—he was the first European to describe a bison—and the rites and traditions of its inhabitants, all told from the perspective of a *cronista*, a chronicler, who was attracted to this brave New World. There were other cronistas in those years, primarily chronicling their adventures in Mexico and South America, but what made Cabeza de Vaca unique was his compassion for Native Americans.

**Quiz Buster #1:** *La relación* was written 66 years before Captain John Smith—of Pocahontas fame—penned *A True Relation of Such Occurrences and Accidents of Noate as Hath Happened in Virginia Since the First Planting of That Colony*, which is usually regarded as the first American book.

> ## Living La Vida Literaria
>
> "The Indians ... have the custom from the time in which their wives find themselves preg-
> nant, of not sleeping with them until two years after they have given birth. The children
> are suckled until the age of twelve years, when they are old enough to get support for
> themselves ... Asked why they reared them in this manner ... they said because of the
> great poverty of the land ... the children were allowed to suckle that they might not fam-
> ish; otherwise those who lived would be delicate, having little strength."
>
> —from *The Narrative of Alvar Nuñez Cabeza de Vaca,* a 1907 English translation of
> Cabeza de Vaca's text

# Seven Cities of Gold

Cabeza de Vaca did not tell a tale-told-by-a-fool. Literate, well-versed in the popular literature of his time, and with a great deal of biblical knowledge, he fashioned a realm as
magical and alluring as Harry Potter's Hogwarts. The allure worked. Even before *La
relación* was published, eager conquistadores in Mexico had heard about Cabeza de Vaca's
adventures. Soon, scores of explorers took off for El Norte.

Donning suits of armor and helmets, or wearing habits and holding crucifixes in hand,
Spaniards trekked north from New Spain (what Mexico was called at the time). In 1539,
Fray Marcos de Niza explored the territory of New Mexico, searching for the legendary
cities of gold, the Seven Cities of Cíbola. Reaching a village, the friar enthusiastically
reported that he had come across a metropolis as large as Mexico City. It was a highly
exaggerated claim, but no one in New Spain knew this and everyone accepted the Friar's
report as gospel truth. It was this report that prompted Coronado's famous expedition.

**Quiz Buster #2:** In 1540, Francisco Vázquez de Coronado led more than 1,000 men into
the region of Cíbola. There, the explorer did not find a city of gold but a small village
that was home to 200 warriors, warriors who were not happy to see the Spanish and soon
enough challenged them to combat. The battle, which took place in July, was the first major
armed confrontation in the United States between the organized forces of a European
power and Native Americans.

Winning the battle, Coronado continued his exploration of the territory, dispatching his
men in all directions. One of the officers, Captain López de Cárdenas, was the first European
to cast eyes on the Grand Canyon, and another, Hernando de Alvarado, toured present
day Albuquerque. Coronado himself wandered into Texas, Oklahoma, and even central
Kansas.

> **Para Tu Información**
>
> Cabeza de Vaca, which means cow's head, is not a surname but a hereditary title awarded to Alvar Nuñez Cabeza de Vaca's ancestors during the Spanish war of reconquest against the Moors (eighth century to the fifteenth). A shepherd named Martín Alhaja found a little-known passage in the Sierra Morena mountains and marked it with the skull of a cow so the Christian army could use the pass to launch a surprise attack on the Muslim forces. A grateful King Sancho of Navarre bestowed upon the shepherd aristocratic rights and the title of Cabeza de Vaca.

# The Pass to the North

Coronado never found his cities of gold. However, his failure did not stop others from heading north. In the 1580s, several friars and explorers journeyed to places such as Santa Fe, Texas, and Wichita, Kansas.

The next big push came in 1598, when the governor of New Spain appointed Juan de Oñate *adelantado*, the pathfinder, of an expedition to settle New Mexico. Accompanied by 600 soldiers, women, children, Indians, and Africans, Oñate claimed for Spain the region in present-day El Paso. Naming it El Paso del Norte, he then sailed up the Rio Grande to New Mexico, where he founded the village of San Juan de los Caballeros.

Life in New Mexico was not easy. The settlers were not always happy with Oñate's dictatorial administrative style, and there were ongoing conflicts with Native Americans. Eventually, in 1680, the Pueblo Indians staged an uprising, pushing the settlers out of New Mexico and driving them south to El Paso. (Twelve years later, Spanish forces were able to retake New Mexico.)

> **Hablas Español**
>
> Adelantado means pathfinder, and was the name given to the leader of an expedition, who was usually rewarded with whatever riches he found.

In El Paso, the transplanted New Mexicans founded the villages of Ysleta and Socorro, Texas' first towns. In 1691, a governor was appointed to manage the area, and the Catholic Church established several missions, of which the most important was the mission of San Antonio, founded in 1718 and housing The Alamo.

# California, Here I Come

In the late 1700s, not only was California beckoning Spain but it was also beguiling Russia, which had expressed interest in securing the land. So, in 1769 two expeditions took off for the North, one by sea, heading for the bay of San Diego, and one by land.

The land contingent was led by an army officer named Gaspar de Portolá and by the Franciscan Friar Junípero de Serra. Their adventure was the stuff of movies—in fact, the story of their adventure was made into a movie titled *Seven Cities of Gold*, starring Mexican-American legend Anthony Quinn. The expeditionaries endured sand storms, food shortages, and skirmishes with Native Americans. Finally, in the summer of 1769, Friar Serra planted a cross on a San Diego hill and began the construction of the first mission in California.

Next, Portolá and the friar went on a search for the bay of Monterey where the missionary wanted to establish another mission. The dynamic duo arrived in Monterey in May, 1770. Again, Friar Serra erected a cross on a hill and began the construction of the mission. Then the mission-bent missionary continued exploring California, establishing seven more missions in the state.

# Kino Can Do

While Oñate was organizing New Mexico and Serra was evangelizing California, a quiet but determined figure was quite busy in Arizona. His name was Eusebio Kino.

Educated in Germany, Kino was a Jesuit missionary who traveled to Arizona in 1691 in search of the sources of the Colorado, the Gila, and the Rio Grande rivers. Traveling on a horse, he founded five missions and taught the Native Americans new agricultural techniques as well as how to plant wheat. An astronomer and mathematician, Father Kino proved that Baja California was not an island but a peninsula.

# Go West, Young Man

By the end of the 1700s, the Spanish territory on the West coast included present day Arizona, California, New Mexico, Texas, and parts of Colorado, Nevada, Utah, and Washington. In the 1820s, when Mexico gained its independence from Spain (take a look at Chapter 9), those states became Mexican provinces.

A few years later, eager Americans—or Anglos, as they were called—from the East made their way to these Mexican provinces, setting up farms and small businesses. While they got along with some of their Mexican neighbors, the Anglos didn't like living under Mexican rule. Religion was an issue: the Mexicans were very Catholic and the Anglos were not. Law was an issue: the Spanish courts didn't use a jury, but a judge, and assumed you were guilty until proven innocent—quite the

**Para Tu Información**

Manifest destiny was the belief that the United States should rule all of North America. It maintained that as a growing and powerful nation, the United States needed to expand from the East to the West. It was popular during most of the nineteenth century.

opposite of what Anglos were accustomed to. Also, the Anglos believed in the concept of manifest destiny, which was the dream of forging the West and East coasts into one land and one nation, undivided.

Tensions between the Mexicans and the Anglos simmered, and eventually boiled over. The United States and Mexico went to war (for more about the war, see Chapter 11), with the United States eventually defeating its southern neighbor. As the saying goes, "to the victor goes the spoils," and the "spoils" in this case was the Mexican territory north of the Rio Grande. Thus, the Mexicans living there became American citizens, taking on a dual identity as Mexican-Americans.

# Comings and Goings

The second half of the nineteenth century was the age of the railroad, the building of new cities, and the rush for the gold on the hills. Workers were needed. And they came: Over 120,000 Mexicans entered the United States from 1888 to 1900.

More came during the first two decades of the twentieth century, as 700,000 Mexicans escaped the revolution ravaging their country. Many were members of the middle and upper classes, and because they were intensely loyal to Mexico and considered their country the most beautiful in the world, they were nicknamed the Mexico Lindo generation.

World War II brought about the creation of the Bracero program, already discussed in Chapter 2, which resulted in the immigration of over 300,000 Mexicans. This migration went on until 1964.

# Back on the East Coast

Before the Floridian presidential election fiasco of the Bush vs. Gore campaigns, there were several other campaigns that ended in fiasco in Florida. They all occurred in the sixteenth century.

The first took place in 1513. That year explorer Juan Ponce de León, rumored to be searching for the Fountain of Youth, discovered the sunny peninsula. So taken was the Spaniard by the plush vegetation that he uttered "Florida," meaning filled with flowers and plants, in admiration. The natives, however, observing from behind the very same vegetation, were not as taken by the visitor. They took to their bows and arrows and proceeded to attack Ponce de León and his men. The explorer had no choice but to retreat to his ships and sail away to Puerto Rico, already colonized and Spaniard-friendly.

Ponce de León returned to Florida in 1521. This time, he was determined to overpower the Native Americans, colonize Florida, which he believed to be an island, and introduce Christianity to the natives. The natives, however, had other plans; they attacked Ponce de León and his men, fatally wounding him.

**Para Tu Información**

The story about Ponce de León searching for the Fountain of Youth is more of a legend than a fact. The explorer might have been interested in coming across such a fountain (Wouldn't you be? Think: Viagra!), he was too experienced a traveler and too educated to really believe it existed. He was more interested in finding gold and gaining recognition and favors from the Spanish crown than in the Fountain of Youth.

# The Spanish John Smith and Pocahontas

The next chap to come along was Pánfilo de Narvácz. In 1527, Narváez and his men landed in Tampa, journeying inland from there. Meagerly provisioned, overpowered by the flora and fauna, and harassed by the restless natives, the explorer wandered too far from the coast and his ships, getting lost. Building barges by felling trees with swords and knives, Narváez and his men planned to reach Mexico by sailing along the coast of Florida and present-day Alabama and Mississippi. Once the improvised fleet was put on the water, Narváez sailed off to the horizon. He vanished, and no one heard from him ever again. But people did hear from one of his officers, Cabeza de Vaca. Remember him?

It was Cabeza de Vaca's stories that ignited the imagination of still another explorer. Hernando de Soto landed in Tampa in 1539, where he soon came across one Juan Ortiz, a survivor of the Narváez's expedition.

**Quiz Buster #3:** Ortiz told de Soto that Native Americans had captured him and that his life had been spared because the daughter of a chief had interceded on his behalf. Thus, as scholar José Fernández points out in *The Hispanic American Almanac*, "Spanish Florida had its romance story some sixty eight years prior to that of John Smith and Pocahontas."

Hernando de Soto and his men spent four years traveling through Florida, Georgia, the Carolinas, Tennessee, Alabama, and Arkansas. Exhausted, with little food, and fighting disease as well as Native Americans, the explorers headed for Mexico via Texas. By the time they reached their destination in 1542, their leader was dead and, of the 650 who had made up the expedition, less than half had survived.

## St. Augustine Before Jamestown

Success finally came in 1565. That year the king of Spain decided that Florida had to be settled and protected from other European powers and threats, who were beginning to explore Florida. To that end, commander Pedro Menéndez de Aviles and 800 soldiers and colonists disembarked at a bay that offered shelter, seemed easy to defend, and was near a river.

**Quiz Buster #4:** Because the landing occurred in the month of August, Menéndez named the site St. Augustine, founding the first permanent European settlement in the United States, decades before the building of Jamestown.

*Reconstruction of a Spanish settlement in St. Augustine, Florida.*

**Para Tu Información**

Some Latino scholars claim that the first Thanksgiving took place in St. Augustine, explaining that shortly after erecting the fort, Menéndez celebrated mass followed by a feast to which the local Native Americans were invited. The natives accepted the invitation, commencing a peaceful coexistence that lasted for years.

Menéndez kicked French explorers out of Florida and turned St. Augustine into a prosperous town with a fort and a main street that still stands today—portions of it, anyhow. St. Augustine helped to assure the Spaniards the possession of Florida for two centuries. In 1763, however, Spain traded the peninsula to the British in exchange for the city of Havana, Cuba, which the British had captured for a short while. Then, in 1783, Spain recaptured Florida. In 1821, this Spanish colony was sold to the United States for five million dollars.

# Nueva York

Fires of rebellion against Spanish rule began spreading throughout Latin America in the nineteenth century (see Chapter 9 for more on these). These wars of independence propelled thousands of immigrants to the United States, specifically the East coast.

In the 1820s in Philadelphia, and later on in New York City, there were Latinos from Argentina, Cuba, Colombia, Ecuador, and Venezuela. Mostly middle class *criollos*, direct descendants of Spaniards, they were political exiles. They published newspapers and pamphlets advocating their cause and frequented bookstores, at least one in Philadelphia and one in New York City, that sold Spanish classics and afforded the exiles the opportunity to meet other Latinos with pro-independence stances. As their countries achieved independence during the 1820s, most of these conspirators returned home. Remaining were the Cubans and Puerto Ricans, whose struggle for independence lasted until the end of the century.

From the 1870s to the 1890s, around 100,000 Cubans left the island, seeking temporary residence in Europe and the United States. In New York City, where many affluent Cubans set up small hotels and businesses on Fourteenth Street and along Fifth Avenue, Cubans and Puerto Ricans joined ranks in their fight against the Spanish monarchy . The heart and soul of these revolutionaries was the Cuban poet and propagandist José Martí, who in hundreds of speeches and articles promoted independence and the establishment of democratic governments on the two Caribbean islands. Martí obtained financial backing from Latinos of all walks of life, from factory workers to bankers, and he used the funding to support the insurgents back home. The largest bulk of the money came from the *tabaqueros*, the cigar makers, of Tampa.

The tabaqueros arrived in Florida from Cuba sometime after 1868. Settling initially in Key West, they moved on to Tampa where a Spanish tycoon named Vicente Martínez Ybor founded the suburb of Ybor City. The suburb teemed with life. There were over 150 tobacco factories and dozens of shops, theaters, and cultural centers.

The tabaqueros were well-versed in current events and were familiar with the literature of the time. For as they rolled tobacco leaves in the factories, a lector, a reader, read to them newspapers articles as well as history books and novels. About 4,000 Cubans worked as tabaqueros; today, their descendants, many of whom still live in Tampa, are called *Tampeños*.

### Hablas Español

**Criollos** are the offspring of Spaniards born in the New World.

### Living La Vida Literaria

The Latinos who lived in Philadelphia during the 1820s were highly cultured and literate. One of the first novels about Latin America, *Jicoténcal* by Cuban exile Félix Varela, was written and published in Philadelphia in 1826.

### Hablas Español

**Tabaqueros** are cigar workers who make cigars by hand, and still practice their trade in Tampa, Miami, and in some communities in New York and New Jersey. **Tampeños**, born and raised in Tampa, are the descendants of the tabaqueros who arrived in Florida towards the end of the nineteenth century.

# From the Caribbean, with Love

In 1898, the United States declared war on Spain. Known as the Spanish-American War, the conflict lasted less than six months. It resulted in victory for the United States, humiliation for Spain, and independence for Cuba, Puerto Rico, and the Philippines. Cuba went on to become an independent nation, while Puerto Rico became a territory of the United States.

In 1917, Puerto Ricans were granted citizenship by the American congress, facilitating their entry into and exit from the United States. However, mass Puerto Rican migration did not take place until World War II when agricultural employers from New York and New Jersey recruited nearly 20,000 laborers from the island to replace the farmers who had gone off to war.

In the 1950s, Operation Bootstrap, created by Luis Muñoz Marín, the popular governor of Puerto Rico, changed the economic structure of the island as American investors set up businesses that attracted more skilled workers from the island. The less skilled and educated were unable to find jobs and flew north to places like New York and New Jersey. By 1950, there were over 300,000 Puerto Ricans living in the mainland, mostly in New York City. Twenty years later, the figure had increased to a million and half.

Cuban mass immigration didn't get started with any vigor until 1959, when rebel leader Fidel Castro overthrew dictator Fulgencio Batista. Welcomed at first by all segments of Cuban society, Castro soon implemented radical reforms that displeased members of the upper and middle classes. Within the first five years of the revolution, 300,000 Cubans—the wealthy, middle class, and professionals—went into exile. From 1965 to 1980, another 500,000 Cubans, representing all segments of Cuban society, left the island. In 1980, about 125,000 participated in the Mariel Flotilla, when in a period of 3 months or so, Castro allowed Cubans from the United States to sail to the island and pick up their relatives at the port of Mariel. Since 1994, over 40,000 asylees have made their way north on homemade vessels, or balsas.

## Para Tu Información

Until 1995, the United States welcomed Cubans, automatically designating them political refugees and granting them permanent residency. In 1995, President Bill Clinton removed the refugee tag and mandated that Cubans wait for visas before entering the United States. There's a loophole, though: the law allows Cuban balseros who reach American shore to stay, but those stopped by the Coast Guard on the high seas are sent either to the U.S. Guantanamo Naval Base on Cuba or back to Cuba proper.

## Should I Stay or Should I Go?

Immigrants of the nineteenth and early twentieth century rarely returned to the old country. Even if an Irish immigrant did save enough money to pay for fare back to the Emerald Isle, the hard-working immigrant probably couldn't afford to take the several months away from work or family that such a journey involved.

Thanks to advances in technology and the proximity of most Latin American countries to the United States, returning to the old country is a realizable dream for most contemporary Latino immigrants. The flight to Yucatan, in Mexico, from Miami Beach takes about an hour. A trip to Santiago, Chile, is a bit longer—over 12 hours—but it's still doable even for someone with only a week or two of vacation.

Some Latinos even dream of returning to the old country for good.

Immigrants who used to come to the United States to make money and sent most of the money home or took it back with them, were dubbed "raiders." Today, the more gentler and kinder term is "transnationals," meaning they make money in one country but call another country home. Many Dominicans living in New York are transnationals, expecting to return home to open businesses with the fruit of their labor in New York.

The term transnational also describes those who go back home regularly—once a year or at least every other year—for a stay of two weeks or two months. Mexican workers are known for this form of transnationalism, especially at the end of the harvest in the United States and the beginning of local fiestas and Christmas holidays in Mexico. Thousands of Mexicans drive south in the fall, undisturbed by the border patrol whose mission is to detain illegal immigrants dashing north, but never from driving south.

Of course, some immigrants are never going to return to the old country, whether by choice or by necessity. Some, like Cuban-Americans, might visit Cuba for a brief vacation, but will not stay as long as Fidel Castro remains in power. Others, like economic immigrants, have gotten used to the material comforts of this country and would not give it up.

The reality is that most Latinos in the United States are staying for good, just like the Irish, Chinese, Germans, and others before them who left behind established lives, friends, and cultures to start new lives in the United States.

## The Least You Need to Know

- ◆ Latino presence in the United States predates an Anglo presence.
- ◆ Most of the West coast was once a Mexican possession.
- ◆ Puerto Ricans are American citizens.
- ◆ Until 1995, Cubans were automatically considered political refugees.
- ◆ Though many Latinos will go back home, most will stay in the United States, just like other immigrants before them.

# Chapter 4

# You Say Hispanic, I Say Latino: Latin American Identity

## In This Chapter

◆ What Latinos are called in Latin America

◆ The Hispanic vs. Latino debate

◆ The sounds of Spanish and Spanglish

"It's a puzzlement!" That's the line uttered by the king of Siam, in the musical *The King and I*, whenever he is confronted by life's complexities. While the king wasn't a Latino or a Hispanic, the expression he coined is applicable to the complexities covered of this chapter. When it comes to deciding which term to use, either Hispanic or Latino, you might as well say, "It's a puzzlement."

We'll try to piece the puzzle together in this chapter. We'll look at an array of terms used in the United States and Latin America to describe people from the region. We'll study the controversy over Hispanic vs. Latino and see how all of it is connected to language. Then, we'll talk a bit about the use of language by Spanish-speakers and the colorful changes taking place in the Spanish language in the United States.

Are you *listo?* Are you ready?

# You Say Potato, I Say Patata

A rose by any other name might still be a rose, but a Latino by any other name ... maybe not!

Referring to people from Spanish-speaking countries can be a very confusing endeavor. Even people we usually turn to for the answers—government officials, corporate executives, and college administrators—are still scratching their heads over this knot of a problem. For example, a university dean, who cares about her student body, might ask her students to clarify what designation they prefer: Hispanic or Latino? After the students argue and disagree with each other, they might turn to their favorite professor and ask him which term to use. The professor, in turn, phones a colleague at a nearby university to pose the question, thus, kicking off an eternal merry-go-round.

**Para Tu Información**

In this book, I am using the term Latino to refer to people who originate in nations conquered and colonized by Spain, thus keeping cultural and national issues easier and simpler to understand.

Finally, to stop the cycle, a consultant is brought in to conduct a poll, analysts analyze the data, and commentators comment on the conclusion. So, what's the conclusion?

To find out, let's turn to the source: Latin America.

# South of the Border

The people in Latin America identify themselves by their country of origin: Someone from Argentina is an Argentine; someone from Ecuador is an Ecuadorian; a Venezuelan comes from Venezuela. When the need arises to describe themselves or each other in generalities, the people in Latin America use either Latinoamericano or Hispanoamericano.

**Para Tu Información**

In the early 1500s, a letter written by Amerigo Vespucci describing his travels in the New World was published and sold throughout Europe, becoming something of a best seller. A mapmaker named Martin Waldseemüller was so impressed by the letter that he suggested the New World should be called America, to honor the explorer. Since then, maps of the world have identified the lands as America.

Latinoamericano refers to two concepts: America and the Latin language. America is the name of the whole continent, from the tip of Alaska in the north to the tip of the Tierra del Fuego in the south. The word is a variation of the Christian name of explorer Amerigo Vespucci, who was the first to realize that the lands discovered by Columbus were not islands off the coast of Asia but a new territory altogether. Latino alludes to the Latin roots of the Spanish language used by the colonizers of the New World.

The first part of the term Hispanoamerica refers to Hispania, which was the ancient name of Spain during the time of the Roman Empire. It also refers to the

Spanish language and acknowledges the dominant influence of Spanish culture and civilization in Latin America. The second part of the term, of course, refers back to our friend Amerigo Vespucci.

# Get Hip to the Language

In the United States, an Argentine is still an Argentine and an Ecuadorian remains an Ecuadorian, but other designations pop up, too. These terms acknowledge the uniqueness of the diverse nationalities that make up Latin America. Here are some of the terms you might want to keep in mind:

- **Boricua**   A Puerto Rican. Borinquen is the Native American name of Puerto Rico.

- **Caribeño**   Someone from the Spanish-speaking Caribbean.

- **Chicano**   A Mexican-American who identifies with his Mexican and Native American heritage.

**Hablas Español**

An **Anglo** is a white American. It is not a condescending term.

- **Cubiche**   A Cuban, regardless of whether he is in Cuba or in the United States.

- **Hispanohablante**   A person who speaks Spanish.

- **Dominican York**   A Dominican from New York City.

- **Jewban**   A Cuban Jew.

- **Jíbaro**   Puerto Ricans from the countryside.

- **Marielito**   A Cuban political refugee who arrived during the Mariel boatlift of 1980.

- **Mejicano**   A Mexican. The use of the "j"—instead of "x"—differentiates a Mexican who lives in Mexico from a Mexican who lives in the United States. The "j" is used in the United States.

- **Nuyorican**   A Puerto Rican from New York who cherishes his or her New York background as much as his or her Puerto Rican heritage.

- **Norteño**   As used in the United States, a Mexican from the north of Mexico. In Mexico, it might refer to a Mexican who lives in the United States.

- **Pachuco**   A tough guy—maybe even a gang member—from Texas.

- **Quisqueyano**   From the Dominican Republic; quisqueya was the island's original name.

- **Sudamericano**   A South American.

- **Tampeño**   A Cuban-American whose ancestors came to Tampa at the end of the nineteenth century to work as cigar makers.

- **Tejano**   A Mexican-American born and raised in Texas.

- **YUCA**   Stands for Young Upwardly Mobile Cuban-American.

---

### Living La Vida Literaria

Chicano became popular during the Civil Rights Movement and connotes identification with the underdog. The word is a derivative of Mechicano, from the Nahualt language. Some people also suggest that Chicano is a variation of "Mejicano," without the first two letters, as if someone were rushing through the word, saying "jicano." The term probably earned its social and political coloring in 1928, with the publication of the Mexican-American novel, *Las aventuras de Don Chipotes*, in which the main character referred to himself as a Chicano in a gesture of solidarity with the common man.

---

With so many terms and words to keep in mind, and so many nationalities to recognize, government officials and others wanted a more general term to refer to everyone from Latin and South America. Thus, all the nationalities and names were transformed into a generality, a sweeping expression that crowds everyone under an umbrella term. Even that umbrella term has been transformed, as people began to recognize the power of labels and the importance of identifying terms.

# Are You Talking to Me?

Hispano was one of the first umbrella terms used to refer to Spanish speakers and their descendants. It was used mainly in the West coast, especially in the New Mexico area, during the nineteenth century. Referring specifically to the descendants of the Spanish conquistadores who came north from Mexico, the term makes a direct connection to Spain, and it indicates a clear separation from Latin American countries.

A Hispano is someone whose parents were both white folks from Spain—they are not of mixed heritage, for example, having a Spanish father and a Mexican mother. Today, this term is used only in New Mexico, and it is used to differentiate someone of Spanish descent, who considers him- or herself white, from someone of Latin American descent.

### Cuidado!

In Latin America the word Hispano refers to someone who comes from Hispanoamerica. Unlike in New Mexico, where the term is used to indicate whiteness, in Latin America the word echoes of the cultural heritage of many Latin Americans.

In the first half of the twentieth century, the label "Spanish" was used exclusively to describe an individual who was either from Spain or of Spanish descent. Because at the time Anglos had a preference for things European, an individual of European descent did not experience as much discrimination as a person from Latin America. Thus, many Latinos identified themselves as Spanish to avoid being discriminated against. The term was used a lot more on the East coast than out west.

In the 1950s, the U.S. Census introduced the category "Spanish-surname" to tabulate all Spanish speakers and people of Latin American, South American, and Spanish descent. The Census used a list of about 700 recognizable surnames, such Fernandez, Perez, and Rodriguez, but did not count Latinos with non-Spanish last names, such as Higgins. Consequently, Latinos who had Anglicized their names—Carr for Carrasca, for example—were not counted as a Latino. Furthermore, the Census did not distinguish between people of different national origin, so people from Mexico, Cuba, South America, and Spain were lumped together in one general category. The Census used the "Spanish-surname" category for two decades.

From around 1920s to the 50s, the term "Latin" was used to identify Latinos. The word alluded to the language, that is, the linguistic roots of Spanish and all romance languages. It was also short for Latin American. It conveyed the image of the Hollywood Latin Lover: dark, handsome, suave. It was not connected to a particular country, but to a type. Though it still shows up now and then, Latin fell out of popular use around the 1960s.

## In This Corner, Hispanic

In the 1960s, the Census once again took up the challenge of counting and naming people of Latin, South American, and Spanish descent. This time, it chose the word Hispanic to identify these people. The Census was not alone, *The New York Times* and several other papers used it as well. However, cultural and civic organizations had used the term way before the Census. In New York, there was the Hispanic Society—a library and museum organization—that was founded in 1904. In 1929, the Hispanic Chamber of Commerce was established in San Antonio, Texas. Whereas the Hispanic institutions emphasized culture, the media used it to suggest race and color.

The term "Hispanic" refers to ancient Hispania and the Spanish language. It is an English word, created by the British during their confrontations with the Spanish in the nineteenth century because they couldn't pronounce España. It is a term created by English speakers for an English-speaking audience, and today use of the label Hispanic often carries a conservative inflection. Hispanics who accept the term tend do so because the word hints of middle class values. A civil rights activist once said that Hispanic is for those who have or want to have money.

> ### Living La Vida Literaria
>
> According to Earl Shorris in *Latino, A Biography of the People*, "... in 1980 the U.S. Census was on the verge of choosing Latino as the correct word when someone said that it sounded too much like Ladino, the ancient Castilian now spoken only by descendants of the Spanish Jews who went into exile in the fifteenth century. Latino was replaced by Hispanic in the census ..."

## In That Corner, Latino

Latino is a Spanish word chosen by people of Latin American descent to identify themselves. It has gender: Latino for male, Latina for female. It is short for Latinoamericano, thus it looks more towards Latin America than to Spain. It refers to the salad bowl of Latin American culture: it has a Spanish flavor, Native American condiments, and African spices. In the United States, the term was not coined by the gringos, but emerged from the gente, the people themselves.

People who call themselves Latinos often do so as a political act of self-expression, and those who use it tend to be liberals. For instance, author Sandra Cisneros takes pride in describing herself as a Chicana, a Mexican-American, and a Latina, but never a Hispanic.

### Hablas Español

A **gringo** is an American. The term probably evolved during the Mexican-American War when American soldiers rode into Mexico singing the song, "Green Grows the Lilac." What Mexicans heard was, "Green Gos the Lilac." Soon, the Mexicans held on to the "Green Gos," made it into one word, and used it to poke fun at the soldiers. Gringo carries a derogatory connotation, but recently Mexican author Carlos Fuentes used it in his novel, *The Old Gringo,* in a gentler and even romantic manner.

## A Passion for Language

The use of Hispanic and Latino is not a neutral exercise; rather, it is much closer to a volcanic eruption. That's how volatile the matter can be. Those who call themselves Hispanic usually bemoan the use of Latino. Those who prefer Latino often criticize the choice of Hispanic.

The editors of the magazine that bears the name *Hispanic* experienced the wrath of Latinos when they reported that the vast majority of Hispanics disliked the appellation Latino. The editors arrived at this conclusion after conducting a poll in the fall of 2001 that asked 1,200 participants which term they preferred. Soon enough, Latinos wrote complaint letters, suggesting that the poll was rigged to express the magazine's conservative viewpoints.

At some universities, there are faculty members who promote awarding scholarships to students who identify themselves as Latinos but not as Hispanics. And if you're a politician in Dade County, Florida, you have a better chance of getting elected if you call yourself a Hispanic.

## Can't They Stop Speaking in Spanish?

The Hispanic-Latino controversy is more than a battle over names, though. The conflict is about power language and the struggle of minority people to name themselves, rather than let others decide what labels to use.

The persistent use of the Spanish language is a salient characteristic of the people from Latin America. It is a characteristic that draws comments such as, "Why don't they learn English? My parents did." Resentment of the use of Spanish even reached the political arena a few years ago in Miami, when county officials approved a law prohibiting the use of Spanish in government buildings. The public library, for example, was not allowed to publish flyers in Spanish promoting services, which were in English, to the Spanish-speaking community. And a Spanish-speaking worker at a supermarket, where the manager was eager to enforce the anti-Spanish legislation, was fired for speaking in Spanish to another worker. Nationally, the resentment was one of the contributing factors in the birth of the English Only movement (check out Chapter 20 for more on this movement).

Social commentator and author Richard Rodriguez objects to the use of Spanish in public for a more philosophical reason. He considers the language of Cervantes to be a language of intimacy and family and sees English as a public language. For him, the use of Spanish outside the house is betrayal of privacy. Likewise, conservative thinker Linda Chavez objects to Spanish in public spaces. She once suggested that Latinos maintained their language as a strategy to stay out of the mainstream and remain a minority, the better to receive government benefits.

## Speak Trippingly on the Tongue

That's one take. There are others. For one, people from Latin America treasure Spanish fluency. One of the top movie stars in Latin America is the comedian Mario Moreno, better known as Cantinflas (you can catch him in the 1956 American film, *Around the World in Eighty Days*). Known for his gift for juggling the Spanish language the way Abbot and Costello do English, his films are constantly shown on Spanish-language television and his videos are very popular, even though the performer is dead and had stopped making movies a generation ago.

Cantinflas used alliteration, words with double meanings, and long sentences that twist and turn, leading nowhere. In one of his monologues, about the law of gravity, Cantinflas explained that the law is quite grave and the force of gravity on a falling body leads to an early grave.

Another manifestation of language appreciation is in courtship. Traditionally, a macho man in Latin America is expected to win a lady's heart not by his looks but by the way he

## Cuidado!

People often mistakenly assume that people from different Latin American countries speak variations of Spanish. Although this is true in a few countries, such as Brazil, where Spanish is not the national language, everyone else speaks the same Spanish, regardless of whether they come from Guatemala or Uruguay. A Bolivian in Manhattan will have no trouble communicating with a Uruguayan or a Costa Rican.

## Para Tu Información

One of the requirements to become a naturalized U.S. citizen is that you must speak English. But many Puerto Ricans, who are American citizens by birth, speak only Spanish. That makes Spanish a language as American as English.

speaks and can recite poetry. A political leader is often evaluated by his language prowess as well. That's how it was with General Juan Domingo Perón in Argentina 50 years ago, and with Fidel Castro shortly after he took over the Cuban government in 1959.

Cubans in the United States, to name but one group, often assess an individual by that person's ability to speak Spanish correctly and creatively; not to master the language could be interpreted as a sign of weakness. This is how Oscar Hijuelos portrays one character's inability to handle the language in the novel *Our House in the Last Country:*

> "His Spanish was unpracticed, practically nonexistent … saying a Spanish word made him think of drunkenness. A Spanish sentence wrapped around his face, threatened to peel off his skin and send him to the floor …"

Spanish continues to thrive in the United States in part also because of the constant influx of new immigrants, who keep the language fresh and alive. If Alfred forsakes his Spanish for the sake of English, newly arrived Gabriela brandishes her Spanish while at the same time learning English. Gabriela gets her news and information from Spanish radio and television stations, keeping her Spanish up-to-date while at the same time assuring the Spanish stations a loyal fan.

# Hablas Spanglish?

But not all the Spanish you hear is Spanish. There is a marriage of English and Spanish that is dubbed Spanglish. The sentence, "cierra la window porque esta rainando" (close the window because it's raining), with its mix of English and Spanish words, is an example of Spanglish.

Older Latinos and recent arrivals do not approve of the use of Spanglish, which they perceive as a corruption of their native tongue. They maintain that a person must speak either correct Spanish or Standard English, but not mix the two. It is sort of a linguistic generation gap.

Here are few Spanglish words:

◆ **cachear**   to catch

◆ **espelear**   to spell

- ◆ **frizado**   frozen
- ◆ **frizar**   to freeze
- ◆ **lonche**   lunch
- ◆ **lonchar**   to have lunch
- ◆ **la marketa**   the market
- ◆ **pichear**   to pitch
- ◆ **pisue**   pay-for-piece work
- ◆ **taipiar**   to type

A more difficult aspect of Spanglish is the Anglicizing of Spanish syntax. A speaker might be using Spanish words but the sentence could be a direct translation of English. A perfect example is the use of the verb "to return." In Spanish, the word is "devolver" but that verb has been transformed into the English equivalent of to "give back." Thus, instead of hearing "devolver," you hear "doy para atrás," meaning "I give it back to you." The simple verb now becomes a long and awkward phrase.

Another variation of Spanglish is code switching. That means the insertion of a Spanish word or phrase into an English sentence or vice versa. Code switching is sometimes done intentionally by the speakers to indicate familiarity or as a sign of bonding, while keeping intruders out. But sometimes code switching occurs because the speaker forgets a word in one language and substitutes it with another word in another language or because the word in the other language describes the thought far better.

Practitioners of code switching and Spanglish tend to be young. As they get older, they move away from Spanish and use English a lot more. Even those Latinos who might be bilinguals tend to favor English. A while ago, essayist Richard Rodriguez said that to be successful in the United States you had to speak English, the language of the banker. Well, we all go to the bank, don't we?

What it all means is that given world and time enough, the Spanish speakers who are now speaking Spanish will one day conduct all their businesses in English. If not them, their children will. That's the way of all immigrants.

# Round and Round It Goes

So, what's the final answer? Do you say Hispanic? Do you choose Latino? Well, if you're in Florida, you can use Hispanic. If you're in New York, you might try both Hispanic and Latino. In the West coast, Latino will serve you well. In New Mexico, well, that takes you back to Hispano.

In business, Hispanic might be the way to go. At universities and colleges, however, the trend is for Latino. In your own particular community, you might have to ask your neighbors.

Overall, that's the safest approach: consult your gente. Talk to your students, your coworkers, your clients, your friends, and ask them what term they prefer. The answer might just surprise you.

## The Least You Need to Know

◆ Hispanic and Latino can be controversial terms, and are not universally accepted.

◆ People in Latin America describe themselves as Argentines, Colombians, Guatemalans, and so on. When describing themselves in a larger context, they use either Latinoamericanos or Hispanoamericanos.

◆ All Spanish-speakers speak the same Spanish with some variations in vocabulary.

◆ It is likely that a Spanish-speaking Latino youngster will use more English and less Spanish as he or she grows older.

◆ Ask your Spanish-speaking friends and acquaintances how they prefer to be addressed.

# Part 2

# We're the World: The Latino Universe

To appreciate the rich history of Latinos in the United States, you must begin at the very beginning. Legendary heroes, heroic fools, bloody battles, confusing compromises, acts of love and betrayal, and supreme sacrifices have all shaped Latinos throughout the centuries.

We'll discuss Columbus and Cortés, Bolívar and Juárez, Díaz and Perón. We'll see armies going into action: fighting against Spanish troops, fighting against French invaders, fighting against nature to a build a highway of water where there was no water.

The finished product? Latinos: heroic, revolutionary, enterprising … and above all, dreamers.

# Chapter 5

# What Pueblo Are You From?

## In This Chapter

- ◆ Latino diversity par excellence
- ◆ Iberian Latin America
- ◆ Europeans south of the border
- ◆ Barrios, Chinos, and Japanese communities
- ◆ Judíos
- ◆ Moros and Cristianos

The dinner guest at a Chinese restaurant was taken aback when the host and the Chinese waiter talked to each other in Spanish. How could that be so? It turned out that the waiter was Chinese, but he grew up in Panama.

Latinos of Chinese origin are not as rare as many people think. As a matter of fact, there are thousands of Asian-Latinos in Latin America and in the United States. There are also Latinos whose parents are Jewish or who are descended from Muslims. And let's not forget Latinos whose ancestors came from Europe.

Yes, Latinos are not only racially, culturally, and economically diverse, their ancestry is diverse, too.

And that's the theme of this chapter.

# We're Many

The story has it that moros, or Moors, sailed to the New World with Columbus. The story also has it that upon reaching the Caribbean, one of the moriscos, as the Moors were also called, spoke to the Siboney Indians in Arabic. Scholars question the validity of this colorful story, but there's no disputing the fact that as soon as Columbus arrived at the New World, it was the beginning of diversity in Latin America.

### Hablas Español

People from the Middle East were generally referred to as **moros** or **Moors. Morisco** is another word for moros.

### Hablas Español

**El Cid** was a Spanish knight who fought against the Muslims in medieval times. The word *cid* now refers to a person who is strong and brave. **Ojalá** means the desire for something to take place. **Olé** is an exclamation of admiration.

### Para Tu Información

The Moor, or Islamic, Empire in Spain lasted from 711 to 1492. The Moors in Spain invented algebra and introduced paper to Europe. Greek philosophy and classical literature was translated into Arabic and Spanish. Splendid mosques were built, of which the Great Mosque of Cordova still stands with 80 pillars of the original 1,200.

## Diversity Back in Europe

Diversity was already present on the Iberian Peninsula of Europe, even though for several centuries the Spanish chose to ignore the many cultures that formed Spanish civilization. Spain was shaped by the Romans, who invaded the peninsula and who introduced Christianity to the region, and by the Visigoths, from Germany, who invaded and took over the country in 573. Then came the Muslims, a mighty force who conquered almost all of Spain, founding cities, constructing buildings, creating arts and music and philosophy, conjuring a world of marvel. And even more marvelous was their level of tolerance. For the Muslim warriors allowed Jews to coexist side by side with them.

These three cultures—the Christian, the Muslim, and the Jewish—shaped the Iberian universe, whether in love, in war, or in peace. From Christianity came the Catholic faith and the urge to build cathedrals. From the Muslims came heart-pounding music and words … lots of words: *olé*, a transformation of Allah; *ojalá*, adapted from a Moorish expression meaning "to hope that it happens"; and *El Cid*, the name of Spain's greatest hero of all time, a name that means Lord in Arabic. From the Jews came financial institutions and the funding for trips across the ocean to the Americas. What better illustration of the three cultures exists than in the music gypsies play and the dance Flamenco dancers dance?

Yet, two of these cultures were denied—the Moor and the Jewish—the result of The Inquisition, an institution of the Catholic Church that sought to eradicate ideas and beliefs that were seen as a threat to Catholic doctrine at the time. But these cultures were not forgotten.

# Across the Ocean Blue

The Spanish conquistadores overtook America. Many of them came from the province of Extremadura, an arid land of cold winds and hardness. The *colonizadores*, or colonizers, came from other provinces and regions: Andalucía, Cataluña, Galicia, and the Canary Islands. They settled all over South America, except for Brazil, which was a Portuguese colony.

### Para Tu Información

By the end of the sixteenth century, there were 200,000 Spanish colonizers in the Americas. They founded over 250 cities and through war, usurpation, and disease wiped out 12 million Native Americans, according to a contemporary account written by Father Bartolomé de las Casas. Two hundred years later, Spanish colonizers were killed during the wars of independence and/or were shipped back to Spain after independence. But the ties were not severed, and between 1850 and 1900, Latin America welcomed back the Spanish—about 2 million of them—except that now, they were returning as immigrants, not as rulers.

## Fear of Color

Aware that South America was a vast territory and there were more Native Americans and slaves in the colonies than Spaniards, the Spanish Crown proposed limited European immigration to the New World with the intent of keeping the region "white" and Catholic. By the 1600s, there were in the Americas immigrants from France, Italy, Germany, and Ireland. These immigrants were occupied in trade and shipping.

After the wars of independence (see Chapter 9), immigration from Europe continued. Venezuela needed laborers for its vast *latifundios*—large land holdings belonging to one person or family—and thus it beckoned over 60,000 immigrants from the Canary Islands. Argentina, eager to cultivate the pampas and raise cattle, called out to Italians, and nearly 4 million sons of Italy journeyed to South America between 1825 and 1900. Paraguay attracted Germans, and in the late 1800s, a German Mennonite community of about 6,000 settled in the Chaco region, a stretch of land between Paraguay and Bolivia. A few years after the Spanish-Cuban-American War of 1898, the republic of Cuba welcomed about 900,000 Spanish immigrants.

### Para Tu Información

Latin America is quite diverse, and this diversity is visible in the many languages spoken south of the border. Over 300 million Latin Americans speak Spanish, and about 150 million speak Portuguese. A million or so people in Central America speak Nahualt, the language of the Aztecs. In South America, you can still hear Quechua, the language the Inca rulers spoke at the time of the conquest. After Spanish, Guaraní is the official language in Paraguay.

Immigration from Europe continued during the 1900s. In Argentina, from about 1910 to 1920, three out of four residents of Buenos Aires had been born in either England or Italy. After World War II, about 300,000 Italians relocated to Argentina as well as hundreds of Germans. Ex-Nazis also traveled to Paraguay, moving into remote regions in the countryside. By 1958, there were 75,000 people from England, France, and Italy living in Paraguay.

In Chile, by the 1950s there were over 100,000 immigrants from England, France, Germany, Ireland, Italy, and Yugoslavia. In the Chilean region of Valdivia, a German community of 30,000 thrived, farming and running businesses in German. During the 1920s and '30s, about 1,000 immigrants a year entered Venezuela, and from the late '40s through the 1950s, over 350,000 *europeos*, or European settlers, settled in this nation. The majority of these immigrants came from Spain, followed by Italy, and then Portugal.

## From Asia

The Chinese traveled to Latin America the same way they came to the United States: as indentured servants. By the mid-1800s, an employment agency in China recruited, contracted, and transported Chinese workers to the New World. The contract committed the Chinese to eight years of labor, after which the worker could go back home or remain in Latin America and find another type of employment. Subjected to the hard labor of the sugar cane fields and mines, many of the workers didn't survive their eight-year commitment. Historian Luis Martínez Fernández points out in *Fighting Slavery in the Caribbean*, "A small portion … survived the duration of their terms, and even a smaller portion managed to return home. Many … succumbed to the numbing fumes of opium, the evasive promise of games of chance, and the ultimate escape offered by suicide."

### Para Tu Información

One area where the Chinese culture and Caribbean traditions joined together was in the kitchen. For example, the Chinese adapted some of their traditional dishes to Cuban tastes. Thus, they added pork, beef, shrimp, and egg to fried rice, and it was served with *croquetas*, croquettes, and *platanitos fritos*, fried bananas. There are variations of this culinary theme in the Dominican Republic and Puerto Rico.

By the end of the 1800s, there were about 40,000 Chinese in Mexico, about 150,000 in Cuba, and an equal number in Peru. With time, Chinese immigrants worked as street vendors and opened their own shops and restaurants. In Havana, they established an economic enclave—"el barrio chino"—packed with *fondas*, eateries, markets, movie houses, and vaudeville theaters.

**Hablas Español**

A **fonda** is a casual restaurant, often serving Chinese cuisine.

*Chinese workers in nineteenth-century Cuba.*

The Chinese suffered extensive discrimination and persecution in Latin America. During the Mexican revolution, many Mexicans resented Chinese merchants and turned against them, accusing them of spreading diseases, encouraging opium addiction, and preying upon the Mexican women. Many Mexican patriots thought it was their duty to call for the expulsion of the Chinese from Mexico, which in fact happened in 1931. Some of the expelled Chinese relocated to Cuba, Central America, Ecuador, and Peru.

## The Japanese

The vast majority of the Japanese in Latin America settled in Brazil, where they worked in coffee plantations; however, towards the 1890s, a group of about 1,000 Japanese men and women arrived in Peru. After working initially in agriculture, they moved to cities and towns, where they found employment as servants and set up cafeterias, barbershops, and ice cream businesses.

Prior to World War II, the Japanese-Peruvian community numbered fewer than 5,000. Many Japanese men married Peruvian women and, upon marriage, they converted to Catholicism and often changed their names. They were relatively well to do, kept abreast of developments in Japan, and established contacts with their compatriots in the United States. It was surprising, therefore, that after the attack on Pearl Harbor Franklin D. Roosevelt was so worried about the Japanese presence in South America that he ordered their capture and transfer to the United States. The Peruvian government obliged, and about 2,000 Japanese families—those who had not assimilated completely into Peruvian society—were shipped to the United States for detainment.

After the war, the Japanese continued to prosper in Peru, even producing a president, Alberto Fujimori. Today, there are about 100,000 Peruvians of Japanese descent, and the nation has strong commercial and cultural ties with Japan.

**Para Tu Información**

About 30,000 people from Latin America live in Japan. They are mostly recent arrivals, having moved to Japan within the last 10 years, and they live near major cities all over Japan. Ninety percent work in factories, clocking in six days a week, 10 hours a day.

## Judíos

*Judíos*—Jews—were not encouraged to come to Latin America during colonial times (see Chapter 14 for more on this). The situation was unchanged during the years immediately following the wars of independence. However, towards the end of the nineteenth century, as the need arose for laborers in rural areas and merchants in growing towns, and Latin American leaders were influenced by French liberalism, anti-Semitism grew more restrained, and Jewish immigration was encouraged.

Argentina was a favorite destination for Jews. From 1890 to 1900, about 30,000 Jews arrived in that country. By 1917, there were about 150,000 Jews—mostly from Central and Eastern Europe—in Argentina. About 20 percent of the Jewish immigrants came from North Africa and the Middle East.

---

| **Living La Vida Literaria** |
|---|

In *La Capital*, Jonathan Kandell describes the execution of Mexican Jews in sixteenth-century Mexico:

> The thirteen Jews marked for death [by the Inquisition] were … brought … to the plaza for execution. Twelve of them were garroted after yielding to the crowd's exhortations to … die as Christians … one of the victims, Tomas Trevino de Sobremonte, refused … to renounce his Jewish faith and was burned alive. As the flames seared his body, he shouted out: 'Throw on more wood—after all, I'm paying for it.'

Between the two world wars, over 100,000 Jews sailed to the Americas. Besides Argentina, they settled in Cuba, Central America, Mexico, Venezuela, and Uruguay. At the height of World War II, about 10,000 Jews arrived illegally, obtained visas, and then headed north to the United States. After 1948, with the establishment of Israel, many Jews from Latin America returned to their Promised Land.

Jewish cultural life thrived in Buenos Aires, Mexico City, and Havana. Yiddish poetry bloomed in Mexico a few years after the Mexican Revolution. Havana became the center for *Ladino* (the language written by the Sephardic Jews who were originally from Spain ) publishing until the advent of Castro's government in 1959. Buenos Aires was home to important Jewish writers and journalists, the likes of Samuel Pecar and Jacobo Timerman.

### Hablas Español

The **Ladino** language was spoken by Sephardic Jews who settled in the Middle East, Turkey, Greece, North Africa, and the Balkans after their expulsion from Spain in 1492. It is a form of archaic Spanish where instead of saying "hijo"—son—you say "fijo," for example. Sephardic Jews wrote poetry, stories, and religious essays in Ladino.

### Cuidado!

As in the United States, the subject of race and color is a sensitive matter among Latinos. It's a confusing and more complex subject than in the United States, where a bipolar racial system regards those with some traces of blackness as black, while Latinos tend to view color as dependent on a range of hue and pigmentation. For example, light-skinned Dominicans who regarded themselves as whites back home are surprised when Americans describe them as blacks. There are Central Americans and Mexicans who take pride in their Indian heritage, while there are others, especially in New Mexico, who boast of their Spanish conquistadores roots. What's the advice here? Be sensitive to your Latino friends and their views on race.

## Muslims and Moros

Historians believe that many Muslim Africans came to Latin America as slaves during colonial times, although it's hard to narrow down the figure. Most scholars suggest that about 15 to 20 percent of the slaves were Muslims.

### Hablas Español

A neighborhood or a community is a **barrio**; **arabes** is Spanish for Arabs and **turcos** is Spanish for Turks. Therefore, a **barrio arabe** is an Arabic community or neighborhood and a **barrio turcos** is a Turkish neighborhood.

### Para Tu Información

In 2001, a military expedition into the countryside of Peru discovered what might be a Muslim community in the middle of the jungle. The town features a mosque and small houses constructed in a Middle Eastern architectural style. The people who were roaming about were dressed in robes and were wearing turbans.

In the nineteenth century, moros from Syria and Lebanon settled in South America, establishing economic enclaves dubbed as *barrios moros*, *barrios arabes*, or *barrios turcos*. There were communities in Cuba, Colombia, Ecuador, and Peru. In Central America, particularly Panama, the moro residents had originally come from Pakistan and India. Many opened jewelry and clothing stores, though the vast majority worked as artisans and agriculturists. Again, it's difficult to determine the number of moros, because they were regularly pressured into baptism in the Christian faith, and it was a lot easier to blend in with the Christians than face persecution and high taxes.

Still, discrimination persisted, at least in the shape of resentment. Poor people envied the success of enterprising moros. For example, in Gabriel García Márquez's novel, *Chronicle of a Death Foretold*, which is based on an actual crime, a young man is murdered not only because he was accused of seducing a young woman in town but also because he was wealthy and from the Middle East.

Today, about 4 million Muslims live in South America. It's estimated that about 40,000 Latino Muslims reside in Chicago, New York City, and Washington, D.C. Many of these have converted from Catholicism or Protestantism.

# Discrimination

During colonial times, colonial aristocracy conjured a scheme of power and prestige based on color or national origin. In essence, the closer you were to Spain and Europe, the better person you were perceived to be. Years later, the scheme was adjusted to reflect color. In the conversion, the whiter you were, the better life was for you.

The social scheme worked like this:

◆ *Gachupines* were recent arrivals from Spain. As were *chapetones* and *peninsulares*. They were regarded as rude and ill-mannered and weren't liked by the aristocrats who lived in the Americas.

◆ *Criollos* were anyone born in the Americas but of 100 percent European extraction. The Spanish aristocracy viewed those in this group as second-class citizens.

◆ *Gente decente* were aristocratic criollos who had money.

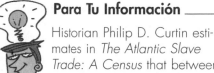

**Para Tu Información**

Historian Philip D. Curtin estimates in *The Atlantic Slave Trade: A Census* that between 8 and 10 million African slaves were brought to the Americas from colonial times to the abolition of the slave trade in the 1860s.

The racial scheme was arranged in this manner:

◆ A white person was on top of the world. This individual was either European or of European descent.

◆ *Mestizo* was the child of a European—or person of European descent—and a Native American. To become whiter, a mestizo was encouraged to marry a white person. A mestizo was regarded as a second class citizen.

◆ *Mulatto* was the child of a white person with a black person. A mulatto was perceived belonging in class lower than a mestizo.

**Hablas Español**

◆ A Spaniard or European recently arrived in Latin America is a **chapetón**.

◆ **Gachupín** or **cachupín** is a Spanish immigrant who settles in Latin America.

◆ **Gente decente** means decent people; **gente** is Spanish for people, though it can be used to refer to one person.

◆ A person with a father or mother who is white and a father or mother who is Native American is a **mestizo**.

◆ **Mulatto** is the child of a black-and-white union.

◆ Someone who comes from a peninsula is a **peninsular**; sometimes the word connotes a person who is closed-minded.

# Happy Coupling

Despite discrimination and racism, there was still a lot of mingling and mixing. It was a reality of the colonial experience. The initial waves of conquistadores and colonizers reached the New World without the company of ladies. Whether they were married or not, the Spanish invaders found the Caribbean and Mexican women attractive. Hernén Cortés coupled with Malinche, his translator, and they had a son, the first Mexican of the modern age, as author Carlos Fuentes dubbed him.

As Cabeza de Vaca walked his way through the United States, it's believed that he was probably accompanied by a Native American woman, though modest as he was he made no reference to any such liaison in his chronicles. The conquistadores who trekked north from Mexico into Texas and California came alone. And yet, populations of mestizos flourished. Obviously, something was going on between the beautiful ladies who inhabited those territories and the lusty Spanish explorers.

Centuries later, when the Chinese were contracted to work in the Americas, they came without their families. The need for companionship and love inspired them to court African slaves and black women in the Caribbean, and Indians in Central America and the Andean region of South America. The moros married each other, but also joined in matrimony with Criollas, often converting to Christianity and modifying their surnames to sound less exotic.

## What's in the Mix?

Some countries experienced more diversity than others. Here's a brief incursion into the territory of race and ethnicity:

- Argentines think of themselves as mostly European, emphasizing their European heritage in the national and popular culture.
- Chileans and Uruguayans are descendants of Europeans, though the Chilean population has traces of Araucanian Indians in their blood.
- There are a lot of Indian roots in the family tree of people from Central America and countries in the Andean region, most noticeably in Guatemala and Bolivia.
- The Caribbean, Colombia, Panama, and Venezuela have touches of Spain, Africa, and China.

It is this mixing that makes Latinos both exotic and bland, fair and dark; it's a mixing that defies easy categorization, adds to the confusion in attempts at describing the racial characteristics of Latinos, and above all, makes the whole discussion of Latino race and heritage and culture a lively engagement.

## The Least You Need to Know

- Like the United States, Latin America was and is a land of opportunities for immigrants.
- After Native Americans, the first people to come to Latin America were explorers from Spain.
- During colonial times, Spain invited Europeans to settle the vast colonial territories.
- Chinese came to the New World during the nineteenth century.
- Latinos are happy configurations of many cultures, nationalities, and races.

# Chapter 6

# The Lay of the Land: Mapping Latin America

## In This Chapter

- ◆ Mapping Mexico
- ◆ Touring Central America
- ◆ Navigating South America
- ◆ Sizing up notable Latin American isles

A few years after the Conquest, European theologians were convinced the New World was the original site of Eden, the biblical land of the beginning. Over the centuries, that notion lost its credibility, but the allure of the New World remained. During the 1800s, Latin America beckoned explorers who came armed, not with swords and muskets, but with quills and diaries. One such traveler was Alexander Von Humbolt, who is often referred to as America's second discoverer. He fell in love with the exotic flora and the beguiling fauna, writing extensively about South America and enticing other writers and explorers to come see it for themselves.

Sherlock Holmes creator Arthur Conan Doyle also succumbed to the magic, writing that if there were still dinosaurs around, the creatures would live in the lush jungles of Venezuela. He wrote about the region in *The Lost World*, which has been adapted several times for the big and the little screens. Even today, with increasing population levels, development, and depletion of the rain forests, Latin America still harbors forbidden landscapes and elusive creatures.

There is neither time nor space in this book to do justice to the geography of Latin America. But, in this chapter we'll scratch the surface of the terrain that covers the lands south of the border.

# An Awful Lot of Land

Latin America is huge. It extends south from the U.S. border all the way down to the frigid tip of the *Tierra del Fuego*, encompassing a total of 8,000,000 square miles, an area similar in size to the landmass occupied by the United States and Canada. This vast New World can be cordoned into three major areas: Central America, South America, and the Caribbean. Should we include North America as well? You bet, for Mexico is in North America, which is a little detail we often forget.

> **CAUTION**
>
> **Cuidado!** _____
>
> If you book a trip to Latin America expecting to find palm trees and beaches, make sure you do your research first, or you could end up in a chilly mountain village instead!

Obviously, with such an abundance of land, you get a lot of diversity in climate, flora, and fauna. And you get lots of mountains, valleys, and rivers.

# Making It to Mexico

Mexico is located just south of the United States. It consists of six areas:

- **The Pacific Northwest** Resembling the American west, the Mexican Pacific Northwest is a thin corridor of rolling mountains and deserts, and it includes the peninsula of Lower California.

- **The Plateau of Mexico** The Plateau of Mexico encompasses most of Mexico, and it is the birthplace of the majority of Mexican immigrants who come to the United States. Mexico City, founded on the ancient Aztec capital, Tenochtitlan, stands on this plateau, and the Sierra Madre Mountains, a range that covers about 75 percent of Mexico, frames it.

- **The Gulf Coast** Far on the east is the Gulf Coast, where many of Mexico's rivers flow into the sea.

- **The Southern Uplands** A region of mountains and gorges where the Aztecs mined gold. The famous resort town of Acapulco is located here.

- **The Chiapas Highlands** The Chiapas Highlands rise 9,000 feet above the sea, and on its top are flat stretches of land—called tablelands—that are still being farmed by the Mayas.

♦ **The Yucatan Peninsula** This landmass juts into the Gulf of Mexico and has a terrain of limestone and tropical forests. The popular beach town of Cancun is in the Yucatan.

## Para Tu Información

Mexico is a land of volcanoes. In 1943, it afforded geologists the opportunity to witness a volcano in the making. It happened one night in the town of Paricutín, to the south of Mexico City, where a farmer who was working in the fields suddenly heard a growling noise and saw a hole open up before him. Within seconds, steam was hissing through the hole which grew bigger and bigger. The farmer did the wise thing: he ran for his life.

By dawn, the hole had grown into a cone that was 150 feet high. Ten days later, the cone was an erupting volcano, spilling out lava and obliterating the town. It was the first time ever geologists were able to record the birth of a volcano.

Forests cover about 20 percent of Mexico towards the south, while the desert dominates the north. In the forests, azaleas, orchids, and poinsettias are abundant, whereas hundreds of species of cactus plants spike the northern desert. Mountain lions and deer make their homes in the forests; in the desert, wild coyotes howl and deadly rattlesnakes shake their rattles. Parrots, hummingbirds, and herons take to the sky almost everywhere in Mexico, while multi-colored quetzals lend their beauty and grace only to the forest. A wide variety of agricultural products, including bananas, chili peppers, corn, coffee, mangos, oranges, pineapples, potatoes, and tomatoes thrive in Mexico's fertile soil.

Over 700,000 square miles in size, Mexico has both a temperate and a tropical climate. If you travel to the capital in the winter, you will need a sweater. But if you visit Cancun during the same time of the year, you will probably want to cool off in the Caribbean Sea.

Mexico has one of the largest populations in the world—101,879,171, according to the *World Almanac 2002*—and is also home to the biggest city in the world. This is one reason why so many Mexicans migrate to the United States.

### Living La Vida Literaria

"Sprawling across a 7,500-foot-high valley surrounded in every direction by even taller mountains, Mexico City is poorly endowed as the industrial and commercial hub of a nation. The closest seaports lie hundreds of miles away, at the end of curving, tobogganing mountain roads. Unable to supply its hydraulic needs, the city must pump hundreds of millions of gallons of water ... from distant, lower-lying terrains ... the huge crush of new inhabitants [has] wiped out much of the valley's farmland ..."

—Jonathan Kandell, describing Mexico City in *La Capital*

# South to Central America

To the south of Mexico is the isthmus, or narrow land bridge, that makes up Central America. Today, Central America is home to Guatemala, Honduras, El Salvador, Nicaragua, Costa Rica, and Panama. Mountains form the backbone of Central America, with high ranges, steep gorges, and dozens of volcanoes—Guatemala alone has 14 major volcanoes.

On the West coast of Central America, the mountains plunge, as if in a hurry, into the Pacific Ocean. On the east, the lowlands climb gradually towards the mountains. The breeze from the Caribbean Sea blows in clouds, creating ideal conditions for rain and humidity, which, in turn, nurture the tropical forests. These forests are classified into two types: the rain forest, which is on the coast and is made up of massive trees; and the cloud forests, which paint the interior mountains and dormant volcanoes in a cover of solid green. Temperature depends on the altitude; the higher you go, the cooler it gets. Overall, though, Central American nations are described as experiencing an eternal spring.

### Hablas Español

Costa Rica means rich coast, reflecting the hopes of the conquistadores, who thought they would extract a lot of gold and silver from this nation. El Salvador is a religious allusion to Christ, the Savior. Honduras comes from hondo, or deep, and it's reflective of the deep valleys in between high mountains.

Swamps dot the East and West coasts. There are large lakes in Nicaragua and Guatemala to the east, and deserts to the west. Earthquakes are frequent, as are volcanic eruptions. The countries are small—El Salvador is smaller than New Jersey, and Nicaragua is smaller than Florida.

Jaguars, pumas, and deer inhabit the forests, and more than 700 species of birds are native to the region. Central America produces beans, cocoa, corn, and sugar cane, with coffee and bananas accounting for nearly 50 percent of the exports from the area.

## The Countries of Central America

| Country | Population | Capital |
| --- | --- | --- |
| Costa Rica | 3,710,558 | San Jose |
| El Salvador | 6,122,515 | San Salvador |
| Guatemala | 12,639,939 | Guatemala City |
| Honduras | 6,249,598 | Tegucicalpa |
| Nicaragua | 4,812,569 | Managua |
| Panama | 2,808,268 | Panama City |

Central America covers over 200,000 square miles. Towards the south, the landmass is a little more than 40 miles wide.

# The Deep South of South America

Traveling further southward, we move from the small Central American landmass to the vast continent of South America. The fourth largest of the world's continents, South America covers an area of 6,878,000 square miles. On the Pacific side, the Andes Mountains serve as the continent's backbone. On the Atlantic side, as if trying to match the scope of the Andes, the Amazon basin discharges the most fresh water in the world and is home to the biggest rain forests in the world. And then there's the Amazon river, all 4,000 miles of it, second in size only to the Nile on the other side of the globe. Pretty big, eh?

**Para Tu Información** _____

The Andes is the world's longest chain of high mountains, extending over 5,000 miles, nearly equivalent to the distance from New York to California and back.

*(Map by Armando H. Portelo)*

Geographers often divide South America into three distinct zones: 1) Amazonian region, 2) The Andes, and 3) The Southern Cone.

## Flying Down to Rio

We won't spend much time on Portuguese America. Why? Because we're dealing with Latinos from Spanish-speaking countries, and the folks from Brazil don't fall into this category. It gets complicated, but here is the logic: as noted in Chapter 4, Latino heritage is the marriage of the New World with Spain. The heritage of Brazil is a product of the mingling of the New World with Portugal. Brazilians speak Portuguese, and their holidays, celebrations, and their very history, is bound to Portugal, not Spain. Because the area covers a very large portion of the continent, you should know at least a little bit about it, though.

Brazil is one of the largest countries in the world: over three million square miles! Mountains dominate the eastern coast of Brazil, while the interior is home to the Amazonian rain forest. The Amazon River has many tributaries, including the Negro, the Xingu, and the São Francisco, which Brazilians have harnessed as a source of hydroelectric energy. Flatlands and swamps surround the Amazon River and are cyclically flooded by the mighty stream. The area is home to such exotic animals as the flesh-eating piranha, the slow moving sloth, and the mythic giant anaconda.

The nation's principal crops are coffee, soybeans, and sugar, as well as lumber. It is also the world's largest producer of iron.

---

### Living La Vida Literaria

"… under the bow of [the boat] there appeared a triangular head and several feet of undulating body. It was a giant anaconda. I sprang for my rifle as the creature began to make its way up the bank and … I … smashed a .44 soft-nosed bullet into its spine. As far as it was possible to measure, a length of forty-five feet lay out of the water, and seventeen feet in it, making a total length of sixty-two feet."

—Explorer Percy H. Fawcett's encounter with a giant anaconda, as recorded in *Lost Trails, Lost Cities*

---

Brazil is home to 174,468,575 inhabitants. Most people mistake either Rio de Janeiro or São Paulo as the country's capital, but it is Brasília.

## Climbing Up to the Andes

The Andean region is located on the northwest of South America, and it consists of the countries of Bolivia, Colombia, Ecuador, Peru, and Venezuela. The region includes some of the highest peaks in the world, such as Mount Aconcagua, which is over 20,000 feet tall, as well as tropical forests. Deserts can also be found in the Andean region near the mountains.

Most of the Andes look as if they were the continent's vertebrae, running through the center, but some of the ranges extend out to the Caribbean Sea, going right through Colombia.

*A Bolivian village at the foot of the Andes.*

*(Photo by Erica G. Polakoff)*

Geographically speaking, the Andes are made up of three separate ranges: the Cordillera Oriental, the Cordillera Central, and the Cordillera Occidental. The Cordillera Oriental is located in Venezuela. The Cordillera Central has many volcanoes, and its volcanic soil yields coffee beans, cultivated by the folks from Colombia. The long Cordillera Occidental flanks the West coast of the continent, forging a narrow coastline. The weather there depends on the altitude, and rainfall varies from one area to the next.

**Hablas Español**

In Spanish, a mountain range is called a **cordillera**.

**Para Tu Información**

One of the most majestic animals in the Andes is the Condor. Black, with white on the tip of the wings and around its neck, the Condor is about 54 inches long, with a wingspan of 10 feet. Soaring high over mountains and valleys, the stately bird flies effortlessly and elegantly, almost resembling a stealth fighter.

The puma and the jaguar reside in the Andean region, as do the armadillo and the llama. Aside from coffee, the region also produces cotton, cocoa beans, potatoes, and sugar, as well as marijuana and cocaine, made from the coca shrub. There are also vast *llanos*, flat lands, where cattle graze and, on the Peruvian side, harbors teem with fish and marine life.

Colombia is the only Latin American country that has a coastline both on the Pacific Ocean and the Caribbean Sea. Bolivia is land-locked, without even a river to connect it to the world. Venezuela is a country of geographic contrasts: It is home to the high mountains of the Andes as well as a good chunk of the Amazon forests.

## The Countries of the Andean Region

| Country | Population | Capital |
| --- | --- | --- |
| Bolivia | 8,300,463 | Sucre |
| Colombia | 40,349,388 | Bogota |
| Ecuador | 13,183,978 | Quito |
| Peru | 27,483,864 | Lima |
| Venezuela | 23,916,810 | Caracas |

### Living La Vida Literaria

"To the south lay the swamps, covered with an eternal vegetable scum, and the whole vast universe of the great swamp … had no limits. The great swamp in the west mingled with a boundless extension of water where there were soft-skinned cetaceans that had the head and torso of a woman … The ground became soft and damp, like volcanic ash, and the vegetation was thicker and thicker, and the cries of the birds and the uproar of the monkeys became more and more remote … in that paradise of dampness and silence …"

—Gabriel García Márquez, describing a South American swamp in *One Hundred Years of Solitude*

## Rolling On to the Southern Cone

The third region of South America is known as the Southern Cone. Argentina, Chile, Paraguay, and Uruguay (also parts of Brazil) comprise the cone. The flatland, called the Pampa, is one of the famous features in the region.

The Pampa is an extensive grassland located smack in the middle of the Southern Cone, stretching between Argentina and Uruguay. The air is humid in the east and dry in the west of the region. The soil in the Pampa is good, and it receives adequate rainfall, providing ideal conditions for raising cattle and growing sunflower seeds, peanuts, soybeans, and wheat.

The Pampa's Central Valley is known for its wines. It is an area that is cool and humid in the winter, warm and dry in the summer. Much of central Chile is located in the fertile valley.

Windswept and arid Patagonia is located to the south of the Central Valley. Remote and rocky, Patagonia is ideal for sheep herding, although the recent discovery of oil and natural gas has lead to industrial development in the region.

Finally, *Tierra del Fuego* sits at the very tip of the continent, separated from Patagonia by the Straits of Magellan. This icy territory, a polar post far from civilization, is the very antithesis of what people think Latin America looks like.

Argentina, Chile, Paraguay, and Uruguay have temperate climates, though Paraguay is the warmest of the four. The summers are mildly warm and the winters are snowy—the further south you travel in the winter, the more snow you will find. The seasons are the opposites from the seasons in the United States. So, if you go south in July, take your skis. If you book a trip in February, don't forget to pack your bathing suit.

**Hablas Español**

**Llano** is Spanish for something flat and plain. **Pampa** is the Spanish adaptation of the Quechua word for plain. It refers to the treeless plains in Argentina. **Tierra del Fuego** means the land of fire. This was what explorer Magellan called the territory when at night he saw the natives lighting many fires to stay warm.

## The Countries of the Southern Cone

| Country | Population | Capital |
|---|---|---|
| Argentina | 37,384,816 | Buenos Aires |
| Chile | 15,328,467 | Santiago |
| Paraguay | 5,734,139 | Asunción |
| Uruguay | 3,360,105 | Montevideo |

Argentina looks like an elongated and very trim triangle. Chile is pencil thin. Paraguay, resembling an amoeba, is landlocked. Uruguay is a misshaped square, only slightly bigger than Georgia.

# Cruising the Sunny Caribbean

The Caribbean countries are a group of islands between the United States and the South American continent. These islands tread the Caribbean Sea, which is nearly 900 nautical miles long and extends from the United States to the coast of Mexico to the northeast of South America. The Latinos who fly or sail to the United States from the Caribbean come from three islands: Cuba, Hispaniola, and Puerto Rico.

*(Map by Armando H. Portelo)*

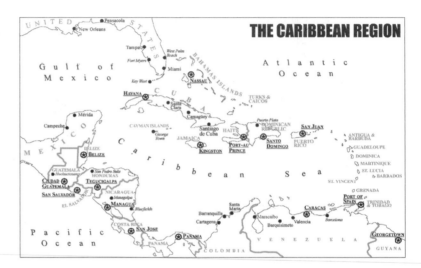

**THE CARIBBEAN REGION**

Cuba is the largest of the Caribbean islands. Shaped like a crocodile, the island is 42,800 square miles and lies directly under Florida, 90 nautical miles away. It is a green island of plains and valleys. The Sierra Maestra range, where Castro hid during the revolution, is the highest elevation on the island, rising to of 7,872 feet at its highest point. In the summer, the temperature is about 90 degrees Fahrenheit; in the winter, the temperature seldom dips below 70 degrees. It's warm enough to swim almost all year long, but the sea tends to be rougher during Octo-ber and November, the time for hurricanes. Sugar and tobacco are the major crops. The Zum-zum, the smallest hummingbird in the world, makes Cuba its home.

The island of Hispaniola is home to two countries, the Creole and French-speaking Haiti and Spanish-speaking Dominican Republic. Hispaniola is formed by the peaks of two underwater mountains, one coming from Cuba, the other from Jamaica. The Cordillera Central range runs through the country, going from the west to the east. Most of Dominican Republic is mountainous, but its eastern end tends to be flat; sugar cane is cultivated in

**Para Tu Información**

Caribbean comes from **Caribe,** the name of the aborigines who lived on the southwestern most islands when Columbus arrived. The Caribes came from South America. Fierce and feared warriors, the Caribes invaded the islands sometime around 1300 B.C.E. They were said to eat their victims.

the south of this area. Tobacco is planted on the slopes of the northern range of mountains, called the Cordillera Septentrional.

*Caribbean forest.*

*(Courtesy of North Wind Picture Archives)*

A rare rat-like species lives in the Dominican Republic. Called solenodon, it runs about on the edges of its feet and is described as having a friendly face. Only a handful of people have recently spotted this tiny mammal.

At 3,435 square miles, Puerto Rico is the smallest of the Spanish-speaking Caribbean islands. North of the island, the sea drops 30,000 feet below sea level. On the south, there is an underwater channel that is 16,000 feet deep. From a plane, Puerto Rico looks like a massive rock shooting upwards from the bottom of the sea. A mountain range, the Cordillera Central, runs from the east to the west on the southern part of the island. Sugar cane grows on the south of the island. The coqui, a tiny and almost transparent frog, is a rare species found only in Puerto Rico.

## The Island Countries of the Caribbean

| Country | Population | Capital |
| --- | --- | --- |
| Cuba | 11,184,023 | Havana |
| Dominican Republic | 8,581,477 | Santo Domingo |
| Puerto Rico | 3,808,610 | San Juan |

# Latin American Isles

There are a few islands in Latin America that have become famous either because of their geography or history.

◆ **Falklands (or Malvinas), Argentina:** Though this island of rocks and cold winds is located in Argentine territory, it belongs to the British. And that's why the island is famous. The Argentines claimed it during colonial times, but the British took over the island in 1833. Since then, the two nations have argued over possession. In 1982, Argentine troops landed on the island and tried to take it, but the British repelled the invasion. People in Latin America refer to the island as Las Islas Malvinas.

◆ **Galapagos, Ecuador:** A group of islands made up of volcanic peaks. Charles Darwin visited them in 1835 and wrote about the mysterious creatures that live on the islands. Some of these creatures include giant turtles that weigh more than 500 pounds, birds that can't fly, and giant iguanas. During the nineteenth century, mutineers from ships were often abandoned on the island.

◆ **Isla de la Juventud, Cuba:** This island, The Island of Youth, was originally named Isla Evangelista by Christopher Columbus. Later on, the name was changed to Isla de Pinas. Novelist Robert L. Stevenson used it for the setting of his adventure novel *Treasure Island*, dubbing the island la Isla del Tesoro.

◆ **Vieques, Puerto Rico:** Often in the news, this island is owned and is used by American armed forces for training and war games, including bombing campaigns. Puerto Ricans object to the military use and have invaded the island on several occasions, trying to stop army maneuvers from taking place.

Even though today we know that the world south of the border is not Eden, it might as well be. For its beauty continues to invite tourists and haunt the memories of those who left, planting in their hearts a desire to return one day, to journey south, following the path that ancient nomadic tribes took centuries ago.

## The Least You Need to Know

◆ Central America, South America, the Caribbean, and parts of North America make up Latin America.

◆ Mexico is as much a North American nation as the United States.

◆ Latin America has a wide range of climates and geographies.

◆ When it's summer in the United States, it's winter in the Southern Cone, and vice versa.

◆ Latin America gets a lot of sunshine, but it also gets a lot of snow.

# Mayas, Aztecs, and Incas: America's Pre-European Civilizations

## In This Chapter

◆ The glory that was Middle America

◆ Maya's shining moment

◆ The ascent of the Aztecs

◆ The road to the Incas

◆ The fruit of ancient labor

It's windy. It's frigid. Ice extends before you like a gigantic corridor made up of sparkling silver. Then, you see dark figures on the horizon, heading your way, growing in size. It's a herd of mammoths, dozens of them. Behind them, there are men dressed in bison furs, tracking the mammoths, hoping to catch one of the mammals for a polar picnic. These hunters make their way across the Bering Strait to North America. Some head for the Midwest, others continue south to the Southwest and then Mexico, Central America, and South America.

This was the scene about 40,000 years ago when nomadic groups from Europe and Asia migrated to the New World. During the Ice Age, the sea between Europe and Alaska was a frozen land bridge that connected the two continents and the ancestors of the ancient people of the Americas migrated to the New World crossing over the frozen Straits of Bering. Get ready to join the migration and meet the descendants of the first immigrants.

# Oh, MAI: The Mayas-Aztecs-Incas

*Three.*

That's the magic number. There were three advanced civilizations in the Americas when Columbus arrived. How advanced? As advanced as Ancient Egypt and Ancient Rome, and more advanced than Spain and Portugal in 1492.

The three civilizations were, in order of first appearance, the Mayas, the Aztecs, and the Incas.

## The Maya Flower

The first major, and longest lasting, civilization in pre-1492 Americas was that of the Mayas, who flourished for 2,000 years in *Mesoamerica*, or Middle America, an area that encompassed Mexico and Central America. Descendants of the Olmec, a people who sculptured giant faces out of monoliths, the Mayas erected soaring pyramids that played tricks on the eyes: for at a given moment during the year, the sun would cast shadows on the edifices, shadows in the shape of snakes—due to the positioning of the steps—that seemed to slither down the pyramid.

**Hablas Español**

**Mesoamerica** means Middle America. Meso comes from the Greek for middle.

**Para Tu Información**

The Mayas believed that men and women were made of corn. According to Mayan beliefs, God had creatures made out of clay, then wood, followed by straw. But God was not satisfied with his creation and destroyed them all. He was only happy when he made men and women out of maize.

The Mayas also designed accurate 365-day calendars, invented the concept of zero, practiced accounting, and kept written records—in the form of hieroglyphs—on vases, pillars, and monuments that described religious practices, adventures of ancestors, and family genealogies.

There were two Mayan civilizations. The first lived in Guatemala. Known as the Classic Mayas, scholars regard them as sages because they studied the arts and astronomy and were peaceful by nature. The Classic Mayas created cities, with large temples atop pyramids, buildings with many rooms, huge open plazas, and ball courts where a type of basketball game was played. Historians believe that about 10,000 people lived in the Maya city of Tikal, a sprawling urban center.

Maya cities had their own government and were ruled by members of the same family. Sometimes, a city administered the villages in its vicinity, but overall the Mayas didn't have a central government, the way the Aztecs and the Incas did later on.

## Maya Decline

The Classic Maya civilization lasted from 250 to 900 C.E. Sometime around 800, the Mayans left their cities, including Tikal. No one knows why, but theories abound. One explanation is that cities were overpopulated, and their inhabitants set out to look for greener pastures. Another theory is that the exhaustion of natural resources, coupled with disease, toppled the cities. A third possibility was that a rebellion against a ruling family, and the subsequent political fallout, drove the people away. Who knows?

*An ancient pyramid in Chichén Itzá.*

Around 900, the Mayas moved to Yucatan, where they merged their culture with that of the Toltecs, who were originally from northern Mexico and had migrated to the Atlantic coast, probably running away from the Aztecs. Together, the two peoples built the city of Chichén Itzá. A tall pyramid dominated this city, erected near a deep well where it's believed sacrificial victims were dumped. Near the well there was a ball yard and a large palace with many rooms, as well as numerous sculptures of gods worshipped by the Toltecs. Chichén Itzá was administered by a group of advisers, probably a combination of priests and warriors.

**Para Tu Información**

The Mayas played ball. The game took place in a long courtyard, flanked by tall walls. Attached to the walls, at opposite ends of the field, were two loops. The object of the game was to get a ball, made of leather or tree roots and weighing eight pounds, to pass through the loop. Neither feet nor hands could be used. Players had to push and propel the balls forward with their heads, shoulders, even hips. As you can imagine, it was very difficult to score, so the moment a team managed to get a ball through the loop, the game was over. It's theorized that the losing team was a big time loser, for they were sacrificed.

By the way, in case you want to try the game, the ancient ballpark in Chichén Itzá still stands.

By now, the Maya civilization was in decline. Around 1200, there was a revolt against the Maya-Toltec rulers, and people again left the city. When the conquistadores arrived in the 1500s, they found the abandoned temples and pyramids of Chichén Itzá and Tikal.

A brief chronology of Mayan Civilization is as follows:

- **800 B.C.E.:** Mayas build pyramids.
- **250 B.C.E.:** Classic Maya civilization blooms.
- **800 C.E.:** Mayas stop erecting cities.
- **900:** Classic Maya era comes to an end. Mayas move to Yucatan.
- **1200:** Chichén Itzá declines.
- **1400:** Maya Empire breaks down into provinces.
- **1500:** Spanish conquer the Mayas.

# The Eagle and the Serpent

The Aztecs were the rulers of central Mexico at the time of the conquest. Like the ancient Romans, they were warriors. Like the ancient Romans, they adopted the cultures of the people they conquered. And like the ancient Romans, they were doomed.

Arriving in Mexico sometime in the 1200s, the Aztecs journeyed from a place in the north called Aztlán, located somewhere in the United States, perhaps even in Utah. Guided by divine providence, in a Mesoamerican version of Moses and the journey of the people of Israel, the Aztecs looked for the promised land and found it in a valley where, in 1325, they built the city-state of Tenochtitlán.

Tenochtitlán consisted of several small islands connected to man-made isles of woven, pressed roots, plants, and piles of mud, fortified with rocks. Dozens of temples and pyramids, decorated with intricate carvings, were erected on the islands. There was also an aqueduct, built miles away, and a viaduct that brought drinking water to the city. The design and sophistication of the city demonstrate the Aztec's knowledge of architecture and engineering, and the murals and carvings on the walls of the temples told, through pictograms, the history of the Aztecs.

Two hundred years after the founding of the city there were 300,000 Aztecs living in Tenochtitlán, more people than in any city in Europe. No wonder the Spanish were dumbfounded when they first caught a glimpse of the Valley of Mexico!

> ### Living La Vida Literaria
>
> In *La Capital,* Kandell describes how the Aztecs found the promised land: "[the god] Huitzilopochtli ... ordered them to continue their quest for the promised land, which they would recognize at a lake with a small island where an eagle perched on a cactus plant was devouring a snake. This divinely appointed scene unfolded on a lake in the Valley of Mexico, and it was there that the Aztecs built their great city-state ..."

# The Fighting Aztecs

The Mexican valley wasn't empty of people when the Aztecs arrived. People already settled in the area pushed the Aztecs out of the valley, calling them nomads. The Aztecs stayed put, often hiring themselves out as mercenaries and thus learning the art of war. As they became skilled fighters and as their population grew, the Aztecs developed a reputation for bravery and cunning. They even used spies to learn about the people surrounding them; for example, when a merchant passed through the valley, an Aztec would follow him home and then would come back with information about the merchant's village. Based on the intelligence, Aztec warriors would attack the village. In this way, merchant-by-merchant and village-by-village, the Aztecs built their empire.

Aztec warriors didn't fight to kill. Their objective was to capture prisoners who could be sacrificed. The Aztecs worshiped many gods, and some of the gods demanded the pulsating heart of a living victim. It's reported that at one time, the Aztecs sacrificed 20,000 prisoners during one gigantic and drawn-out celebration. When Hernán Cortés and his men entered Tenochtitlán, they were taken aback by the sight of fresh blood on the temple walls and the scent of rotting flesh.

> ### Cuidado!
>
> The Aztecs didn't call themselves by that name. They used Mexica instead. The Mexicans told the conquistadores that they came from an area called Aztlán, but the conquistadores thought the Mexicans were telling them that they were Aztecs. Thus, the origin of the name. Today, people in Mexico use Mexica to refer to the Aztecs, but throughout most of the world people are still using Aztec.

The sacrifices made the Aztecs detestable to other Indians in the area. The neighboring Indians, seeing themselves as potential sacrificial lambs for the Aztecs, joined forces with Hernán Cortés and his men to fight against the Aztecs. The way these Indians saw it, they were neither helping the Spanish nor betraying their country, but were fighting against an evil empire.

# A Doomed People

Superstitious to the core, the Aztecs were fatalists. They believed that existence was cyclical and that their world consisted of five suns, or eras. The last era, called the fifth sun, signaled the end of the world.

Just before 1519, the Aztec astronomers saw a comet in the heavens. Then, one night the waters of the lake bubbled up. There was also a report of a woman wailing in the middle of the night, begging for the return of her missing children. To top it off, a high priest prophesied the return of the white god Quetzalcoatl, sailing in from the east.

Who happens to sail in just about now? Hernán Cortés, whom the Aztecs took for a god and their enemies took for an ally. Everything was set in motion. Cortés captured emperor Moctezuma, who almost to the bitter end believed the conquistadore was a god, and took over Tenochtitlán without a struggle. But in 1520, the Aztecs, who viewed their emperor as too weak, staged a rebellion against Cortés and when Moctezuma tried to pacify them, his former subjects shot arrows and rocks at the emperor, killing him. Cortés and the Aztecs then battled each other. But not for long; by 1521 the Aztecs were defeated, and the glory of the empire was no more.

Though outnumbered by the Aztec warriors, the Spanish were better equipped. The Spanish had horses and guns, the equivalent of an armored tank back then. They also had double-edged and sharp-pointed swords. The Aztecs' swords were blunt, not designed to kill and maim but to render the enemy unconscious, so he could be captured and sacrificed. In essence, a blow from a conquistadore meant death or the loss of a limb. Furthermore, the Spanish had a secret weapon, one that historians think was more potent than all the others: they inadvertently carried the smallpox virus with them. With no anti-body in their system, the disease annihilated thousands of Aztecs in a matter of days.

A brief chronology of the Aztec Empire is as follows:

- ◆ **1100:** Aztecs migrate from Aztlán.
- ◆ **1200:** Aztecs reach Valley of Mexico.
- ◆ **1325:** Founding of Tenochtitlán.
- ◆ **1400:** Expansion of Aztec Empire.
- ◆ **1519:** Arrival of the Spanish.
- ◆ **1520:** Capture of Aztec Emperor.
- ◆ **1521:** Destruction of the Aztec Empire.

# Inca, Inc.

The road to hell was paved by the Incas. Or so it seemed. For it was a road engineered and constructed by the Incas that led the Spanish conquistadores to the very heart of Peru, where they captured the Inca emperor.

The Incas rivaled the Aztecs in splendor and power—though the two groups didn't know of each other. They ruled one of the richest and largest empires in the world: 25,000 miles of a territory that included parts of Colombia, Ecuador, Peru, Bolivia, Chile, and Argentina.

*An Inca Descendant.*

*(Photo by Erica G. Polakoff)*

The territory was administered through a bureaucratic structure in which groups of families were ruled by a chief, an administrator similar to a mayor. A group of chiefs was overseen by a governor; and the governors were accountable to the emperor and his advisers. The inhabitants of the towns and villages conquered by the Incas were instructed to follow this political system. Carlos Fuentes comments on the skills required to succeed at governing such a large system in *The Buried Mirror*; "… to unite and govern this immense, variegated land required enormous gifts of statesmanship and a most energetic organization. Ancient Peru had both."

The Inca Empire began in 1438, when the Incas defeated rival tribes and started to expand their kingdom to the south of present-day Cuzco. For the next 50 years or so, the Incas ventured into Chile and Argentina, conquering both lands.

# Power Of Persuasion

The Incas were skilled soldiers and strategists. Upon seeing the enemy, they first tried to persuade their leaders to become friends and allies. If this didn't work, the Incas would attempt to bribe them by offering them jewels, food, and slaves. If this failed, then the Inca generals would harangue the enemy while parading the Inca troops, as if saying, "don't be a fool, don't fight against us."

If the adversaries turned out to be fools, then they had to contend with a well-planned attack that consisted first of archers and sling men shooting arrows and rocks, followed by lancemen shooting spears, and, finally, by the infantry descending upon them with axes and blunted swords. Before the final attack, the Inca commanders would gather intelligence to figure out just how large the opposing forces were and who were the leaders. For the Incas, fighting was not a gut reaction. It was a planned effort, with a structure and rules of behavior.

Like the Aztecs, the Incas didn't fight to kill their enemies. Instead, they fought to make them part of their empire and to civilize them. You see, the Incas had good self-esteem and they wanted to shape the world in their own image.

> **CAUTION**
>
> ### Cuidado! _____
>
> The Incas didn't refer to themselves as Incas. In fact, there were many nations with many different names under the rule of the Inca Empire. The word "Inca" meant emperor or ruler. The Spanish mistakenly thought anyone who lived in Peru was called an Inca.

# The Way of the Incas

The Incas had a mail delivery system. They used the decimal system to arrange their society into groups of tens, hundreds, and so on. They also had an accurate method of computing. It was called the "quipu," and it consisted of a horizontal cord with other braided cords branching from it. Knots on the cords indicated a numeral value, let's say number 10, number 100, etc. By tying a stick to a cord, you could keep a running count of just about anything. And they even composed religious, historical, and personal poems.

The Incas constructed cities, fortresses, and giant artwork. Cuzco, the capital, was arranged like a chessboard, with two plazas in the center. The emperor lived in one plaza in a building that had large rooms and was decorated with gold figurines, ceramic jars, and woven

> **Living La Vida Literaria**
>
> The following is an excerpt from a personal poem:
>
> Two enamored doves
> Sigh, weep and grieve
> For the snow separates them
> On a dry, woodwormed tree trunk.

fabrics with geometric drawings. Machu Picchu, an Incan city that still stands today, was a fortress of stones and large rocks built atop a mountain. Nazca was a larger-than-life natural canvas where the Incas drew pictures of giant creatures—a spider and a jaguar, to name a few. These pictures were not visible from the ground—only from the sky.

# A Fatal Flaw

The Incas practiced a form of socialism—everything was owned by the state, and the state provided for everyone. For example, when a child was born, the state gave the family a plot of land. When someone died, the state took away from the family a plot of land. All in all, it was a pretty good political system … with one fatal flaw.

Only the emperor could choose the next ruler, and if the emperor died without identifying his successor, the court would plunge into intrigue and even war. That's what happened when the Spanish arrived in the sixteenth century.

Just before the conquistadores reached Peru, dying emperor Huayna Capac couldn't decide who would be the next ruler: son number one or son number two. So, he made the two brothers—Huáscar in one corner, Atahualpa in the other—the top cheeses of the empire. That was a bad decision. For the two brothers went to war against each other and the victor, Atahualpa, was still solidifying his base (his dead brother had many supporters) when in marched Francisco Pizarro in 1532. The rest is history. Pizarro strangled the emperor, found a demoralized country, and took over the Inca Empire.

A brief timetable for the Incas is as follows:

- **1100:** The Incas arrive in Peru.
- **1200:** Cuzco is settled.
- **1438:** The birth of the Inca Empire.
- **1527:** Civil War breaks out between Atahualpa and Huáscar.
- **1532:** Atahualpa kills Huáscar. Spanish reach the empire. Pizarro murders Atahualpa.

### Cuidado!

Back in the 1970s, self-described "scholar" Eric Von Danniken suggested in his book, *Chariots of the Gods*, that the sophisticated architecture and sculpture of the Aztecs, Incas, and Mayans was the result of outer-space intervention. In other words, that Martians were responsible for the wonders of pre-Columbus civilizations. Aside from pure nonsense—though fascinating—the suggestion was highly insulting to Latinos. For them, it meant that a European regarded people from Latin America as too inferior and primitive to be able to construct such wonders.

# Other Civilizations

The big three are the most famous pre-Columbian civilizations. But there were others as well:

◆ **Araucanian Indians** were from the Southern Cone— Chile and Argentina. They fought the Spanish for nearly three centuries.

◆ **Caribes** were warriors from the Caribbean islands. Presumed to be cannibalistic, the Caribes were feared by the Taino Indians (more on them later).

◆ **Chavíns** preceded the Incas. They lived near Cuzco, Peru, and it's believed they were the first people in the Americas to live in cities.

◆ **Patagones** were hunters from the tip of South America. The region called Patagonia is named after these Indians.

◆ **Tainos** were Indians of the Caribbean. They lived near the sea, which yielded its bounty to these peaceful Indians. The Tainos were the first Native Americans to encounter the Spanish.

◆ **Tarascan** were fishing people from Mesoamerica. It is believed they migrated from north of Mexico with the Aztecs.

What we know today about pre-Columbian civilizations comes from numerous sources. Years after the conquest, a descendant of emperor Atahualpa, a writer by the name of El Inca Garcilaso de La Vega, wrote a chronicle of his ancestors, based on factual information. Priests also chronicled information gathered from newly converted Mayas, Incas, and so on. Over decades of research, archeologists have deciphered hieroglyphs and pictograms engraved by the Aztecs and Mayas. Murals have also yielded snap shots of major events as well as of daily life in ancient America.

# Gifts from the Past

Some of the pyramids and temples built by the Maya, Inca, and Aztec still stand. You need only travel to Mexico and Central America to witness their splendor. But the ancient people left more than ruins behind. Just a few of the legacies left by these early Latin Americans include the following:

◆ Emperor Moctezuma loved to sip a drink that was dark brown and a had a pleasant aroma. It was called xocolatl; today we call it chocolate.

◆ If you happen to have Irish ancestors who were potato farmers, you might find it hard to believe that before the conquest of the Americas they didn't grow potatoes. Potatoes originated in the Americas, cultivated by the Incas.

◆ Did Italians pour tomato sauce over their pasta in 1492? No, not really. Tomato was planted in the Americas by the Aztecs; its name was xitomatl.

◆ Probably the most famous product to reach Europe after the discovery was tobacco, which Columbus first saw in use when he reached Cuba in 1492.

Latinos take great pride in the ancient cultures of the Americas, and it's easy to see why.

*Potatoes and other products that originated in ancient Latin America.*

## The Least You Need to Know

◆ The Aztec, Inca, and Mayan civilizations were more advanced than Spain, Portugal, and most of Europe at the time.

◆ The destruction of the pre-Colombian empires was more the result of the introduction of diseases, such as smallpox, than actual combat.

◆ Lots of chronicles, diaries, and architectural wonders help us reconstruct the life and times of the Aztecs, Incas, and Mayas.

◆ Such daily staples as tomatoes and potatoes originated in the Americas.

# The Spanish Are Coming, the Spanish Are Coming: Colonization and Conquest

## In This Chapter

- ◆ Surprising and enterprising ladies
- ◆ Clash of Titans: The Christians and the Muslims
- ◆ The not-so-flat world
- ◆ Cortés, Pizarro, and company
- ◆ Don't cry for me, America

According to legend, no one believed Christopher Columbus when he said the world was round. In reality, no one was laughing at the sailor for his claims about the shape of the Earth—most of the people who Columbus was dealing with in the royal court were educated and knew the world wasn't flat. What they doubted were his estimates as to how near Asia—his destination—was to Spain, and his claim that it was possible to reach it by sailing west.

In this chapter, we'll retrace the path of the Nina, the Pinta, and the Santa Maria, making our own journey of discovery to find out who won and who lost in Europe's encounter with the Americas.

# A Mighty Queen and a Daring Explorer

Way before the modern Women's Movement there was a woman who caused a great deal of movement: from the North to the South and from the East to the West. Like Helen of Troy, the lady-in-question launched a thousand ships, with thousands of soldiers on board those ships. Her name was Queen Isabella.

*Pre-Columbus Caribbean.*

### Para Tu Información

Ferdinand and Isabella shared duties evenly, as described in their motto, *Tanto monta, monta tanto, Isabel como Fernando,* a figure of speech that can be translated as Isabel rides a horse as well and as often as Ferdinand.

### Hablas Español

**La reconquista** is the noun for the reconquest, from the verb reconquistar, to reconquer.

Queen Isabella, of the kingdom of Castile (located in present-day Spain), was a devout Catholic with a calling: to reconquer Spain from the Moors and to expand her kingdom. She married King Ferdinand, of the kingdom of Aragon (also in present-day Spain), and together they formed a mighty force that set out to push the Moors out of the peninsula. The Moors, who were Muslims, had invaded Spain in the early 700s, occupying a territory bigger than Texas. Bit by bit, the Spanish rebelled against the Moors, calling their effort *La reconquista,* for the conquered ones were trying to conquer the conquerors. (Remember Cabeza de Vaca's ancestor from Chapter 3? He was a participant in La reconquista.)

Through four centuries of fighting, the Spanish gained ground, retaking cities from the Moors. By the 1400s, the Moors' last stronghold was in the city of Granada. A determined Isabella and Ferdinand planned a massive assault on Granada. In 1492, after a long and arduous campaign, the Christian army reconquered the last bastion of Moorish power, civilization, and culture on the peninsula.

# An Offer You Can't Refuse

Soon after the retaking of Granada, a chap with an idea caught Queen Isabella's eyes and piqued Ferdinand's curiosity. It was a simple idea: "I can sail west from Spain, and not only am I not going to fall into the abyss, I'm going to reach Asia." Intoxicated with their defeat of the Moorish empire and the unification of Spain into one kingdom, the Catholic couple, who needed a new pet project, nodded their approval. Why not?

It was a cheap enterprise, after all: it only required three ships and the promise to make the fellow an admiral, give him some wealth, and throw in a heritage for his descendants for good measure. That was not a big deal, considering he might disappear in the fearsome sea of mystery. Thus, in October 1492, the former Cristoforo Columbus, but now called Cristobal Colón to demonstrate that he had become a Spanish subject, set sail upon the blue sea.

*Christopher Columbus.*

### Para Tu Información

Queen Isabella was a tough cookie—tough and shrewd. As a youngster, she survived the back-stabbings that went on in court, didn't let her brother, who was the king of Castile, boss her around, and stopped his daughter, who was her niece, from ascending to the throne. As a young queen, she fought off suitors and chose her own groom, with whom she formed a loving marriage, not a requirement for a successful monarchy. She and her husband divided their labor; she concentrated on national matters, and he administered foreign affairs. The queen did make a few major blunders. One was the creation of the Inquisition. The other was the expulsion of the Jews from Spain in 1492, creating a brain drain that lasted for centuries.

You probably already know the plot of this adventure, including many "facts," which just happen to be fiction. Before checking on the progress of our fearless admiral's journey, let's take a second to quench a few rumors about Colón, a.k.a Christopher Columbus, and the queen:

♦ Queen Isabella was not in love with Colón.

♦ Queen Isabella did not have to pawn her jewels to finance the trip. She had money to pay for it, and there were a few other investors interested in the enterprise.

♦ Colón didn't sail with a crew of crooks, fresh out of jail. A trained and experienced navigator, he signed on 90 professionals, including physicians, linguists, map makers, priests, servants, and a secretary.

♦ Colón didn't become a celebrity in his own time. There are no contemporary portraits of him and nothing, not even a baño, was named after him during his lifetime.

# Calling Off Columbus

Colón—okay, let's use Columbus for a while—Columbus made four journeys to the New World:

♦ **1492–1493:** Lands on the islands of San Salvador, in the Bahamas, Cuba, and Hispaniola (present-day Dominican Republic and Haiti).

♦ **1493–1496:** Disembarks on Puerto Rico.

♦ **1498–1500:** Reaches Trinidad and sights Venezuela and the Orinoco River.

♦ **1502–1504:** Sails to Martinique and travels along the coast of Central America.

After his return to Spain in 1504, Columbus didn't take to the sea again. He died two years later, half believing that he had found a route to Asia, and half suspecting that he had found another continent. Contrary to common belief, Columbus didn't die poor. For although he had been reprimanded for being a weak administrator, allowing the Native-Americans on the island to be mistreated by his men, he kept much of the wealth the monarchs had bestowed on him. His titles were passed on to his descendants, who are still a noticeable presence in Spain.

### Para Tu Información

Admiral Columbus tried to colonize the island of Hispaniola. But he was a navigator and an explorer, not a manager. To keep his men happy, he allowed them to enslave the Taino Indians. Eventually, a rebellion broke out which Columbus quelled. Learning about trouble in paradise, Queen Isabella sent an investigator, who was not friendly towards the admiral. When the investigator saw that Columbus had imprisoned the leaders of the rebellion against him, he released the prisoners and arrested Columbus, chaining him. In Spain, Columbus was freed and forgiven by the king and queen.

Sometime after the admiral's death, other dreamers sailed the sea of blue, arriving in the New World like bats out of hell to suck the gold—and life itself—from the Native-Americans. Two of the most famous were Hernándo Cortés and Francisco Pizarro.

# Oh, Lucky Man

He came. He saw. He conquered. That sums up the career of conquistador par excellence Hernándo Cortés.

In 1519, Cortés prepared to set sail from the Spanish colony of Cuba to Mexico, a country that had been discovered a few years earlier. Before departing, Cortés assembled an expedition of 500 soldiers, some horses, and muskets and cannons. Cortés was in search of gold and something equally as precious to him: GLORY, in capital letters. In *The Buried Mirror*, Carlos Fuentes writes that Cortés "... had come to fashion his own destiny, a destiny of power, wealth, and glory, achieved through ... personal determination, aided by a bit of good luck."

And, boy, was he lucky! To begin with, when he disembarked in Mexico, the Aztecs thought Cortés was Quetzalcoatl, the white god who had promised to return to Mexico. Then, he met a Native-American princess named La Malinche, who told the conquistador about the emperor and the riches that lay in the heart of the land, in a magical city called Tenochtitlán, adding that the emperor was a tyrant and that many tribes wanted to get rid of him.

*Hernándo Cortés.*

## Into the Valley of Death

Cortés knew he was no god, but certain that God was on his side, he made straight for the magical city. But before doing so, he had to persuade his men that they could overrun the Aztec empire. Sure, they were strangers in a strange land, but that was no problem: they had guns, they had swords, and they were determined—at least, he was.

There was some understandable hesitation on the part of the men; some were even tempted not to follow their leader to what they thought might be their demise. But Cortés had a clever strategy: he burned their ships. Now, there was only one way out, and that was into the valley of death.

Here, the story picks up pace. Cortés and his soldiers fought off a few tribes, reaching the valley of Mexico with relatively little trouble. The emperor welcomed the Spanish with open arms. Interpreting the *mi casa es tu casa* offer like any back-stabbing double-dealing conquistador would, Cortés and his men imprisoned the emperor, battled the Aztecs, ransacked their city, and destroyed the empire. It was the stuff of legend: 500 men against thousands of warriors. The whole drama took two years from beginning to end.

> ### Living La Vida Literaria
>
> "… [The Aztecs] with swords and shields and other arms larger than swords, such as broadswords, and lances, how they pressed on us and with what valour and what … shouts and yells they charged upon us! The steady bearing of our artillery, musketeers and crossbowmen, was indeed a help to us, and we did the enemy much damage …"
>
> —Bernal Díaz del Castillo, one of Cortés's soldiers, describing the battles with the Aztecs

# P for Pizarro and Peru

Eleven years later, a reenactment of the Mexican conquest occurred, this time farther to the south. It had a similar cast of characters: on one side stood an emperor, Atahualpa, the emperor of Peru; and on the other side stood a glory- and gold-hungry conquistador, Francisco Pizarro.

Pizarro marched into Peru in 1532. The land of the Inca was recovering from a cruel civil war in which Atahualpa had murdered his brother, who was supposed to co-rule the empire with him. Taking advantage of the chaos and strife, Pizarro took over a city that was near a field where Atahualpa had set up camp. The conquistador invited the ruler to visit with him, but with one condition, don't bring weapons. To Pizarro's surprise, the ruler—no one knows exactly why—accepted the invitation. As Atahualpa walked into the center of the town, Pizarro unleashed his men on the unsuspecting emperor and his followers. The Spanish killed all of the Indians save their leader, and not a single Spaniard perished in the ordeal. Pizarro held Atahualpa for ransom, but even though the emperor's subjects gave Pizarro enough silver and gold to fill a chamber, the conquistador executed the emperor anyway.

The conquest of Peru took a lot longer than the conquest of Mexico. The conquistadores had to fight in hundreds of encounters over a 40-year period before solidifying their power over the Incas. In the long run, the Incas didn't have a chance. They couldn't fight against the technology of the day: armored soldiers on armored horses.

# Lesser Luminaries

Though the spotlight shines brightest on Cortés and Pizarro, other conquistadores played supporting roles in the conquest of the New World:

◆ **Pedro de Alvarado** (1485–1541) conquered the Mayans in Guatemala and in El Salvador. At the advanced age, for the times, anyway, of 56 he returned to Mexico, where, while battling rebellious Indians in the province of Zacatecas, a horse fell on him. Alvarado died a few days later.

◆ **Pedro de Valdivia** (1500–1553) set out to conquer Chile. He founded the cities of Santiago and Valparaiso. He battled constantly against the Araucanian Indians and was unable to defeat them. The Araucanians captured him during a skirmish and tortured him to death by pouring molten gold down his throat. (And you thought having a horse fall on you sounded bad!)

◆ **Gonzalez Jiménez de Quesada** (1501–1579) traveled throughout Colombia, looking for El Dorado, a fabulous king who was said to live in a city of gold. In 1538 he reached Bogotá, where his soldiers fought against the Native-Americans. When the Native-American king of Bogotá was killed, Jiménez de Quesada named the surviving brother ruler, but with a catch: that he would give the Spanish the royal treasure. The newly appointed sovereign did so and was summarily executed by Jiménez de Quesada.

## Other Conquests

The chronology of the conquest and settlements of the rest of South America is as follows:

◆ **1500s:** Honduras, Venezuela

◆ **1510s:** Panama

◆ **1520s:** Colombia, El Salvador, Guatemala

◆ **1530s:** Ecuador, Paraguay, Southern Chile

◆ **1560s:** Costa Rica

◆ **1570s:** Nicaragua

◆ **1580s:** Argentina

◆ **1720s:** Uruguay

**CAUTION** **Cuidado!** _____

Neither Cortés or Pizarro lived happily ever after. Pizarro's rule over Peru ended when he lost his life as a result of a war with another conquistador. As for Cortés, the Spanish Crown accused him of strangling his wife and stealing money from the monarchy. He finished his life in obscurity, in a small village far from Mexico City.

## After the Conquest

The exciting age of conquest was followed by the quieter period of colonization; quiet, yes, but just as deadly for the Native-Americans. The *colonizadores*, colonizers, were dull and bland, everyday people sent from Spain to make money for Spain and for themselves. To do so, they had to extract ore from the mines, agricultural products from the fields, and timber from the jungles. But the colonizadores didn't plan to do the actual work. Not when there were Native-Americans around.

To help the colonizadores, the Spanish Crown established the system of *encomienda*, the first instance of systematic slavery in the New World. The colonizadores demanded tributes from Native-Americans and forced them to farm and work in the mines in order to earn the money to pay up. In return for the tribute, the colonizers were supposed to look after the Native-Americans and convert them to Christianity. But there was more of a chance of a camel going through the eye of a needle than of the Spanish treating the natives kindly.

In 1524, friar Bartolome de las Casas rallied support for the abused Native-Americans. In a book titled, *The Devastation of the Indies*, published in 1552, he lobbied the Spanish Crown to abolish the encomiendas and reprimanded the colonizers for their inhumane treatment of the Native-Americans. Insisting the Indians had a soul and were as human as their oppressors, the friar proved a nuisance for many. The Spanish Crown was won over by de las Casas' arguments, however, and 10 years after the publication of his book encomiendas were abolished.

> **Hablas Español**
>
> **Colonizadores,** from verb the colonizar, means to colonize. A colonizador is a pioneering settler.
>
> **Encomiendas** was the judicial and economic system which led to the enslavement of Native-Americans.

## Not By Bread Alone

During colonial times, government officials, the Catholic Church, and land and mine owners oversaw the administration of the colonies. Though the king of Spain appointed royal administrators to manage the territory, the vast distances from one town to another encouraged local rule, resulting in the evolution of town bosses, or *caudillos*, and self-government, as well as a great deal interest in local matters rather than national affairs. Years later, the practice of local government and self-rule would sow the seeds for independence from Spain.

Representing the Catholic Church, Jesuit missionaries came to Latin America, first to Peru in 1567 and then to Mexico in 1572. Compassionate, the Jesuits acknowledged what Bartolome de la Casa had acknowledged before them: Native-Americans were as human as anyone else. These missionaries established small villages just for Native-Americans. Once converted to Catholicism, the Native-Americans lived under the spiritual guidance of the Jesuits, who taught them music and how to read. By the end of the 1700s, the Jesuits had baptized over 700,000 Native-Americans and had sheltered them from abusive colonizers, blessing them with a touch of paradise.

> **Hablas Español**
>
> A **caudillo** is the local boss in a rural community or small town. During colonial times, caudillos often had the final word in local conflicts.

**Para Tu Información**

The conquest and colonization of Latin America is a gory event that is filled with fury, bravery, and a lot of blood—in other words, the stuff of Hollywood. These videos make for a good night at home:

◆ *Captain from Castile* (1947)    The conquest of Mexico, starring Tyrone Power and Cesar Romero.

◆ *Kings of the Sun* (1963)    Yul Brynner is the lead actor in this film about the Mayas.

◆ *The Mission* (1986)    Jeremy Irons plays a Jesuit missionary in South America.

◆ *The Royal Hunt of the Sun* (1969)    Tells of the capture of Atahualpa. Chistopher Plummer plays the emperor and Robert Shaw suits up as the conquistador.

# Pretty Words, A Pretty Woman

The Jesuit presence in Latin America makes it clear that the sixteenth and seventeenth centuries were not just about guts and gore, wealth and power. There was another aspect to the Americas: this brave New World was beginning to develop its own sense of identity, art, and culture, one separate from the Old World.

In the late 1500s, the epic poem "La Araucana" captured vivid images of the war between the Araucanian Indians and the Spanish in Chile. Its author, Alonso de Ercilla y Zúñiga, a Spanish soldier, celebrated the bravery and nobility of the very Native Americans he was combating. In the 1600s, El Inca Garcilaso de la Vega, a descendant of the Inca aristocracy, penned a series of books, among them the *Royal Commentaries of the Incas and General History of Peru*, that told the colonizers all they needed to know, but were afraid to ask, about the soul, the humanity, and the intelligence of the Incas.

A couple of decades later, during the 1600s, a literary style called *Barroco* evolved. Its most talented interpreter was a rarity. Why? During a time when women were expected to be pretty but silent, in stepped a writer who was indeed a pretty woman, but who was certainly not silent.

Sister Juana Inés de la Cruz became a nun so that she could write. Highly intelligent, she penned poems about the passion of Christ, the passion of faith, and the passion of love. (She harbored a forbidden love. Some say she was in love with a married man; some say she loved a woman.) Her poetry was elegant, intelligent, and defiant:

> Do not sing verses that another demands of you
> Except in due season, or if compelled
> By some great prince who commands it.
> In matters that we ourselves have chosen
> All goes very smoothly, but on the contrary
> What is forced on us is hard and rough.

In the 1700s, Cuban poet-soldier Manuel de Zequeira y Arango wrote an ode to a fruit of the tropics. In "Oda a la Piña" (Ode to the Pineapple), the poet gathers the pineapple from a Cuban field and delivers it to Mt. Olympus, where the Greek gods cherish the flavor and beauty of the tropical fruit.

There was in this ode an emerging literary freshness, and a sense of the new, that was equally evident in the works of other Latin-American writers of colonial times. Something was happening: nearly three centuries after the conquest and colonization of Latin America, the children of the conquistadores and colonizadores were coming into their own, with their own likes and dislikes. They were crafting their own Latin-American persona, their own Hispanoamericana identity—the very identity that in the nineteenth century would lead to the wars of independence and in the twentieth century would make Latinos in the United States so resilient.

**Hablas Español**

**Barroco** is a literary style characterized by its intellectual approach to such universal themes as love and mortality. It relies on astronomical imagery and lots of descriptive passages, and it can be extravagant in its use of language.

## The Least You Need to Know

- 1492 was a watershed year in modern history: Spain was reunified and Columbus sailed across the "ocean blue."

- Columbus didn't realize he had come to America; but at the end of his life, he suspected that maybe he hadn't gotten to Asia, either.

- The sixteenth century was a time of violence throughout Latin America.

- The seventeenth century was the period of the settlement of Latin America.

- No matter how you look at the conquest and colonization of Latin America, the bottom line was that Native-Americans were the big losers.

# Chapter 9

# Birth of Nations: Independence for All

## In This Chapter

- ◆ The bells toll for freedom
- ◆ Latin Americans take up arms
- ◆ Independence for one and all
- ◆ Learning how to govern, the hard way

In the nineteenth century there were a lot of *gritos*, or calls to arms; there were gritos in Puerto Rico, Cuba, and Mexico. The grito in Mexico, which took place in September 1810, was the most cinematic.

Grab a chair and check out the screen: an establishing shot shows a panoramic view of a colorful Mexican village called Dolores. The camera focuses on a small church. Now, a close-up of a priest—he's wearing a black cassock and climbing up the church's bell tower. Out of breath, he pulls a thick rope, tolling the bells. The camera zooms back, revealing hundreds of peasants milling in the church's yard and crowding into the sanctuary.

The priest rushes down the tower and up to the pulpit at the front of the now-crowded church. Without mincing words, he tells his congregation that someone has betrayed them—that Spanish authorities have found out about their planned uprising. They have a choice, the priest continues: they can do nothing and let the Spanish arrest them for the planned insurrection, or they can take matters into their own hands and fight for their freedom. Grabbing a banner of the Virgin of Guadalupe, Mexico's patron saint, the *padre* calls out a grito: "Long live the Lady of Guadalupe. Death to the tyrants." Thus begins Mexico's war of independence.

The picture fades from the screen, the lights come on.

# All or Nothing

Time for a flashback to find out why, after three centuries of Spanish rule, Hispanoamericanos were growing dissatisfied:

   ◆ The King appointed Europeans to rule Latin America. Those Europeans felt they were superior to the *criollos*, those born in Latin America from Spanish parents.

### Hablas Español

A **criollo** is the offspring of Spanish parents born in the new world. A child of a white and a Native American is called a **mestizo**.

### Para Tu Información

Latin Americans also resented the Spanish Crown for removing the Jesuits from their land in 1767. The Crown felt the Jesuits were too influential. The act demonstrated that the Spanish Crown was not as religious as it claimed to be, and it also showed that the monarchy was not sensitive to the needs of people in Latin America, who truly admired and respected the Jesuits.

   ◆ Up to the end of the eighteenth century, The King didn't allow criollos and the *mestizos*, the children of Spanish and Native Americans, to take over any administrative post of importance, no matter how much wealth the criollos and mestizos had garnered and how much education they had.

   ◆ Latin Americans were not allowed to trade with any other country except Spain. Even nations within Latin America were forbidden to trade with each other.

   ◆ People in Latin America were not permitted to manufacture their own goods; they had to acquire those products directly from Spain.

   ◆ Spanish subjects were not permitted to criticize decisions made by the Spanish Crown or its representative in Latin America.

   ◆ The Spanish crown imposed oppressive taxes on Latin America.

In other words, in its relation with the colonies, Spain followed a simple rule: all or nothing. All for Spain, nothing for Latin America.

*The Virgin of Guadalupe/
Our Lady of Guadalupe.*

# My Mother, the Tyrant

For a long while, *Latinoamericanos* accepted these conditions. Spain, after all, was the Madre Patria, the mother country. According to Carlos Fuentes, this is how a Spanish viceroy, or governor, of Mexico phrased it, "Let us not forget that this is a colony and that it must depend on Spain, its mother country, and must yield her some benefit because of the protection it receives from her."

What protection? That was the question the loyal subjects posed. In the eighteenth century, the British had attacked and occupied Havana. Early in the nineteenth century, the British, the mother country's perennial enemy, had disembarked in Argentina and marched right into its capital, Buenos Aires. It was the Argentines, not the Spanish troops, who rallied together and revolted against the invaders, capturing 1,200 British soldiers.

## Hablas Español

**Tiro de gracia** is a saying that's the equivalent of "the straw that broke the camel's back." It refers to the bullet that is shot through the head of an executed man, just to be certain he's dead.

Spain's inability to properly protect its subjects was a sign of weakness, the result of its numerous wars in Europe and its reliance on products made in Latin America and sold, at a lower price and at a loss due to poor internal management, to European nations. Then, in 1807 came *el tiro de gracia*: Napoleon Bonaparte sent his troops to Spain and proclaimed his brother Jose ruler.

# Padre Knows Best

Many Spanish officials lent their support to Napoleon's brother and accepted him as the ruler of Spain. Those officials dispatched Napoleonic representatives to the New World. To their surprise, the children of the mother country ousted the French sympathizers and demanded the return of the Spanish king. In undertaking this action, the Latinoamericanos learned two lessons: Spain was a weak country, and criollos and mestizos could work together for independence.

It was now evident that people in Latin America could oust Spain. They knew that the United States had done it with England. They knew that before Napoleon, the French common folks had wrested power and glory away from the French monarchy. Their grito was in the making, if not yet in their throats.

Padre Hidalgo, the priest from the little town of Dolores, was the first to call his country-men to arms. His grito, known as El Grito de Dolores, convinced 90,000 Native-Americans, mestizos, and poor farmers to follow him in revolt. Winning numerous battles, Hidalgo formed a provisional government in Guadalajara. Soon, however, more than 9,000 Spanish troops arrived and attacked the rebels, turning the tide against the padre. Hidalgo was captured and executed, but his grito lived on. The war continued under the leadership of a former officer in the Spanish army, General Agustín Iturbide, who led Mexico to independence in 1821.

---

### Living La Vida Literaria

"[Father Hidalgo] was first brought to trial by the Inquisition, which condemned him as a heretic and ordered him defrocked. He was then convicted of sedition by a royalist court ... On July 30, 1811, he was shot and decapitated. The heads of Hidalgo [and some followers] ... were transported to Guanajuato, and hung for a decade in metal cages ..."

—Journalist Jonathan Kandell, describing the execution of Father Hidalgo in *La Capital: The Biography of Mexico City*

---

# Two of a Kind

Elsewhere in Latin America, two men followed Hidalgo's example. They were Simón Bolívar and José de San Martín. Together, they liberated South America.

If he had been born in this century, Simón Bolívar's looks might have landed him on the cover of *GQ* magazine. Instead, this attractive Venezuelan ended up on the front lines of his country's war for independence. He organized an army and liberated Venezuela. Next, he seized Colombia, taking it away from the Spanish. Finally, Ecuador and Peru threw off their chains. Bolívar led his men into battle almost constantly from 1811 to 1825. His military strategies were dramatic. To defeat the Spanish troops in Bogotá in 1819, he took an army of 2,500 men up the Orinoco River, climbed over the Andes, and descended on the enemy.

Bolívar wasn't the only South American to climb great heights to defeat his enemy. Argentine general José de San Martín, joining forces with the Chilean Bernardo O'Higgins, led an army of 5,000 up the Andes, climbing to an altitude of 15,000 feet. In February of 1817, San Martín surprised the sleeping Spanish troops on the other side of the mountain. When the battle was over, the Spanish had lost more than 500 men. San Martín's casualties numbered 12.

In Peru, San Martín and Bolívar, the two victorious heroes who had wrestled South America away from Spain, met to discuss the fate of the newly freed territories. Respected and admired by the multitudes, they could have divided the continent in two: "You take the North. I take the South." But the leaders had different visions of how to govern—whether to establish a democracy or benign dictatorship—and after their encounter, San Martín, tired of fighting, went home, and Bolívar remained. San Martín sought the solitude of his home in Buenos Aires. Bolívar sought the solitude of power.

> **Para Tu Información**
>
> What about Spain's Central American colonies? When Napoleon invaded Spain, the Spanish colonies of Central America seized the opportunity to declare their independence. So busy was Spain with its internal problems and the emerging wars of independence in Mexico and South America, it didn't send troops to Central America. Thus, without bloodshed, the nations of Central America achieved independence as a group in 1821.

# The Most Faithful Island

By the 1830s, Spain had only two possessions left in the New World: Cuba and Puerto Rico. You would think that the Spanish king and his advisers would have taken to heart their defeats and done anything possible to keep the two islands. But no, they were so sure that Cuba would remain a "faithful island," as they described it, and that Puerto Rico would remain tranquil, that they did nothing to improve situations on the islands.

During most of the 1800s, the two islands conspired against Spain. Many leaders suggested annexing the islands to the United States, and several American presidents, including Jefferson, contemplated the idea of purchasing Cuba. But many Cuban patriots opposed those plans, calling for complete independence. In 1868, a plantation owner named Carlos Manuel de Cespedes let out a grito: El Grito de Yara. Forming an army of freed slaves and criollos, he and his soldiers marched into the mountains. In September of the same year, Puerto Rican patriots made their own call to arms. Known as the Grito de Lares, the insurgents took over a town, defeating the Spanish soldiers stationed at a garrison.

In 1878, a tired Cuba and a tired Spain signed a truce. In Puerto Rico, Spain instituted broader local rule. Spain maintained its remaining colonies, for a little while, anyway.

In 1895, the fires of rebellion were rekindled in Cuba. Its leader was the poet José Martí. From New York, where he lived as an exile, Martí planned the insurrection. He collected money, which he sent to the *mambises*, Cuban soldiers, in Cuba and coordinated the efforts of several Cuban generals. Martí called for a war of liberation based on the love of freedom and not the hatred of the Spanish. He also advocated the establishment of a democratic regime, where people of all races and religions would have equal representation. In January of 1895, Martí left New York City. When he reached Cuba, the mambises proclaimed him president of the island. Eager to take part in combat, Martí joined the mambises during a skirmish. The poet, who didn't even know how to fire a handgun, was the first casualty in the encounter.

### Hablas Español

**Mambises** were Cuban soldiers who fought in the mountain and jungle during the wars of independence; a mambis is a symbol of courage and liberty.

### Para Tu Información

The first country in Latin America to achieve independence was French and Creole speaking Haiti in 1804.

The struggle for Cuban independence dragged on without Martí. In 1898, the U.S. sent the battleship Maine to Havana to protect American interests. While anchored in the harbor, the ship exploded. Accusing the Spanish of sabotage, the U.S. declared war on Spain (see Chapter 11 for more on this war, called the Spanish-Cuban-American War). Soon, more than 60,000 American troops landed in Cuba. Under the leadership of Teddy Roosevelt, a regiment called the Rough-riders charged up San Juan Hill, occupying the heights that overlooked the city of Santiago and the entrance to the harbor, thus making it impossible for the Spanish to defend these positions. In fewer than four months the war was over.

## Latin American Independence Dates

| Country | Date | Country | Date |
|---------|------|---------|------|
| Argentina | 1816 | Guatemala | 1821 |
| Bolivia | 1825 | Honduras | 1821 |

| Country | Date | Country | Date |
|---|---|---|---|
| Chile | 1822 | Nicaragua | 1821 |
| Colombia | 1818 | Panama | 1821 |
| Costa Rica | 1821 | Paraguay | 1811 |
| Cuba | 1902 | Peru | 1821 |
| Dominican Republic | 1821 | Uruguay | 1828 |
| Ecuador | 1819 | Venezuela | 1830 |
| El Salvador | 1821 | | |

### Para Tu Información

The battleship Maine arrived in Cuba in February 11, 1898. Four days later, the ship blew up. Two hundred thirty sailors were killed. The Americans immediately blamed the Spanish. The Spanish, on the other hand, claimed that it was an accident. With Americans in the United States clamoring for revenge, the United States declared war on Spain.

An investigation in 1911 reported that it was possible an object outside the ship had caused the explosion. Subsequent studies suggested that overheated ammunition within ship was the cause. A third theory suggested that either a Cuban or a Spanish anarchist, unhappy with the Spanish empire, had sabotaged the Maine. No one knows for sure.

# One America, One Problem

The newly-liberated Latin Americans made several attempts to create one large republic with many states. The first attempt was the creation of Gran Colombia, the brainchild of Simón Bolívar. It included present day Colombia, Ecuador, and Venezuela. But in 1830 Gran Colombia ceased to exist, and the four countries went their separate ways. Colombia and Panama remained as one country for a few more decades; Panama eventually rebelled against Colombia and formed its own nation.

In 1822, Costa Rica, El Salvador, Guatemala, Honduras, and Nicaragua joined the republic of Mexico. But political differences made these nations opt out a year later. Next, they banded together under the United Provinces of Central America. However, some of the nations wanted a strong central government while others favored autonomy, so by 1838 the nations seceded to create their own governments.

National interests pitted one nation against another. Peru invaded Ecuador in 1828 in an attempt to take over the city of Guayaguil. From 1865 to 1870, Argentina and Uruguay fought against Paraguay in a land dispute known as The War of the Triple Alliance (the third member was Brazil). In the War of the Pacific, which lasted from 1879 to 1883,

Chile battled against Bolivia and Peru over nitrate mines along the Pacific. At the turn of the twentieth century, Peru and Ecuador went to war over an unpopulated area in the Amazon basin.

# Personality Problems

The encounter between San Martín and Bolívar hinted that the leaders of the wars of independence didn't share a common platform for the governing of Latin America after the departure of Spain. The fundamental issue was the form the governments should take: Democracy? Monarchy? Military dictatorship?

In Mexico, military dictatorship became the norm. The two most famous rulers were General Santa Anna and Porfirio Díaz. Santa Anna was the fellow who led the expedition against The Alamo. He was a whimsical leader who, upon losing a leg to amputation, ordered a state funeral for the limb. Porfirio Díaz was a strongman who introduced the modern technology of his time into Mexico, but at a cost of personal freedom: no one was allowed to criticize his actions. Intent in making the nation appealing to Europeans, Díaz forced Native-Americans to wear shoes to make them look "civilized" and kept them out of Mexico City.

In Argentina, General Juan Manuel de Rosas organized death squads to do away with the opposition and ruled the country for 20 years. During his tenure, he managed to keep foreign businesses from exerting control over local economies and encouraged the growth of the cattle industry. In Paraguay, Dr. Jose Gaspar Rodríguez de Francia closed the country from the rest of the world. Calling himself "El Supremo," he didn't allow foreigners to come into the country.

And what about Simón Bolívar, the great liberator? Surely, he didn't yield to temptation? Yes, he did. Not because he wanted to be a dictator as such—although, he did use the title—but because he dreamt of creating one continent rather than many individual nations.

By 1828, Bolívar's creation, Gran Colombia, was beginning to crumble as the member nations expressed interest in local matters and didn't want to share power (remember the preference for local rule that evolved during colonial times?). Fearing the outbreak of war amongst the four nations, Bolívar recommended a new convention that would strengthen the presidency so that stronger measures could be undertaken to keep the union together. But when politicians failed to do so, the former liberator claimed that the original constitution was outdated. He assumed dictatorial powers in 1828, trying to keep Gran Colombia together by sheer personality. His violation of the constitution, for which he had labored years before, angered his opponents, who tried to assassinate him. In 1830, Bolívar resigned, heart-broken over the failure of his dream of unity. He died shortly afterwards. (For more on Bolívar, see Chapter 12.)

# A Mexican Hero

While Latin America was trying to find itself, politically, at least, a European power thought it was time to re-introduce the Old World into the New. In the 1860s, France invaded Mexico.

In 1858, a Zapotec Indian, Benito Júarez, became Mexico's minister of justice. He enacted laws that limited the power of the Church, the army, and the Mexican aristocracy. The laws also instituted a judicial system that treated everyone equally. As a result of these leg-islations, a civil war broke out between the liberals, those who supported the new laws, and conservatives, who favored power in the hands of the few. It ended with the vic-tory of the liberals. Fresh from his victory, Benito Júarez was elected president in 1861 (for more on Júarez and this era of Mexican history, see Chapter 12). Still unhappy with him, conservatives and military officers approached the ruler of France, Napoleon III, and asked for his support in getting rid of Júarez. Meanwhile, the Mexican president had decided to stop paying the country's foreign debt until it could rebuild its financial foundation.

> **Para Tu Información**
>
> When he was 12 years old, Benito Júarez went to live with a priest who looked after the boy as if he were his own son. The padre introduced him to literature and history and hoped Júarez, would join the clergy. But Júarez wanted to be a lawyer, and when he was 22 years old, he bade farewell to the old priest, whom he called godfather.

## The Emperor's New Country

Júarez's decision to withhold payment due to France gave Napoleon III the perfect excuse to invade Mexico. He sent Maximilian of Austria as his representative and to serve as emperor of Mexico, deposing president Júarez. Maximilian didn't make many friends in his newly-adopted country. He angered the conservatives by refusing to do away with the progressive laws enacted by his predecessor. Unhappy with Maximilian's support of Júarez's progressive laws, the aristocrats and the conservatives, who had asked the would-be emperor to come to Mexico in the first place, deserted him—as did many of his officers. To add insult to injury, the United States told Napoleon III to get his cronies out of the Americas, that America was only for Americans. Maximilian was left without the French army to protect him.

The emperor was captured and sentenced to death. Most world leaders realized that Maximilian had been duped, and even the Pope asked Júarez to spare his life. But the Mexican president was aware that Maximilian's soldiers had killed many young Mexicans; not only that, he knew he could not allow an invader to come and go into Mexico as he pleased. Thus, in the name of the country, Júarez had Maximilian executed. According to legend, the emperor requested that Mariachis play the Mexican song "La Paloma" just before he was killed.

*Emperor Maximilian of Austria.*

## The Least You Need to Know

♦ As in the United States, Latin American countries rebelled against their mother country because of lack of representation.

♦ Unlike the United States, where after the wars the generals retired from the army and the government, many of the generals in Latin America refused to surrender power to the people.

♦ Several attempts to create a single united nation out of several countries failed.

♦ In the nineteenth century, there was a preference for strong rulers and local rules.

# Chapter 10

# Cronies and Caudillos: The Twentieth Century

## In This Chapter

- ◆ The digging of the Panama Canal
- ◆ The first revolution of the twentieth century
- ◆ Generals parade through Latin America
- ◆ Castro sets up shop in Cuba
- ◆ The United States declares war on drugs

Newly arrived Latin American immigrants to the United States are often pleasantly surprised by the absence of military personnel in the streets. Sure, after September 11, armed soldiers patrol the airports, and at events of epic-proportions, like the Super bowl and the Olympics, large contingents of police officers and undercover agents abound. But on any given day, at any given time, in any given town, it's a given that you won't find the Marines hanging out at the corner.

That was not so in Latin America during the twentieth century. Anyone from the region who was born before 1990 either witnessed a *golpe de estado*—a coup d'etat—or lived under a military regime. Such was the nature of politics south of the border, and such is the nature of this chapter. As a bonus, you'll learn about an event in which the American armed forces performed a nonmilitary role.

# The Century of the Americas?

The twentieth century has been dubbed the American century—and there is a humongous book by that title to prove the point. That's fine, but how about an amendment? Let's call it the *Siglo de las Américas*, the Americas century, to include Latin America, too.

The logic is simple. Throughout the twentieth century, the United States and Latin America have commanded much of the world's attention.

**Hablas Español**

When a government is overthrown it is known as a **Golpe de Estado**. Golpe means punch and estado refers to a government or state.

## Americas, Americas

In the past century, several events in Latin America helped to change the face of the world. Although scholars and history buffs might quibble over which item is more important than another, most people can agree that the following events altered political balance in the world arena:

- The building of the Panama Canal
- The Mexican Revolution
- The Perón years in Argentina
- The Cuban Revolution
- The era of *los militares*, the military
- The narco-wars

# Can You Dig It?

It was a dream for magicians: to conjure up an ocean where there was none, creating a shortcut from the Caribbean to the Pacific. The conquistadores mused about it, wondering whether it would be possible to turn a narrow stretch of land known as Panama into a watery road. A couple of hundred years after the conquest of the Americas, another traveler, by the name of Alexander Von Humbolt, entertained a similar thought. After all, Panama was less than 40 miles wide: a lot shorter than the distance between Los Angeles and San Diego.

It was a Cuban-American officer of the U.S. Army (a bright engineer named Menocal, whose descendant would become president of Cuba in the twentieth century) who first took digging the canal seriously, but he reported that any attempt would be very difficult. How could the technology of the day dig through rock foundations that were miles deep into the earth? Menocal instead suggested creating the pathway in Nicaragua, taking advantages of lakes and rivers in the region that could be used as natural viaducts.

> ### Living La Vida Literaria
>
> "The creation of the Panama Canal was ... a profoundly important historic event and a sweeping human drama .... it represented the largest, most costly single effort ever before mounted anywhere on earth. It held the world's attention over a span of forty years. It affected ... tens of thousands of people at every level of society and of virtually every race and nationality ..."
>
> —Historian David McCullough in *The Path Between the Seas*

The French, who had established relations with Colombia, had a lot of business interest in the region, and had built a similar canal in Suez, went wild over the idea. The project was undertaken by the very optimistic Ferdinande Marie de Lesseps, the builder of the Suez Canal.

In 1882, de Lesseps, after forming a private company called the Compagnie Universelle, began construction. Twelve years later, de Lesseps was tired, disillusioned, and bankrupt. And the project was abandoned. It turned out that the equipment and tools were not powerful enough to dig through mountains and monoliths. Politicians and investors stole funds from the company. And malaria and yellow fever had decimated an army of laborers.

**Cuidado!**

By 1894, 20,000 of the people hired to help build the Panama Canal had perished.

## American Know How

The French sold their digging company to the American government. When Panama declared itself a republic and broke away from Colombia in 1903, the United States presented the Republic of Panama with a check for $10 million, plus the promise of $250,000 a year for several decades, in exchange for rights to construct and manage the canal. Then, president Teddy Roosevelt sent in the Marines. (See Chapter 11 for a discussion of the United States's role in Panama's independence.)

The men in green came not to fight, but to wipe out disease by clearing the jungles, draining the swamps, and eradicating yellow fever (a Cuban physician named Carlos J. Finlay had demonstrated that the illness was transmitted by mosquitoes and you could get rid of the disease by getting rid of the mosquitoes). Next, army engineers created a new design of the canal by substituting the French plan of joining the two oceans on a sea-level waterway with a construction that consisted of a series of locks. The locks created many compartments that could be flooded to float a ship from one coast to the other.

*The Panama Canal (left) and one of its locks (right).*

*(Courtesy of the Samuels Family)*

The canal was officially opened in 1920. It cost the United States $320,000,000. And it changed the face of the Americas.

# The Teacher and the Tyrant

A few years into the twentieth century an old Mexican dictator named Porfirio Díaz, who had been in power since 1876, announced he was ready to abdicate and allow democratic elections. Once election campaigns were underway, however, Díaz changed his mind. In the process, he jailed a presidential candidate who had proved extremely popular with the masses. Released from prison, thanks to influential friends within the government, the candidate relocated to Texas, from where he planned to overthrow the old dictator.

That's how the Mexican revolution started, the first major revolution of the new century. The leader, Francisco Madero, was a mild-mannered teacher from an aristocratic background. He led an unlikely rebellion that included such courageous leaders as the legendary Pancho Villa in the north and Emiliano Zapata in the south. It swept across Mexico, forcing the old caudillo to give up his throne in 1911. The people then elected Madero president, and the former teacher promised land reform, rights and protection for Mexican Indians, and free unions. But Madero was a dreamer, not a politician, and soon his own advisers, who opposed his reforms, turned against him and murdered him. One ruler after another paraded onto the scene, each overthrown in what was to be the prototype of the golpe de estados that plagued Latin America for much of the twentieth century.

Madero was replaced by his killer, General Victoriano Huerta, who was a representative of the former supporters of Porfirio Díaz. Huerta was overthrown by General Venustiano Carranza in 1914. Pancho Villa and Emiliano Zapata rebelled against Carranza, who was murdered in 1920. General Obregón, who had organized the military against Carranza, was next voted in as president. He was followed in 1924 by general Elías Calles, who closed down Catholic schools and convents and kicked the foreign clergy out of Mexico. In 1928, Obregón was elected president for the second time, but a religious fanatic assassinated him before he took office.

By the end of the 1920s the Mexican Revolution was over, a ruling political party—eventually called the Partido Revolucionario Institucional, Party of the Institutionalized Revolution—was established, and laws that didn't allow presidents to run for re-election were enacted, thus eliminating the likelihood of yet another dictatorship.

Stability came to the nation, although peace came at a price: political dissent was neither permitted nor tolerated. In fact, there was very little opposition to the ruling party, known as the PRI, until the recent election of Vicente Fox in 2001, who was the first politician to win an office without being connected to the party.

### Para Tu Información

The Mexican Revolution produced three romantic figures.

◆ **Francisco Madero**   a member of the aristocracy who gave up the easy life to risk it all for an ideology: a free Mexico. Though Madero defeated Díaz, he was a poor judge of character and kept as his advisers former Díaz supporters. They, in turn, sabotaged Madero's presidency and eventually murdered him.

◆ **Pancho Villa**   a ruthless outlaw who joined the war against the old dictator and proved himself a brilliant general who defeated all who came against him. In the end, though, a jealous husband murdered Villa.

◆ **Emiliano Zapata**   a legendary figure who kept his eyes on the prize: equal rights for Indians and the return to the Indians of the land usurped by the government. In the end, he received neither.

# Don't Cry for Me, Argentina

Generally speaking, after 1940 generals in Argentina did the talking, and the ruling, for nearly four decades. During the 1920s and '30s, democracy in Argentina was fragile, victim to the whims of foreign powers and economic upheavals in the United States and Europe. But in the 1940s, one general's star shone the brightest, promising a better future.

His name was Juan Domingo Perón, and in 1943 this Secretary of Labor and Social Welfare became the vice president of the nation. Perón supported social programs that were situated somewhere between capitalism and fascism. Calling it *justicialismo*, just cause, the programs favored labor unions, promised jobs for the urban poor, and salary increases for those who were already employed. Perón talked about taking over the railroad system and building hospitals, schools, and housing for those in need.

Perceived as a threat by the aristocracy and the military, in 1945 these two groups removed Perón from his government post, placing him under arrest. His mistress, the actress Evita Duarte, came to his rescue, rallying the workers and union members to his support; soon all of Buenos Aires demanded his release. The anti-*Peronista* forces relinquished, and a freed Perón addressed a crowd of more than 300,000 from the presidential palace. He promised that he would always fight for the *descamisados*, the shirtless and poor of Argentina.

> ### Cuidado! ____
>
> Latinos, like everyone else, disagree about who is a dictator and who is a good ruler. Millions still support Castro. Millions supported Pinochet. And twenty years after his death, there are Latinos who regard Perón as a great leader and a good thing for Argentina. A conversation with a Latino about any of these rulers could turn into a heated argument.

Perón married Evita, who was as popular as the political leader, and in 1946 he was elected president. But while outwardly promoting a democratic regime for all and instituting social services, Perón was in fact a strong man who censored the press and silenced the opposition. In 1955, he challenged the rule of the Catholic Church in Argentina, and the unrest that followed resulted in his being ousted from power.

Perón fled to Paraguay; from there, he sought asylum in Spain. Even in exile, Peron remained popular, and 20 years later he returned to Argentina, not as a nostalgic exile coming home, but as a president. The people had elected him to lead them once more.

# Evergreen: Castro

As professional soldiers in Argentina in 1955 were kicking Perón out office, amateur soldiers in Cuba were planning to do the same to General Fulgencio Batista. The general had been ruling Cuba, in one way or another, since the late 1930s. Claiming in 1952 that the country was chaotic, the general had overthrown the legitimate government and replaced it with a dictatorship.

The general's move angered a lot of Cubans, including a would-be representative and attorney by the name of Fidel Castro Ruz. Accompanied by dozens of college students and young members of the aristocracy, Castro attacked a military fortress with the hope of capturing it and calling the people of Cuba to join him in a revolt against Batista. The maneuver failed, and Castro was imprisoned. Two years later, Batista, hoping to improve his public image, paroled Castro, who went into exile in Mexico to plan his next move.

In 1956, Castro and a handful of rebels invaded Cuba. For three years, they fought Batista's army. Castro's battle got a big boost on New Year's Eve in 1958: the American ambassador to Cuba told General Batista that the United States would no longer support his regime. Weary and embattled, Batista threw in the towel and hitched a ride to the Dominican Republic. A heady Castro took over the government, welcomed by nearly all Cubans.

*The landing of Castro and his army in Cuba, 1956.*

*(Courtesy of Department of Rare Books and Special Collections, Princeton University Library)*

## Outside the Revolution ... Nothing

Castro made himself the supreme ruler of Cuba. He had one easy-to-follow rule: either you support my revolution or you're against it. The supporters were dubbed *Fidelistas*; the opponents were called *gusanos*, parasites.

Thousands of so-called gusanos ended up either dead or in prison. Thousand others fled to Florida. In the United States, the exiles plotted an invasion of the island with help from President Dwight Eisenhower and Vice President Richard M. Nixon. D-day was scheduled for April, 1961.

As planned, the exiles landed in Cuba, only to learn that the promised support from the United States wasn't there. You see, Nixon had supported the invasion, but his rival, newly-elected President John F. Kennedy, opposed it. Thus, as Cuban exiles fought on the sands of Girón Beach, in the Bay of Pigs region, Kennedy withdrew military support. The invaders were arrested, as were thousands of sympathizers on the island. This was the first defeat ever of an operation designed, funded, and conducted by the U.S. Army and the CIA.

### Hablas Español

In 1959, Castro described anyone who opposed him as a **gusano,** a worm, or parasite, living off the accomplishments of the revolution. The term is still being used in Cuba, where it's meant to be an insult. But Cuban exiles have appropriated the insult and given it a positive connotation.

A year later, Kennedy had a chance to make amends to the Cuban exiles. Castro, in cooperation with the Soviets, had installed missile warheads on the island. In October of 1962, Kennedy stood firm and told the Soviets to remove the missiles … or else. The Soviets didn't say a thing. Castro was fidgety. Kennedy paced round and round the Oval Office. The world watched as millions of Americans stood in line outside churches, waiting to go into the confession booths, eager to cleanse their sins before dying. Was this the end of the world?

It wasn't, as you know. The Soviet Union withdrew the missiles, and Kennedy promised never to attack Cuba. An upset Castro threw a tantrum; how could the Soviets negotiate with the Americans without his consent? But then he calmed down. After all, Kennedy had said that there would no invasion of the island ever again.

The way Castro came to see it, he had won two major battles: the Bay of Pigs and the Cuban missile crisis. The exuberant Cuban leader now felt free to send his soldiers and technicians to other Latin American nations, where he supported guerrilla activities, meeting a promise he had made to himself: to export his revolution to the rest of Latin America.

# The Night of the General

In Chile, a new president extended a hand of friendship to the Cuban dictator. The gesture sealed his fate. The president was Salvador Allende. A socialist, he was elected in 1970, to the displeasure of the military and the upper classes, who feared communists would infiltrate the government. Allende's friendship with Castro gave them further proof that Allende was going to "Cubanize" Chile.

Anti-Allende protests sprang up everywhere and fights broke out between those on the right against those on the left. Finally, one night in September 1973, the military attacked the presidential palace. Allende was killed—some say he committed suicide—and his government was overthrown. Those who had supported the military didn't imagine that a dictator would replace Allende, and that the dictatorship would last 17 years.

---

### Living La Vida Literaria

The niece of Salvador Allende, novelist Isabel Allende, recounts the final attack in her novel *The House of the Spirits*: "The bombing was brief, but it left the palace in ruins. By two o'clock in the afternoon the fire had consumed the old drawing rooms that had been used since colonial times, and only a handful of men were left around the President. Soldiers entered the building and took what was left of the first floor. Above the din was heard the hysterical voice of an officer ordering [the President's men] to surrender and come down in a single file with their hands on the heads. The President shook each of them by hand … They never saw him again alive."

General Augusto Pinochet settled in as the supreme ruler of Chile. He imposed a state of siege that allowed him to imprison thousands of Chilean students, intellectuals, and supporters of Allende, and it's estimated that nearly 6,000 were either murdered or kidnapped, never to be found again.

In the 1980s, as the Cold War was coming to an end and Castro was no longer able to promote revolution in Latin America, the United States, which had plotted against Allende and aided Pinochet, withdrew its support of the dictator. Elections were called in Chile, and Pinochet was defeated. During his regime, more 300,000 Chileans left the country, a good many of them settling in the  United States.

# The Dirty War

In Argentina, another general, a friend of Pinochet, derailed the legitimate political process. In 1976, General Jorge Rafael Videla, prodded by the army, overthrew the government of Argentina. The president was Isabel Perón, the third wife and widow of the ever-popular General Perón. Perón had been re-elected president in 1973, but had died in office. His wife, who was his vice-president, had taken up his duties. A poor administrator, President Isabel Perón was perceived as steering the country into economic chaos. To rescue Argentina, the military stepped in.

Whereas in the past, the military had forced its way into the government to support a single dictator who was seeking power, in this instance, the military's action was based on the perceived need to create an economic system that would benefit the nation. The generals worked as a group, or junta, and once they were in power they chose one of their own as the head of the regime. But this dictator owed his power to his colleagues.

A year after the military had taken the reins of the nation, over 15,000 people—suspected subversives—were missing or murdered. The army ruled until 1982, when Argentina attempted to retake the Malvinas/Falkland islands from the British, who had taken the isles away from Argentina during the nineteenth century. The war was a complete fiasco, resulting in defeat for Argentina. A weakened Argentine army was rebuked by the people, and elections took place, thus ending the rule of the generals. Videla was arrested, was accused of killing thousands of people, and was sent to prison.

**Para Tu Información**

General Juan Perón, a man thought to represent the macho spirit in Latin America, relied heavily on two women. Evita Perón, who was his mistress and then became his second wife, was a key player in his administration during his first term, influencing his political decisions. When Evita died of cancer in the mid-1950s, Perón married an Argentine dancer named Isabel. During his second term in office, Isabel was his vice president.

# The End of the Road

By December 31, 1999, the ruling generals of Latin America were alive and well only in movies and books. The exception, of course, was Castro, who was still ruling Cuba after 40 years and was still donning military regalia.

Castro, Perón, and Pinochet might be the best-known dictators of Latin America during the twentieth century, but there were others, including the following:

♦ **Venezuelan Juan Vicente Gómez** (1908–1935). Described as the wealthiest politician in South America during his life time, Gómez overthrew the government in 1908 and rigged presidential elections over and over again to remain in power. An extensive spy network and the support of the army kept him in office unopposed.

♦ **Paraguayan Alfredo Stroessner** (1954–1989). Stroessner took over the goverment in a military coup and controlled the courts and the legislation, which ratified his long presidential term. Those who opposed him were usually arrested; many were murdered.

♦ **Nicaraguan Somoza Clan** (1936–1979). The Somoza clan consisted of the father Anastasio and his two sons, Luis and Tachito. They exiled opposition leaders, tortured political prisoners, and controlled the press, shutting down opposition newspapers while taking over large holdings of land and businesses.

♦ **Dominican Rafael L. Trujillo** (1930–1961). Trujillo seized power in a revolt against the elected president and remained in power by placing the army under his direct rule—through the appointment of family members to key military positions—and the elimination—through murder and exile—of anyone opposing him. He, his relatives, and friends amassed huge fortunes by stealing money from the government and appropriating the businesses of their opponents.

## Para Tu Información

The advisers that were usually dispatched to Latin America were either CIA operatives or army personnel. Their roles were to instruct the host government on ways of dealing with the crisis at hand, such as how to stop the exportation of drugs and the destruction of drug-related crops, and to keep the American government abreast of local developments and potential foes.

# Narco Wars

By the end of the twentieth century, the era of the generals was a thing of the past. Medals and military parades were out. Drugs were in.

Drugs grown and manufactured in Colombia were shipped north to the United States through Panama. To curtail the trafficking, the United States sent advisers to Colombia, a nation torn by war on three fronts: two competing guerrilla groups—one Marxist, the other inspired by Castro and the Cuban Revolution—and the drug lords. Immensely powerful, resourceful, and ruthless, there were times when the guerrillas and bandits controlled 40 percent of Colombia and flaunted their financial support of presidential candidates.

The narco-war consisted of U.S. and Colombian soldiers raiding traffickers' strongholds, persecuting and jailing drug lords, and destroying farms where coca leaf—used for cocaine—was cultivated. For their part, the guerrillas and drug-traffickers kidnapped and murdered prominent personalities and blew up buildings and planes, targeting civilians. By the end of the 1990s, the narco-war was still raging without a clear winner, Colombia was virtually paralyzed, and thousands of Colombians had fled to the United States.

## Operation Just Cause

The United States fought the drug war on other fronts, too. In December 1989, the United States invaded Panama. The name of the operation was Just Cause, which had nothing to do with justicialismo: the objective was the arrest of general Manuel Noriega, a strongman who was trafficking in drugs and eliminating the opposition by murdering or placing his critics behind bars. His refusal to cooperate with the United States, even after being indicted on drug violations in 1988, prompted the offensive. After several weeks of occupying Panama, the United States captured Noriega. The general was shipped to Miami, as if he were a bag of coffee beans, where he was put on trial and sentenced to 40 years in prison.

The century ended as it had started: with the United States participating in and shaping historic developments in Latin America. Latin Americans were not surprised by the turn of events. By now, they were used to the idea that in one way or another, the United States would always make its presence felt south of the border.

### Hablas Español

Justicialismo comes from justicia, meaning justice. It means the practice of a political system that is based on legal justice and equality for all.

## The Least You Need to Know

- For nearly 90 years, Mexico had only one ruling party.
- Generals ruled much of Latin America during the last century.
- Castro is the longest ruling dictator in the Americas.
- Thousands of victims of the military dictatorships in Argentina and Chile have never been found.
- By the 1990s, the democratic process was in full swing in Latin America.
- Latin American politics is a hot-button issue for many Latinos.

# So Far from God and So Near to the United States

## In This Chapter

- ◆ American intervention in Latin America
- ◆ How Mexican territories became American states
- ◆ Cloak and dagger south of the border
- ◆ Walker's walk to Nicaragua
- ◆ The mixed legacy of the United Fruit Company

Relations between Latin America and the United States have not always been easy, especially during the 1800s and much of the 1900s. Much of the tension had to do with a difference in worldview. To the United States, Latin America was a child capable of great deeds but given to tantrums and whimsical behavior. Seeing itself as a daddy—a big one—the United States felt that it had to nurture, guide, and punish the child as needed. Latin Americans saw the United States as a giant who was a little too eager to flex his muscles and do whatever was necessary to make things go his way.

Naturally, there were conflicts. Some of the clashes didn't show the United States in a good light. Others did. In this chapter, you can be the judge.

# So Near to the United States

It's the nineteenth century. President Porfirio Díaz, who ruled Mexico for 34 years, is in his office, looking out the window at the distant mountains and volcanoes surrounding Mexico City. The clouds are high over the atmosphere, making the sky seem far away. Turning to a map of Mexico and the United States, Díaz sighs: "Poor Mexico, so far from God and so near to the United States."

Díaz's lament echoed the concern of many Latin Americans during the 1800s. Even Cuban poet José Martí, a gentle and loving soul, once referred to the United States as a monster.

### Para Tu Información

Manifest Destiny was the belief that the American way of life was superior to anything else in the New World, and that the United States had the right, and duty, to expand westward. The Monroe Doctrine was a political posturing best summarized as "America and Latin America for the North Americans."

He did not mean that the giant north of Mexico was a monster; he was referring instead to the ogre-ish strains within the American psyche: a predisposition towards imperialism and the temptation to use force.

The fears expressed by Díaz and Martí were not unfounded. They lived in an era when Americans believed in Manifest Destiny—the notion that the United States had the right to expand towards the West, no matter the opposition. Furthermore, the United States government had put into practice the Monroe doctrine, which claimed the U.S. could intervene in Latin American affairs whenever it saw fit to do so.

# War Against Mexico

In 1846, the Monroe Doctrine was already in full swing. That year the United States declared war against Mexico. It was the inevitable result of the Alamo, remember? Ten years before, Texas had decided to sever its ties from Mexico. To end the rebellion, Mexican general Santa Anna marched on San Antonio and attacked 183 rebels, who had barricaded themselves behind the walls of a mission called the Alamo. All the rebels were killed, but a few days later, American general Sam Houston defeated Santa Anna's army at the battle of San Jacinto, in Texas.

The brief war left everyone bitter. Mexico didn't recognize the newly independent Texas, and Texas resented Mexico's attitude. When the United States annexed Texas in 1845, the Mexican government regarded it as an act of usurpation and threatened to take action. Mexico, however, didn't declare war, as if it was hoping for a peaceful resolution.

Then another dispute arose, this one over the location of the border between the United States and Mexico. The United States said the Rio Grande was the dividing line between the two nations. Mexico maintained the border was actually on the Nueces River, further to the north. Deciding action was more effective than words, the United States sent an army of 3,000 men, under the command of General Zachary Taylor, to the Rio Grande. Mexico interpreted the move as an invasion of Mexican territories. The American and Mexican forces clashed on the waters of the Rio Grande. Newspaper headlines across both nations proclaimed that Mexico and the United States were at war.

*General Santa Anna.*

## Short War, Long Memory

While General Taylor fought in the northeast of Mexico, 10,000 American soldiers disembarked at Veracruz and battled their way into Mexico City, which they occupied in 1847. A year later, the two countries signed a treaty to end the war. Called the Treaty of Guadalupe Hidalgo, the town where the negotiations took place, the pact gave to the United States the territories of Arizona, California, New Mexico, Texas, and parts of Colorado, Nevada, and Utah.

The United States celebrated the victory, but many, including an attorney named Abraham Lincoln, felt that politicians in Washington had manipulated the situation to force Mexico into a war it couldn't win. In a matter of years, Americans forgot the war, but Mexicans didn't. Even 150 years after the first shot was fired across the Rio Grande, some Mexicans in Mexico feel that they were duped into the war and that a good chunk of their country was stolen from them.

*The Mexican-American War.*

Abroad, the Mexican War made people in Latin America leery of the United States. At home, the war added fuel to the fires of the slavery controversy: were the new territories to be pro-slavery or free from slavery? Many historians believe that the dispute over the slavery issue in the new states further divided the United States and stirred sentiments that could only be resolved through a violent confrontation.

The battles of the Mexican War served as training ground for many officers who later would fight on opposite sides of the Civil War. Those officers included Ulysses S. Grant, Robert E. Lee, William T. Sherman, and Jefferson Davis.

---

### Living La Vida Literaria

Here is a bit of the Monroe Doctrine, as stated by President James Monroe in 1823: "... the American continents, by the free and independent condition which they have assumed and maintained, are henceforth not to be considered as subjects for future colonization by any European powers ... The citizens of the United States cherish the most friendly sentiments in favor of the liberty and happiness of their fellow men on [this] side of the Atlantic ... We owe it, therefore ... to declare that we should consider any attempt ... to extend their [European] system to any portion of this hemisphere as dangerous to our peace and safety ..."

---

# A Splendid Little War

The Spanish-Cuban-American War was another manipulative American production. After the United States defeated Spain (see Chapter 9) in a battle that took place in and around Cuba, it gained the territories of Guam and Puerto Rico. In Cuba, the mambises, Cuban soldiers, and politicians who feared the United States would annex Cuba, managed to keep the country independent. But Cuban independence came with a price: it was called the Platt Amendment, after its sponsor, Orville Platt.

The Platt Amendment, which was added to the Cuban constitution as well, gave the United States the right to intervene in Cuba whenever activities on the island threatened American interests. Further, the amendment allowed the United States to oversee Cuban foreign policy and for the construction of an American naval base off Guantanamo Bay with an open-ended lease.

In 1934, Cuban politicians lobbied successfully for the removal of the Platt Amendment. The 30 years or so of American presence on the island had turned many intellectuals and scholars against the United States. In 1959, Castro tapped those sentiments to sanction his anti-American stance and to support his anti-American policies.

**Para Tu Información**

Teddy Roosevelt is regarded by historians as the person responsible for the manipulation of events that lead to the Spanish-American war. He is also regarded as the force behind the construction of the Panama Canal.

### Living La Vida Literaria

Upon returning from exile in 1899, Cuban poet Bonifacio Byrne was heartbroken to spot the American flag flying next to the Cuban flag in Havana harbor:

> Upon returning from a distant shore
> Weary of heart and somber
> I searched for my flag anxiously
> And saw another flying beside her
> With the faith of an austere soul,
> In this conviction I have grown-
> That two flags should not be flown
> When one is enough: my own!

# The Revolution Without Bloodshed

You might recall from Chapter 10 that the United States bought from the French the company responsible for digging the Panama Canal. At that time, Panama was still a province of Colombia. So, in order to take over the Canal project, the United States needed to get permission from Colombia. However, the Colombian government was not pro-United States, and wanted a lot of money for the territory. It occurred to the United States that things could turn out differently if Americans could negotiate directly with Panamanians ... only if, Panama somehow gained independence from Colombia ...

This is how it happened. The United States assured Panamanians that if they were to rebel against Colombia, it would support them. Several aristocratic families and officers, all of whom were related to or friends with American officials, plotted the rebellion.

CAUTION **Cuidado!** _____

The independence of Panama is still controversial. Colombians deem it as an act of defiance against their country. The way they see it, Panama was a province that broke away from Colombia, in the same way the South tried to secede from the North during the Civil War. Panamanians, on the other hand, maintain that Colombia was oppressing Panama and not allowing them to participate in world events.

In 1903, the commander of the Colombian army in Panama was taken prisoner by Panamanian rebels, with the help of the American superintendent of the American railroad. Later on, an American naval ship sailed into port, ready to fight against the Colombians. But before the Colombian government, and even most of the people in Panama, realized what had taken place, the U.S. government recognized the new Republic of Panama. Thus, with American soldiers and finance, the Panamanians had won their revolution without firing a single shot.

With Colombia out of the way and no longer able to make monetary and political demands, the United States worked out a deal with Panama, giving the new nation much-needed cash for the right to build the canal and to control it. For many years, Colombians felt that the United States had stolen Panama from their possession.

# Tell It to the Marines

In 1911, a ruler in Nicaragua by the name of José Santos Zelaya dreamt of building a canal without the Americans. To accomplish this objective, he approached the Germans and the Japanese. Since the Monroe doctrine didn't allow for the presence of foreign governments in the Americas, the United States conspired with the Nicaraguan opposition and sent in the Marines. The ruler was ousted. But the Marines remained—for 30 more years.

The Marines stayed because the country was unstable and the United States wanted to protect its business interests and assure the establishment of governments that were American friendly. In the 1920s, the United States helped to rewrite election laws in Nicaragua to assure a more democratic voting process.

By 1926, some Nicaraguans had grown tired of the American presence and started an anti-American movement, led by a General Augusto César Sandino. For years, the marines attempted to track down the general, but they were unable to find him in the mountains of Nicaragua. In 1933, President Calvin Coolidge decided to withdraw the Marines, but only after training Nicaragua's National Guard in the art of modern warfare. Glad to see the Americans go, Sandino let down his guard and was tricked by Anastacio Somoza, the general of the National Guard, who persuaded him to give up fighting and then murdered him.

Though the United States had no direct connections with Sandino's death, Nicaraguans, and many others in Central America, believed that was not the case and that the Americans had been involved in the planning of the assassination. Sandino became a symbol of rebellion against imperialism and American influence. In the 1970s, another rebellion broke out in Nicaragua and the rebels called themselves Sandinistas, after Sandino.

# Central Casting

Nicaragua and Panama weren't the only Central American republics that were of great interest to the United States during the 1900s; actually, all of Central America was central to American foreign policy, even more so after the building of the canal.

In the 1950s, the United States was convinced that a Guatemalan president was planning to sabotage the canal. President Jacobo Arbenz was democratically elected. Leftist and with connections to Moscow, Arbenz implemented rural reforms, nationalizing one million acres of land owned by the United States-based United Fruit Company. At about the same time, the CIA learned that Russia was shipping arms to Guatemala.

The United Fruit Company was angry. The U.S. government was nervous. It was an epoch when the Soviet Union seemed intent on becoming an empire. Americans believed in the domino theory, which was the notion that after one nation turned communist, others would follow, as had happened in Europe after World War II and was happening in Asia in the 1950s. What was the United States to do? Easy, send in the Marines.

## The Name Is Bond ... James Bond

Well, the Marines didn't come at first. The CIA did. The involvement was initially coordinated by James Bond types—in spirit, anyhow—who plotted activities to destabilize the Guatemalan government. The CIA organized a counter-revolutionary army, led by Carlos Castillo Armas. In 1954 the CIA-sponsored army invaded Guatemala. When president Arbenz tried to rally support against the invasion, his own army, with strategic input from the CIA, persuaded him to give up and resign. The president fled the country.

Colonel Castillo Armas took over the presidential reins. Though he was assassinated a few years later, Castillo Armas paved the way for other military rulers who were friendly towards the United Fruit Company and the United States.

**Hablas Español**

The standard and routine way of performing a job is described as a **modo de operaciones**.

The nature of the clandestine operation in Guatemala became the standard *modo de operaciones*, normal procedures, of subsequent participation in Latin American events, including the following:

- In Bolivia, during the 1960s, the CIA trained the national army, and provided them with sophisticated equipment (such as photographic sensors that detected human heat from long distances) to pursue left-wing insurgents. The obvious success of the operation was the capture of revolutionary Ernesto Che Guevara, who had left Cuba and had gone to Bolivia to plan a revolution.

- In Uruguay, in the 1970s, American agents taught the police methods of interrogation and helped the government in its fight against the urban guerrillas, the *Tupamaros*, who had murdered an American official.

- In Cuba in 1961, the CIA planned—from inside Cuba, Washington, and Miami—the Bay of Pigs invasion, imitating the strategy used in Guatemala against the Arbenz regime. The CIA didn't count, however, on Castro's own counterintelligence activities, which resulted in the arrest of thousands of *gusanos*, anti-Castro conspirators, the moment the Cuban leader learned the invasion was on its way. (See Chapter 10 for more on the failed Bay of Pigs invasion.)

**Para Tu Información**

Tupamaros were urban guerrillas in Uruguay. Mostly college students from affluent families, they named their group after the Inca rebel Túpac Amuru, who had led a rebellion against the Spanish during colonial times.

- In Chile in 1973, the CIA supported a truckers' strike against Pinochet, and the United States offered the military funds for their *golpe de estado*, the coup d'etat against the socialist president.

# Santo Domingo: Not Such a Holy Sunday

Both undercover agents and American troops took part in an armed conflict in the Dominican Republic in 1965. After the death of dictator Rafael Trujillo—he was the one who murdered, among thousands of others, the famous Mirabel sisters (see chapter 12)—in 1961, democratic elections were held and author and intellectual Juan Bosch was elected. In 1963 the military, who opposed Bosch's social agenda, overthrew him, establishing a military junta.

In 1965, Bosch supporters attempted to overthrow the junta, and civil war erupted. The United States watched the developments with great concern. There were three possible roads for the Dominican Republic to take: 1) establish a democratic government, 2) establish a right-wing dictatorship, or 3) establish a Castro-like repressive regime.

President Lyndon B. Johnson was convinced that communist elements within the Bosch camp would win the day. The American president stated his position: the establishment of another communist system in the Western hemisphere would not be tolerated. Five hundred Marines landed to protect American interests. A month later, 20,000 American troops were stationed on the island. Criticism of the United States, seen as too eager to implement the Monroe doctrine, prompted Johnson to seek support form the Organization of American States. The result was the creation of a multi-national force, under the leadership of a Brazilian general, dispatched to the Dominican Republic.

**Hablas Español**

A **junta** is a small group of high ranking army officers who takes over a government and rule by decree or force. The junta might rule for a short time while setting up another government or might rule indefinitely. The noun comes from the verb *juntar*, which means to bring together for a meeting.

As Johnson interpreted the turn of events, the large American presence deterred the country from sliding into chaos or a communist regime. The bigger-the-better model used in the Dominican Republic encouraged him to enact a similar strategy, oceans away, in a place called Vietnam.

# Return Engagements

The American participation in the Dominican Republic was not the first time the United States had intervened in the country; it had done so already in the 1910s. As a matter of fact, during the twentieth century the United States was often a repeat offender throughout Latin America. Check this out:

- **Cuba:** Spanish American war in 1898; on and off military interventions from 1906 to 1922; Bay of Pigs Invasion in 1961; Cuban Missile crisis of 1962.
- **Panama:** Building for the canal from 1900 to 1914; invasion of Panama in 1989.
- **Nicaragua:** Military intervention and occupation from 1910 to 1925; participation in military activities from 1926 to 1933; covert activities from 1981 to 1986.
- **Dominican Republic:** On and off military intervention and occupation from 1912 to 1924; invasion in 1965.
- **Guatemala:** Overthrow of Arbenz regime in 1954; military support of dictator regimes from 1954 to 1986.
- **Chile:** overthrow of Allende in 1973; support of military regime until 1976.

# A Walk to the Past

The United States' will to intervene in Latin America dates back to the nineteenth century, when Americans glorified the adventures of brave men who set out to conquer Latin America for the United States. Though there was a hint of glory in their enterprises, which often ended in death, there was also a shadow of racism and bigotry. For these adventurers believed that they were superior to the folks from south of the border and that as such, they, and not the natives, should be the rulers.

These adventurers were called filibusterers. They supported Manifest Destiny, were pro-slavery, and were usually financed by wealthy Southerners. There were quite a few of them. There was Pierre Soulé, who wanted the United States to buy Cuba and who tried to take the state of Sonora in Mexico on behalf of American confederate soldiers. There was Charles Henningsen, who participated in the invasion of Nicaragua. And there was the leader of the invasion, William Walker, called "the grey-eyed man of destiny."

An American physician, William Walker led an expedition into Nicaragua in 1857. The nation was in the midst of a civil war between liberals and conservatives, and Walker sought the opportunity to make himself president of the beleaguered country. And that was exactly what he did after capturing the town of Granada.

## The Yankee President

The United States immediately recognized his government. The Yankee president established pro-slavery laws and made English the official national language. Then, he began plans to conquer all of Central America and turn it into one country—his personal country.

Walker forced farmers to work for him and offered large grants to any American who would join his army. But he didn't plan on the Nicaraguans, Costa Ricans, and Hondurans forming their own army to defeat him. This they did, expelling the Yankee president.

The filibuster par-excellence didn't give up his dream of conquest. He returned three more times to Nicaragua before being captured and executed by the Hondurans. His American contemporaries regarded him as a hero, a view that some still maintain today. But in Latin America, he was seen as emblematic of capitalism, imperialism, and racism.

# Fruit of the Labor

Not all American participation in Latin America was through the armed forces or the intelligence community. American corporations had a great deal of power in the region. Sometimes, the power was welcomed, as the corporation poured money into a nation. Sometimes, the welcome wore thin or the corporation overstayed it altogether.

Throughout Latin America, the United Fruit Company is the epitome of the good, the bad, and the ugly of American capitalism. The company, which was created after an American banana planter in Central America merged his company with the Boston Fruit Company in 1899, acquired millions of acres, first in Guatemala and then in nations such as Honduras and Costa Rica. The United Fruit Company had a railroad and a fleet of ships, which the company used to transport the fruit to the United States. It employed thousands of workers and paid them more than the locals would pay, built schools for their children, and houses and hospitals for their families. That was the good news.

---

### Living La Vida Literaria

In *One Hundred Years of Solitude,* García Márquez tells of the arrival of the United Fruit Company at a town in South America: "... The gringos, who later on brought their languid wives in muslin dresses and large veiled hats, built a separate town across the railroad tracks with streets lined with palm trees, houses with screened windows, small white tables on the terraces, and fans mounted on the ceilings, and extensive blue lawns with peacocks and quails. The section was surrounded by a metal fence topped with a band of electrified chicken wire which during the cool summer mornings would be black with roasted swallows."

---

The bad news was that the company didn't negotiate directly with its workers and didn't allow for the establishment of labor unions, threatening to leave the area if one was created. It also used pesticides that proved harmful to the laborers. The ugly side of the equation was the destruction of the land when the company over-planted bananas, poisoned the fields with pesticides, and moved from one location to another, leaving behind ghost town after ghost town.

Because the company hired armies of workers and dished out tons of money to the local and national governments, it had a lot of power and could alter the flow of regional politics. During 1954 in Guatemala, it was the United Fruit Company that encouraged the overthrow of President Arbenz.

### Cuidado!

It was United Fruit Company's initial activities in Guatemala that created the concept and stereotype of the banana republic.

Now owned by Del Monte products, the United Fruit Company no longer has any political clout. But neither the company, nor its legacy, have been forgotten by Latin Americans.

## The Least You Need to Know

◆ The United States has intervened in Latin American domestic affairs for more than a century.

◆ Most countries in Latin America have been impacted by American foreign policies.

◆ Many Latin American nations are still suspicious of the United States.

◆ Filibusters were wealthy American adventurers who tried to conquer Latin America in the nineteenth century.

# 12

# A Few Good Men and Women: Latino Icons

## In This Chapter

- ◆ Heroes and heroines from Latin America
- ◆ For love of country
- ◆ What patriot did what and where
- ◆ Rebels, writers, and teachers
- ◆ Saints and sinners

History tells us of the events that shape a nation. Events don't just happen, however; they are the results of the actions of individuals. Thousands of people in Latin America have given their hearts and souls—and sometimes even their lives—to fashion a better world. This chapter tells the story of a handful of patriots who made contributions that extend beyond the boundaries of their countries. Their accomplishments are celebrated throughout Latin America. Some you've already read about in earlier chapters, others you might have heard of elsewhere. It's worth retelling their stories here.

# Simón Bolívar: 1783–1830

If there is one Latin American patriot whose name Americans recognize, it is Simón Bolívar. Dubbed *El Libertador*, the liberator, Bolívar symbolizes the whimsical nature of politics and the difficulties of transforming idealism into a practical political agenda. Loved by the thousands at the beginning of the wars of independence from Spain, Bolívar finished his life detested by the very people he had freed. Shortly before his death, El Libertador lamented, "[Latin] America is ungovernable. Those who have served the Revolution have plowed the sea."

Bolívar was born in Venezuela into a wealthy criollo family. Losing his parents at a young age, he traveled to Europe when he was 16 years old. In the Old World, he became fascinated by Napoleon Bonaparte, studied the liberal French philosophers of the era, and fell in love and married. Happiness didn't last, though. A year later, his young wife died. In mourning and forlorn, Bolívar longed to be back in Venezuela, and focused his attention on the independence movements sweeping throughout Latin America.

From 1807 to 1810, he plotted with revolutionaries in Venezuela and was appointed colonel of the rebel army. During the next nine years, pro-independence Venezuelans battled against loyalist Venezuelans and Spaniards, with no clear winner. As described in Chapter 9, Bolívar changed this situation in 1819, when he marched 2,500 soldiers to the very foot of the Andes and crossed the range at a spot deemed impassable. It was a brilliant strategy, for the Spanish troops on the other side of the mountain didn't anticipate the attack. Bolívar and his men surprised and defeated the Spanish troops. He then led his army from one victory to another.

### Hablas Español

Libertador, meaning liberator, was probably used for the first time in describing the deeds of Simón Bolívar.

By 1826, Bolívar had liberated the present-day territories of Bolivia (named after him), Colombia, Peru, and Venezuela.

## To Plow the Sea

Cheered everywhere he went, Bolívar tried to set up a federation, creating from the countries of New Granada, Ecuador, and Venezuela one nation: Gran Colombia. But individual rivalries between military leaders and nationalistic interests forced the nations apart, and civil war broke out. To keep his dream from plummeting, Bolívar took over the government of Gran Colombia, proclaiming himself dictator and ruling by sheer force of personality and will power.

In 1828, assassins tried unsuccessfully to murder the liberator-turned-dictator. Two years later, Venezuela and Ecuador broke away from Gran Colombia. With politicians turning against him, friends assassinated, and the general populace divided over their support for or opposition to him, the liberator retired from politics. Broken-hearted and disinterested in life, Bolívar died from tuberculosis two years later.

Bolívar freed much of Latin America from the Spanish Empire, but he couldn't persuade the newly created regimes to work together as one nation—in a manner similar to the United States —instead of many.

---

### Living La Vida Literaria

In the novel *The General in His Labyrinth,* Nobel Prize winner Gabriel García Márquez describes the last moments in the Liberator's life: "Then he crossed his arms over his chest ... and through the window he saw the diamond of Venus in the sky that was dying forever, the eternal snows, the new vine whose yellow bellflowers he would not see bloom on the following Saturday in the house closed in mourning, the final brilliance of life that would never, through all eternity, be repeated again."

---

# Eugenio María de Hostos: 1839–1903

During the wars of independence, many patriots envisioned life without colonial rule. They dreamed about the establishment of governments and the creation of republics. But few thought of education and schools. Hostos was the exception.

Born in Puerto Rico, Eugenio María de Hostos was a lawyer and world traveler who devoted his life to the cause of independence and education. In Spain, the United States, and South America he worked tirelessly for Cuba's and Puerto Rico's independence.

## The Teacher

Like Bolívar, Hostos had a dream: To make one federation out of three islands, Cuba, the Dominican Republic, and Puerto Rico. The dream was shattered in 1899, when after the Spanish-Cuban-American War the United States occupied Puerto Rico. That same year, Hostos asked President William McKinley to grant freedom to his beloved island, a request that was denied. Disillusioned, Hostos retired to the Dominican Republic.

Actively involved in politics all of his life, Hostos also wrote 20 volumes worth of poems, essays, short stories, and scholarly studies. His best-known philosophical book is *Moral Social,* essays on ethics and social responsibilities.

Hostos organized the Dominican Republic's public school system and promoted education for women—not a popular notion at the time. He taught secondary school in Chile and was professor of international law at the University of Chile, in Santiago. He prodded the students to think beyond national confines. Years after his death, a college in New York City was named after this Puerto Rican patriot, thinker, and teacher.

# Benito Júarez: 1806–1872

If you drive around the barrios of California and Texas, you might see a mural with a man dressed in black, with top hat in hands, commanding the center of the canvas. That man is Benito Júarez, who, along with Simón Bolívar and José Martí, is the most admired hero in Latin America.

*President Benito Júarez.*

*(Courtesy of North Wind Picture Archives)*

A Zapotec Indian, Júarez lost his parents when he was three years old and was raised by an uncle, who was a priest, and befriended by a bookbinder. Together, the two men taught the young Júarez how to read and write, and introduced him to arts and philosophy. Expected to enter the priesthood, Júarez instead chose to attend a secular college to study law. Three years after graduating, he attempted to defend the inhabitants of a small village from extortion by a local priest. The priest had influential friends in the armed forces, the leading families in the region, and the municipal government; Júarez not only lost the case, but he was arrested for a short while. The incident taught him about the inordinate power of the Church, the army, and the wealthy.

# What Price Freedom?

Joining the world of politics, Júarez was elected governor of Oaxaca and then served as national minister of justice in the 1850s, drafting the *Ley Júarez*, the law of Júarez, which ended the use of special courts for the military and clergy. Serving as vice president in 1857, he and his president, Ignacio Comonfort, introduced the Constitution of 1857, which finally abolished slavery, ended obligatory military service, banned nobility titles, granted personal freedoms, and established universal voting rights for all males.

The army and aristocratic families opposed the constitution, and civil war broke out. Forcing President Comonfort to resign, the armed forces appointed their own president. Júarez, claiming that as vice president he was the legal successor to the office, set up his own government in Veracruz.

The civil war lasted three years. In 1860, Júarez defeated the conservative forces. In 1861, he returned to Mexico City and was elected president. Inheriting a bankrupt government, Júarez stopped payment of debts to England, Spain, and France. French emperor Napoleon III used the refusal as an excuse to invade and conquer Mexico, doing so in 1863 and setting up Maximilian of Austria as the puppet emperor of Mexico. Júarez retreated from the capital and for the next four years presided from a black coach that took him all over the country as he led the war against the French.

> **Para Tu Información**
>
> Júarez was a most extraordinary man. He attended school at a time when most students were white and from well-to-do families. He became a lawyer when Indians were expected to be nothing more than laborers. And he became president during an era when you usually had to look European in order to serve in a public office.

Pressure from the United States forced Napoleon III to withdraw his troops, leaving Maximilian with a skeleton crew for an army, an army that Júarez's forces proceeded to turn into actual skeletons by routing them in battle, capturing and executing Maximilian. A triumphant Júarez returned to Mexico City and served as president until his death of a heart attack in 1872.

Although he was busy fighting for the very existence of Mexico, Júarez somehow managed to find the time to make Mexico a better country. He was responsible for reducing of the size of the military, thus curtailing its influence; creating a rural national police; constructing a railroad that linked the capital with the port of Veracruz; revitalizing the country's industry and agriculture; and infusing foreign capital into Mexico City.

# José Martí: 1853–1895

Picture this: A dreamer who didn't know how to handle a gun rides into battle astride a white horse. The enemy, the Spanish infantry, waits until he is near its line before taking aim and pulling the trigger. The horse rears up, and the rider falls backward, blood on his chest, his blank eyes staring at the sun.

Years before, the rider had written in a poem about wanting to die facing the sun.

Such romantic death is but one reason why poet and liberator José Martí is, along with Simón Bolívar and Benito Juárez, one of Latin America's most revered heroes. A journalist, a poet, a teacher, and above all a revolutionary, Martí was born in Cuba in 1853, the son of a Spanish soldier. At the age of 16, he was arrested for writing *independentista* letters and pamphlets, was sent to a labor camp, and banished to Spain. From 1871 to 1895, he traveled widely throughout Latin America, though his main residence was in New York City, which is where he plotted against Spain.

### Hablas Español

Independentista is someone who wants independence for his country from a foreign ruling power.

Martí persuaded the diverse Cuban groups in exile, each with a different reason for fighting against Spain, to unite under the banner of the *Partido Revolucionario Cubano*, the Cuban Revolutionary Party. His objectives were clear: to install in Cuba a government chosen by the people, and to build a pluralistic society where the majority would rule. His stand against racism and his fear of the increasing role of the United States in Latin American politics attracted blacks and whites, rich and poor to his cause.

## For Love of Cuba

In 1894, Martí organized a military expedition to the island. Consisting of three ships, crowded with Cuban rebels, the small fleet sailed from Florida but was detained by the American government, claiming that since it was neutral on the growing political conflict, it couldn't allow hostile activities to emanate from American soil. Undeterred, Martí called for an uprising in Cuba for February 1895, while arranging for another expeditionary force to sail to the island.

Reaching Cuba in April of 1895, Martí joined the insurgents, reminding them they were fighting not out of hatred for Spain but out of love for Cuba. He also urged them to fight until victory. Rumors have it that a malcontent challenged Martí, telling him that it was easy for him to send young men into battle, especially when he himself would not venture into the battlefield. It was a challenge that Martí accepted, to Cuba's great loss.

You're probably familiar with at least one of Martí's poems. His *Guántanamera*, a popular Cuban ballad, was made an American hit by Pete Seeger in the 1960s: "Yo quiero cuando me muera/Sin patria pero sin amo/Tener en mi tumba un ramo/De flores y una bandera." Which means: When I die, without a country but without a master, I want on my tomb flowers and a flag.

As an essayist, Martí wrote descriptive pieces about life in the United States. As a poet, he was one of the founders of *modernismo*, the modernist movement in Spanish letters. As a man, he sacrificed family, wealth, and comfort to give his heart and soul to the liberation of Cuba. Today, he is the only Cuban patriot who is admired and respected by Cubans on the island and in the United States. So, even after death, the poet-patriot can still foster a sense of unity.

**Para Tu Información**

*Modernismo* is a poetic style that expresses the poet's emotional reaction to sights and sounds, shying away from somber sentiments, and using free verse or simple rhymes in a sing-a-song pattern.

# Rigoberta Menchú: 1959–

"My name is Rigoberta Menchú. I am twenty-three years old. This is my testimony. I didn't learn it from a book and I didn't learn it alone. I'd like to stress that it's not only my life, it's also the testimony of my people." Thus begins the autobiography, *I, Rigoberta Menchú: An Indian Woman in Guatemala*, a book which became a bestseller in the 1980s and which took its narrator from a village in Central America to Oslo, Norway, where she was awarded the Nobel Peace Prize.

As a child, Menchú worked alongside her family in a *finca*, a small farm, picking coffee beans. It was not paradise, despite the images that come to mind of pastoral serenity and mountains as green as emeralds, but it was a life surrounded by people she loved. Within 20 years, as if in a decades-long nightmare, Menchú's family would be dead: her father, her mother, and her brother would be murdered by the military.

The 1970s were a time of violence against the Guatemalan Indians. As the government fought

In her book, the Guatemalan crusader tells of her mother's death: "When my mother died, the soldiers stood over her and urinated in her mouth … Then they left a permanent sentry there to guard her body so that no-one could take it away … After that, my mother was eaten by animals …"

against communist guerrillas, the Indians found themselves in the middle of the struggle. The government relocated and drafted into the army whole villages of Indians; they were the lucky ones, though, for over 100,000 Indians were murdered. Fleeing to Mexico, Menchú went on a crusade for the protection of her people, lecturing on the atrocities taking place in Guatemala and attempting to train leaders who could return home to organize peaceful opposition against the government.

# For My People

Menchú lobbied the United Nations to defend the Indians of Central America and presided over national conferences that advocated for the rights and protection of indigenous people. With the money she was awarded in 1992, as part of the Nobel Peace Prize, she established a foundation to sponsor the construction of houses in Central America as well as the building of schools and community centers.

In 1996, she witnessed the signing of a peace treaty between the Guatemala government and the rebels. With the treaty, one of Menchú's dream's came true: a commission was created to study the crimes perpetrated by the armed forces during the war against the guerrillas.

Menchú has been accused of helping out the guerrillas during the war and of promoting Marxist ideals. Some people have also argued that many incidents in her autobiography didn't happen at all or were exaggerated. Her defenders maintain that Menchú used her testimony as a tool against oppression. Either way, many indigenous people in Central America receive medical care and have roofs over their heads, thanks to this brave Guatemalan.

# The Mirabal Sisters

At an international feminist conference held in Bogota, Colombia in 1981, the attendees chose November 25 as the *International Day Against Violence Against Women*. Why this date? Because on this day, 20 years prior, a brutal dictator ordered the brutal murder of three sisters.

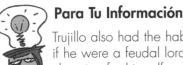

**Para Tu Información**

Trujillo also had the habit, as if he were a feudal lord, of choosing for himself young virgins. He meted out death or imprisonment to anyone who objected to this practice.

Originally, there were four. They were beautiful, they were talented, they were free-spirited, and they wanted freedom for their country. The sisters were Patria, Minerva, Marita Teresa, and Bélgica. Their country was the Dominican Republic.

There was a dictator in the country, and his name was Trujillo. Ruling since 1930, Trujillo annihilated anyone who opposed him. One day, in 1937, Trujillo topped his own record for violence: he ordered the massacre of more than 20,000 Haitian immigrants.

## Butterflies

The Mirabal sisters witnessed the massacre and swore that they would overthrow Trujillo. They made their vow a reality years later when they organized, along with their husbands, a resistance movement. Meeting at Patria's house, the conspirators planned strategies to destabilize the dictatorship. They used the code name, *las mariposas*, butterflies.

Trujillo learned of their work and planned to get rid of the women. Because the sisters were well known and respected, the dictator didn't want to be accused of plotting their execution. His plan was simple: arrest their husbands, imprison them in a remote jail in the countryside, and make sure that the sisters get into a tragic accident on their way to visit their husbands.

Warned about the plan, the Mirabal sisters still decided to make their trip. They couldn't let the ruler intimidate them. So, on November 25, 1960, the sisters were pulled out of the car, tortured, strangled, and pushed off a cliff.

The murder ignited opposition against Trujillo. A year later, while the dictator was traveling in his own car, rebels assassinated him. Today, the Mirabal sisters symbolize freedom in the Dominican Republic and are honored as "the mothers of the nation."

### Hablas Español

**Mariposas** are butterflies. As a feminine noun, it was a perfect label for the Maribel sisters.

### Para Tu Información

The fourth Mirabal sister, Bélgica, nicknamed Dedé, survived because on that fateful day she stayed back to watch her nieces and nephews. After the death of her sisters, Dede raised the orphans. Many years later, she told the Mirabal story to novelist Julia Alvarez, who wrote about it in *In the Time of the Butterflies*.

# Emiliano Zapata: 1879–1919

"My name is Emiliano Zapata." You can hear Marlon Brando mumbling those words as he stands before an actor portraying dictator Porfirio Díaz. Brando looks the part: he has the mustache, the tanned complexion, and the camera angle makes him a dead ringer for the legendary revolutionary. For most Americans, Brando's film is their only exposure to the Mexican revolution and the revolutionary. That's not bad. For the film tells the basic facts about Zapata: he was an Indian of mixed ancestry; he fought for land reform; he didn't compromise his ideals; and he was murdered.

Let's flesh out a few more details. Zapata was not a dirt-poor , as he is sometimes portrayed. He came from a relatively well-known family in southern Mexico that owned a small farm and had cattle. He resented how the government of Porfirio Díaz kept taking land away from the Indians by allowing cronies to farm the lands, and even sell them, without the Indians' consent. In 1910, Zapata, who was intelligent and could express himself well, went to Mexico City to speak to representatives from the government (no, unlike the movie, he didn't meet the dictator) but was arrested and drafted into the army (a common practice by the Díaz regime). A few months later, Zapata was able to leave the army and return home.

## In the Name of Zapata

By now, there was a presidential campaign going on, and when Díaz jailed leading candidate Francisco Madero, revolution broke out (see Chapter 9 for more on the revolution). Zapata organized the villagers in his region and took over a police station. With over 1,000 followers, he moved north, defeating *federales*, federal troops, along the way. When Madero ousted Díaz from power, Zapata realized that the new president wouldn't help the poor Indian farmers from Morelos and continued fighting.

### Hablas Español

The government troops in Mexico during the revolution were called **federales,** because they enlisted in the service of the federal government.

When General Huerta murdered Madero, Zapata still continued his fight, this time helping General Carranza, who seemed to care about the Indians. But when Carranza defeated Huerta, it was clear that the general only cared about power. Joining forces with Pancho Villa, Zapata marched on the capital. But they didn't defeat Carranza, who by now was recognized as a national leader by a population tired of the war, and by foreign dignitaries.

No city slicker, Zapata returned to Morelos, where he continued fighting against Carranza. His position was clear: give the land back to the Indians. The federal government could neither defeat Zapata nor buy him out, as they did with many other rebels, including Pancho Villa. They couldn't ignore him either, so in 1919 government officials asked to meet with Zapata. As the rebel entered a military installation and was invited to review the troops, the federales discharged their rifles. Legend has it that upon seeing its master fall dead to the ground, Zapata's horse took off for the mountains.

The Brando flick ends with a narrator saying that the people in Morelos didn't believe that Zapata was dead because his stallion was seen galloping through the countryside. A bit of Hollywood? Maybe. Maybe not. Seventy years later, Indian rebels rose against the Mexican government. They said they were leading a revolution in the name of Emiliano Zapata.

# A Twist, As Always

Two historical figures are indeed icons, but they're too controversial and even problematic to introduce them as heroes. Yet, we must mention them: Evita Perón and Ernesto "Che" Guevara.

Evita was the wife of General Juan Domingo Perón, a strong ruler who identified with fascist ideology and presided over Argentina from 1946 to 1955 (later on, he made a comeback in the 1970s and was elected president again—see Chapter 10). As Argentina's first lady, Evita championed the cause of the poor, prodded her husband to create social programs, and led a fund-raising campaign to build hospitals and schools.

The problem is that Evita was no saint, and it's believed that she stole a good deal of the money she raised. Rumor has it that Evita was raised in a brothel, and that when she was an actress—years before she met Perón—she moonlighted as a prostitute. Maybe. Maybe not. But the most controversial aspect of her life was the unquestioning support she gave to a ruler who used strong tactics to silence those who opposed him, was anti-Semitic, and created a system that encouraged nepotism and graft. For many in Argentina, Evita and her husband symbolize corruption, greed, and opportunism.

"Che," on the other hand, was not an opportunist. Joining Castro's forces during the Cuban revolution in the 1950s, he helped to topple the dictatorship of Fulgencio Batista, Castro's foe, an admirable deed.

College students, many of whom consider Guevara to be idealist, might not be so gaga over him if they knew a few more details about the famous revolutionary. He played a role in the execution of hundreds of Cubans from 1959–60 after Castro came to power, the arrests of thousands during the early years of the revolution, and he ordered the deforestation of Escambray mountains forests, oversaw the destruction of the cattle and sugar industries in Cuba (in what Guevara regarded as an quixotic anti-bourgeois act).

**Cuidado!**

"Che" is not part of Guevara's name. His full name was Ernesto Guevara. "Che" is an Argentine expression, the equivalent of "Mac" or "pal." In Cuba, the rebels addressed Guevara as "Che" as a cordial act and a way of acknowledging his national origin.

The bottom line is that for an idealist and a humane leader, he did little to protect the rights of those whom Castro saw as marginal to the revolutionary process. So let's a wait a bit before calling Guevara a hero.

## The Least You Need to Know

- Heroic men and women helped to build Latin America.
- The life of Simón Bolívar embodies the mercurial nature of the political world.
- Juárez, Martí, and Zapata are icons of heroism and integrity.
- Not all Argentines consider Evita Perón to be a hero.
- Che Guevara was responsible for hundreds of deaths in Cuba after the revolution.
- Not all heroes from Latin America are free from criticism.

# Part  3

# Body and Soul, Latin Style

The family is the center of Latino life, but when they need spiritual support, Latinos turn to the church and to God. Latinos don't live by faith alone (who does?), though, and Latino families enjoy eating together and eating well.

If you haven't figured it out by now, this chapter is about Latino family, faith, and food ...

# Chapter 3

# Mi Familia: Home and Family Life

## In This Chapter

- ◆ It's all relative
- ◆ Honor thy family
- ◆ Macho macho man
- ◆ Moving toward liberation
- ◆ The American-Latino family

*Novelas*, or soap operas, on Spanish television always come to an end, unlike their American counterparts that seem to go on and on. A novela might last a year, even two, but it will conclude. In the last episode, usually a small celebration takes place. Held at a mansion in Mexico City, or a hacienda in Buenos Aires, on a chateau in the Caribbean, it's peopled with the hero's family and the heroine's family. And aunts and uncles and cousins. In other words, *The Brady Bunch* plus lots and lots of relatives.

Often depicting the struggle of a man salvaging the family's honor or a woman keeping the family together, novelas are as much about romantic affairs as family affairs. If it can be theorized that soaps reflect, and play back on the small screen, the values of a society at a particular instant, the Spanish novelas are reflective of Latinos' interest in the family.

Just how interested, that's what we'll see in this chapter.

# Family Affair

Social scientists call the American family a nuclear family (it has nothing to do with an explosion, even though the family might be explosive), meaning that the nucleus, the parents, are surrounded by the electrons, the children. The nuclear family is the product of the Industrial Revolution. As cities evolved and the nature of jobs changed from families working together at a trade, or a farm, to a single individual working for a company—be it a factory or an office—workers moved away from their parents' homes and established their own residences blocks or miles away. There was no longer a need for a group of family members to support each other. In other words, large families were passé.

### Para Tu Información

The American nuclear family has changed. As recent as 20 years ago, the nuclear family consisted of a husband, a wife, and their two, maybe three, children. Today, the nuclear family might be a single parent with at least one child. Or, it might be a same-sex marriage with children.

But not so for Latinos, for whom large families, called the extended family by social scientists, are still thriving. The Latino *familia* is made up of several generations of family members, as well as siblings. Class and social background determine if the family lives under one roof, near each other, or separately but in constant contact. For example, the Latin American literary classic, *One Hundred Years of Solitude*, by Gabriel García Márquez, is the story of one family and several generations of its members living in the same residence, or a stone's throw away, and struggling together over many years.

## Los Abuelos

In the classic extended *familia*, you have one set of *abuelos* —often the maternal grandparents—the parents, the children, and an unmarried uncle or aunt. If life flows as it's meant to, the grandparents are replaced by the parents, who then become the abuelos, their children the parents, and so on and on.

### Hablas Español

**Abuelos** is Spanish for grandparents. The male singular is **abuelo**, the female is **abuela**. **Familia** means family. The word can also be used as "he's familia" with a non-family member to emphasize closeness.

In the old country, the abuelos helped out around the house by performing chores, cooking, or watching over the children while the father went to work and the mother took care of the housekeeping. That tradition is often carried on by Latinos in the United States, but with the difference that the mother works outside the home. It is estimated that one out of ten Latino grandparents, usually a grandmother, according to a study conducted in New York by The Society for Gerontology, stays home to watch over young children.

*Abuelos from Bolivia.*

*(Photo by Erica G. Polakoff)*

Whether in the United States or in Latin America, abuelos command respect. Their views regarding financial matters, family issues, and the rearing of children are taken into account. They also participate in family outings, so at a soccer game, for example, it might not be uncommon for both grandparents to attend the match.

## Not by Law

You might also spot an uncle or a cousin at the soccer game. These are *parientes*, blood relatives. Parientes are directly connected to the family, no matter how distant that connection might seem. The children of your grandmother's cousin, for example, will be regarded as part of the extended family and will be introduced either as familia or pariente.

There are also family members linked through marriage. The word here is *parentesco*. Notice that in English the word would be "in law," meaning, of course, that the person is related to you by marriage, a legal act. But in Latin America, the person is regarded as a pariente. Law doesn't make your sister-in-law a relative, the heart does.

### Hablas Español

Parentesco comes from the word **pariente**, which is Spanish for relative. **Parenstesco** means relative-like.

## Love and Other Strangers

There are other types of family members who are really not members of the family: they're related neither by blood nor marriage but by adoption—legal or informal adoption.

They're known as relatives of *crianza* (crianza means by rearing, raising as a family member), such as *hermano de crianza* or, *primo de crianza*—something akin to an adopted brother and cousin. In the old country, these hermanos and primos were incorporated into the family for sentimental reasons. For example, someone might help out a friend by raising that person's child until economic conditions improve for that person. It was not uncommon for the children of the adopted siblings or cousins to be considered actual nephews and nieces and to maintain the relations ad-infinitum.

### Para Tu Información

Unlike the concept of "in-law," which hints at an artificial situation created by law and, therefore, with the potential to be terminated by law, the concept of pariente suggests an on-going relation, regardless of circumstances. By considering your brother's wife, or her parents, a pariente, the relation is not determined by legal processes but by kinship, something much stronger than law. Thus, even after the marriage ends, the in-law would still be regarded as a pariente; maybe a distant pariente, but a relation nonetheless.

There are other non-blood relations. They're the *compadres*. These are related through *compadrazgo*, which is the act of becoming godparents. Baptism in the Catholic Church is the formal avenue to compradazgo. The *padrinos*, the child's godparents, are compadres, or co-parents, to the parents. Padrinos are responsible for the religious upbringing of the children, should the parents fail to do so. And if the parents perish, the padrinos are responsible for raising the children. In the immigration process, often parents will ask padrinos in the United States to sponsor their children.

Children treat their padrinos with love, honor, and respect. When a child can't turn to his parents, he is expected to turn to the padrino. As the padrino ages, the child is supposed to help look after him. In the United States, the godchild, known as the *ahijado*, might help his godparents deal with social agencies or medical needs by providing translating services and transportation.

## Comforting Compatriots

In the United States, compadrazgo is also extended to people who come from the same town or the same country. There are many reasons for welcoming a stranger into the familia:

◆ Many Latinos in the United States come without a family or lack an extended family.

◆ As way to reduce isolation. Comments Dr. Ana Nogales in *The Book of Love, Sex, and Relationships*: "Without the cousins, abuelas, sisters, and tios whom we can automatically trust with our personal problems, we feel isolated and alone."

◆ By accepting a stranger, or another family, into the familia, a support system and a network is created.

◆ Life in the United States can be scary for newcomers. Through compadrazgo, immigrants find safety in numbers.

# Children First

Whether blood-related or not, the Latino family cherishes children. Social scientists call it being child-centered. Here is another way to put it: for Latinos, children come first.

You could say that children are important to all loving families, not just Latinos. That's true. But Latinos assign a bit more importance to children. For example, unlike some Asian traditions where the parents are expected to pay more attention to their own parents than their own children, Latinos expect everyone in the familia to nurture the children. And unlike some Anglos, who are relieved when a child goes away to college or moves into his or her own apartment, affirming the tradition of expecting children to leave the nest and become independent, Latinos prefer for the son or daughter to stay home until the wedding day.

According to Lynda Chavez, in *Out of the Barrio*, this emphasis on the child often requires for the mother to stay home. This often has a positive effect on the child. For though the family might earn less money, making it harder to get out of the cycle of poverty, the child experiences nurturing and a sense of belonging.

# Poor, but Proud

Even the poorest familias still do their best to meet children's needs and wants. The best illustration of this commitment is the celebration of the *quince*. A *quinceañera* is someone who is turning fifteen. Such a birthday is a grand occasion, more so for girls than boys.

The quince is something like a sweet sixteen party combined with a bat mitzvah. A hall is rented and a D.J. is hired—in the old days, it used to be a band. The girl's best friends serve as her maids; boys, dressed in tuxes, escort the girls. At a designated moment, the father walks the girl to the center of the hall where they waltz together. After the dance is over, the boy chosen to be the birthday girl's escort takes her hand and dances with her. Then, little by little, the maids and their companions join in the waltz.

**Para Tu Información**

Quinces are big affairs, all right. If all of this is foreign to you and you can't visualize one, try this: think of a wedding without a spouse.

The quince is scaled-down version of a debutante's ball. No matter how Americanized a Latina is, chances are she will look forward to her quince. No matter how economically tight her parents might be, they will maintain the tradition. To do so, they might have two jobs or they might borrow money. And this is where the familia comes in, since many family members will help out the parents.

# Family Values

Familias are united by an emotional link and by values that have been passed on through the generations. The values foster the proper and correct behavior within the family. These values tell family members what is expected of them.

Latinos are oriented towards the group, the familia, versus the individual. The individual— say, the child—is loved, but he is taught that the good of the many comes before a single person. Social scientists call it allocentrism or collectivism. Allocentrism emphasizes the needs, objectives, and points of view of the group. Allocentrism values personal interdependence. Because of this, Latinos are comfortable in groups and communities that are nurturing and respectful.

Children are taught to respect their elders. *Respeto* acknowledges that a certain individual has a certain power over you, based on a social rank, say someone with money, a professional position—doctors, for example—and age. With age comes wisdom and experience, as Latinos see it, anyhow. Children are taught to show respeto towards these individuals by addressing them as Usted—the formal you—not engaging in conversation unless invited to, and avoiding eye contact. And never arguing with an elder, especially an abuelo!

---

### Living La Vida Literaria

For many Latino writers, the grandparents are a link to the old country and an idealized childhood. Here is bit of poem, translated from the Spanish, by Roberto Valero:

> Grandmother sleeps in my wallet
> I know she floats a smile of remembrance
> … And the comfort of walking and walking
> On old streets
> That are used to my steps

---

## Honor Thy Parents

*Honor* among Latinos is highly valued. What does honor mean? At its simplest, honor means not bringing shame to your familia and your family name. The concept might have emerged in Spain during the Reconquest, when a poor Spanish farmer would join the army to earn a salary and to give himself and his family a name. Upon leaving his village for the war, the lad was often told by his dad, "You don't have money. But you have your name. Honor it."

The Aztecs also practiced a form of honor when going into battle. A warrior was expected to fight bravely and die a good death. To show cowardice was to shame the family.

Today, honor means assuring you behave properly, you treat your elders with respect, and you provide for your family.

## Other Values

With honor and respect, comes *confianza*, trust. Confianza is not merely the placement of trust in a person but it's suggestive of a sentiment, a kind of kinship, towards that person. Confianza in the family is the assurance the family will do what is right for you. Confianza also helps to cement friendship with individuals who are not blood related. The act of confianza dictates that business partners don't need legal forms and paper work to seal a deal. A handshake will do. The honor of the family name will suffice.

Another value is *simpatía*. To practice simpatía is to promote pleasant and non-confrontational relations, to treat others with respect, and to keep conflicts and disagreements at a minimum. It is the desire to live in simpatía that prompts many Latinos not to disagree with their supervisor at work or with teachers and doctors. In business, it is this desire that encourages extensive small talks, accompanied by a cup of coffee, or a glass of wine, before plunging into a business transaction.

It all fosters *lealtad*. Here is an example of leal-tad: during the early twentieth century, there was a rebellion in Cuba, led by a close friend of the president in office. When the president, Mario García Menocal, learned of this fact, he met with the rebel leader and negotiated a truce, even though Menocal had the power to quench the insurgents. Asked why he did so, the president said about the rebel leader: "*Con razón o sin ella, el es mi amigo.*" Meaning, right or wrong, he is my friend.

**Hablas Español**

**Confianza** means trust. **Respeto** means respect. **Simpatía** is a sentiment of spontaneous affection and behaving in a likeable manner.

Lealtad is old-fashioned loyalty. To practice it is to stick with your family and friends, no matter what. Thus, you don't allow strangers to criticize your family. Now, is lealtad the same as faithfulness? Not necessarily. For a man might be unfaithful to his wife but see himself as loyal to his family. As long as he provides for his wife and children and protects the family's honor, he's maintaining the code of lealtad.

If you perceive an inherent contradiction in this equation, you're right. It comes about because of a thing called: *machismo*.

# Macho Man

What is this thing called machismo? In certain regions in Spain, a *macho* is a male pig (feminists might find this humorous, so go ahead and smirk). In Latin America, macho means male. Machismo, therefore, has to do with manliness. Now, raise the concept of manliness a few notches by throwing in Jewish and Arabic influences, which dictated that a man was both the bread winner and a soldier, and what you get is a macho man defending and protecting his family at all costs.

**Para Tu Información** _____

The opposite of the macho man is the *niño mimado*, the Mama's boy. The niño mimado expects the world to serve him because his mother has told him that he's special and unique. If he marries, his wife must do everything for him, regardless of whether or not he has a job. Something of a weakling, the niño mimado would shy away from a challenge and would not defend his, or the family's, honor.

That's the Spanish take. The Aztecs also had their own code of machismo. The word they used was *mati*, in Nahualt, the language spoken by the Aztecs, and it meant dying a glorious death in battle, a death that was be rewarded with an eternal presence in paradise. Matism encouraged Aztec warriors to compete with each other, to prove themselves superior to a peer.

The combination created the culture of machismo. This code is not exclusively a Latino invention. Variations and types of machismo are found the world over. It's just that the Latino brand is the most famous.

## The Macho Way

The macho way presumes proper ladies need to be protected and can't fend for themselves. A macho man defends a woman's honor. For instance, in the novel *Chronicle of a Death Foretold*, by Gabriel García Márquez, two brothers are bound by the code of machismo to kill a friend who had gone to bed with their unmarried sister, even though they don't really want to commit the deed.

A macho courts the lady of his dream and, upon marrying her, provides for her and for their children. His wife stays home and doesn't need to work for living. He makes all the decisions, and his decisions are her command.

## The Rules of the Macho Game

This is what the macho man is expected to do:

- Be physically strong; drink without getting drunk; don't ever show pain.
- Dominate others; at the very least, don't let others dominate you, especially women.
- Challenge to a fight anyone who insults you or your family.
- Be the silent type.
- Consider yourself attractive to women.
- When a woman flirts with you, take up the offer, even if you're married.
- Seduce all attractive women that come your way.
- Never jeopardize the family's income by your extra-marital affairs.

This is what the good woman is expected to do:

- Wait for the sweetheart to propose marriage.
- Have sex to have children, not for the sake of having sex.
- Do everything the husband commands.
- Acknowledge his leadership.
- Wait for your husband to get home from work, war, or the arms of his mistress.
- Nurture male children to be just like dad.
- Stick with your husband no matter what; honor his memory after death.
- Remain a widow until your last breath.

> ### Living La Vida Literaria
>
> In *Chronicle of a Death Foretold*, García Márquez describes a woman's perception of a macho man: "Pedro Vicario asked to borrow her husband's shaving implements, and she brought him the brush, the soap … and a safety razor with a new blade, but he shaved with his butcher knife. Clotilde Armenta thought he was the height of machismo."

# The Mother and the Mistress

For the macho man, there are two types of woman: the mother and the mistress. Scholar David T. Abalos, in *The Latino Family and the Politics of Transformation*, sees it like this: "the woman who took care of the [macho man] and procreated [his] children did not have to be the same woman who gave pleasure." In other words, the wife means motherhood and duty; the mistress means pleasure and abandonment.

The mistress is active, a vessel for pleasure, abandonment, and freedom. What the macho man doesn't do with his wife, he does with his mistress. And it's even possible for the mistress to know more about the macho's life, income, and family, than his wife. But there are boundaries, which are well known to the wise mistress. For example, Evita Perón was the product of a liaison between a married man and his mistress. Evita, the illegitimate child, was close to her father, but the day he died, neither she nor her mother were expected to attend the funeral—and Evita and her mother knew so.

## Para Tu Información

Though machismo is part of the Latino experience, not all Latinos practice machismo with the same intensity or at all. In other words, some countries cultivate machismo more than others. In Latin America, it's generally believed that Mexicans are the most machistas of all Latin Americans. Income level has a lot to do with the practice of machismo. More money means more exposure to different worldviews, thus softening some of the more radical components of machismo.

The mother and wife is passive. She is wise and patient and loving—the embodiment of true love, as defined by St. Paul in the *New Testament*. A stoic, the mother tolerates the ways of the macho man while raising the children. She accepts her fate, cooking away and keeping the house spotless. No wonder her children place her on a pedestal.

## Rebels with Cause

Poet-philosopher Octavio Paz observes that the mother-mistress roles are assigned to women by men—without women's input. Which is exactly how the macho man wants it. For as he sees it, the world is his oyster and women are his playthings.

But some women did and do try to rebel. One pioneer was the poet Sor Juana Inés de la Cruz, a nun. More intelligent and better educated than the men she knew in seventeenth century Mexico, Sor Juana decried the power given to these men by society, criticizing the ease with which they dismissed the female gender. She wrote:

> Hombres necios que acusáis
> a la mujer sin razón,
> sin ver que sois la ocasión,
> de lo mismo que culpáis

Meaning, "You foolish men, blaming women without reason, blind to the fact that you create the problems for which you blame them." But such poetry, and posturing, was not tolerated, and the Church, administered by men, ordered her to silence her voice and to stop writing. Which Sor Juana did. Growing mute and growing ill, she withered away in a convent.

There were other rebels. According to Himilce Novas, in *Everything You Wanted To Know About Latinos*, there was a woman in the nineteenth century called Manuela Medina, who fought in Mexico's war of independence, leading an army, and defeating Spanish troops on several occasions. And during the Mexican revolution, there were the "Adelitas," women who went into battle and the bedroom with bandoleers around their shoulders; they were better lovers and better soldiers than most macho guys. In Argentina, during the 1940s, Evita used her sexuality and cunning to obtain power beyond those assigned to her by her husband, the general.

> **Living La Vida Literaria**
>
> Mariano Azuela describes an "Adelita" in his novel *The Underdogs*: "... she was decked out in a silk dress and heavy gold earrings. The pale blue color of the dress accentuated her olive complexion ... She rode with her legs wide apart and her skirt hitched up to her knees ... She wore a pistol across her chest and had her cartridge belt slung across the pommel of the saddle."

## Dump the Guys

But true rebellion by ordinary women didn't occur until the end of the twentieth century. It happened in the United States. And it had nothing to do with ideology but with money—lack of money, actually.

How the rebellion worked out in the Cuban community serves as a good illustration of the process. As middle-class Cubans arrived in the United States in the early 1960s, the men—mostly professionals—couldn't find positions similar to the ones they had in Cuba. Eager to make a good living, couples agreed that both needed to work. Thus, forsaking their traditional roles as homemakers, the wives went outside the home to earn money. Guess what was the outcome? The proper ladies of the house, meant to be protected, defended, and provided by the men of house, managed to make more money than the men of the house.

> **CAUTION** **Cuidado!**
>
> Don't assume that all Latinas are rebelling against machismo. The vast majority still experience it and might not even know it, so much a part of their culture is the macho experience. However, with time and world enough in the United States, Latinas are attracted by the freer ways of Americans and attempt to emulate them.

Initially, the women saw themselves as merely helping out, but 10 years into exile, these Cubanas began to assert their roles in the household, demanding participatory management. By the 1990s, divorce among Cubans in Miami had reached the 50 percent mark as more Cuban women concluded they could make it on their own and dumped old-fashioned, machista husbands.

Working outside the home is now the norm for many Latinas. Comments Ana Nogales, "many Latinas are discovering that in addition to being competent mothers and house-wives, they can also be competent workers, great supervisors, successful entrepreneurs ... they want ... success in a career, and economic independence." The down side is that many macho men experience difficulties with such women. Threatened, especially when the wives earn as much or more than they, the husbands see themselves as failures. For some Latino families, the tension spells disaster.

# The Troubled Familia

Scholar Abalos believes that Latino families are at risk. He observes that many families "are surrounded by the dramas of incoherence and deformation that threaten to destroy the moral fiber of their lives." When the man—the traditional provider—needs the woman to work in order to provide a decent living for the family, the wound to the ego is deep and wide. To dull the ache, and improve their self-image, many Latinos take up drinking, grow distant from the children, and even desert the home.

The children are the victims of the conflict. Writes Abalos, "... Latino children are increasingly born into a world without the merciful container of security ... Because of the breakdown of male/female and husband/wife relationships ... many children are badly hurt." These children do poorly in school. Unable to progress academically, they throw away the opportunities to make themselves a better life than their parents had.

With their hearts breaking, many of these children walk away from their heritage while harboring feelings of inferiority. In most cases, the result is a life of emptiness and the possibility of repeating their parents' mistakes. In the worst cases, some of these youths are attracted to gang life, where they feel part of a group that nurtures and nourishes them—it's no accident that many Mexican-American gang members call their gangs familias.

# A Better Tomorrow?

The good news is that this sad universe of gang life and family neglect is not typical of the overall Latino experience. Furthermore, the attitude towards the code of machismo is changing. Latinos who come to the United States as young children, or who are born here, tend not be as machista as their fathers and are willing to share in the responsibilities of raising a family. Likewise, Latinas who live in the United States more than 10 years tend to reject many of the traditional roles assigned to them by men.

It is a transformation that hopefully will combine the best of Latino family values with the sense of individual freedom American society offers. Call it a marriage between Latin America and the United States.

# The Least You Need to Know

◆ Family life is a crucial to all Latinos.

◆ Latinos prefer extended families over nuclear families.

◆ Some of the values that bind Latino families together are honor, loyalty, respect, and trust.

◆ Machismo is a salient Latino characteristic.

◆ The nature of machismo in the United States is changing due to economics and the influence of the American lifestyles.

◆ Don't assume all Latinos are machistas and all Latinas are subservient.

# Chapter 14

# *Tradición:* Religious Traditions

## In This Chapter

- ◆ Catholic Latinos
- ◆ Pastors and priests
- ◆ Pentecostals
- ◆ The way of all Santeros
- ◆ The life of the Spirit

Fighting alongside Castro in the mountains, during the Cuban revolution back in the 1950s, a few of the hard-core Communists wore around their necks either chains with an image of a Catholic saint or necklaces dedicated to an orisha, an African deity. Though it seemed paradoxical, it wasn't. For even though many of these rebels believed that religion was the opium of the masses—as Karl Marx phrased it—they still didn't want to risk offending supernatural beings. In essence, they believed that there was another universe beyond this world, something that no Communist tract could explain.

Fundamentally, that is how many Latinos view the world. It is composed of the practical and of the spiritual, the ordinary and the magical.

We'll try to understand such paradoxes in this chapter.

# News from Other Worlds

At the end of a recent news broadcast on the Spanish network, the anchorman looked up at the camera and said, "That's it for tonight. We'll see you tomorrow—Lord willing." It wasn't the first time the newsman had ended a program in that manner. Nor would it be the last time. Nor was he the only reporter on the show to allude to the Almighty. As a matter of fact, his colleagues regularly invoked the name of the Lord while covering a news event. For example, during Hurricane Floyd, the weatherman said that the worst of the storm was over, adding, *"Si Dios quiere"*—Lord willing.

Such pronouncements aren't acceptable on the English language television, but on the Spanish networks they are a daily occurrence: the practice is reflective of Latinos' disposition towards religion and spirituality. Most Latinos feel a harmonious relation with the supernatural, a relation that is channeled through participation in organized religion or informal spiritual endeavors.

Traditionally, Latinos are primarily attracted to four religions: Catholicism, Protestantism, Judaism, and Santería.

# The Cross and the Sword

The Catholic Church is big in Latin America. Catholicism came to the New World with the conquistadores. The conquistadores used the sword to conquer the Americas; the accompanying clergy used the Bible to gain the hearts of the conquered. The first priest, a Franciscan monk, arrived in the New World in 1493, with Admiral Columbus on his second journey. Soon, other orders followed. In 1510, the Dominicans and the Mercedarians reached the Americas. The Augustinians arrived three years later. The Jesuits came during the 1540s.

The Spanish Church represented the Spanish Crown, establishing its hold in Latin America without consulting Rome and the Popes. Serving as an administrative unit of the Crown, the Church oversaw the colonization of the Americas. The Catholic bishops dispatched to the New World were responsible for the building of cathedrals, hospitals, and universities. Eager to convert millions of Native Americans, the bishops introduced the printing press so they could publish easy-to-read, often illustrated, books of catechism.

**Para Tu Información**

A lot of the money the Church accumulated during colonial times was used to build hospitals. Three years after the conquest of Mexico in 1521, the Hospital de Jesús was founded in Mexico City. Likewise, more than 10 hospitals were erected in Peru a few years later. The American colonies, on the other hand, didn't have a full hospital until late in the eighteenth century.

*Statue of Christ in Havana.*

*(Photo by William Luis)*

The Church accumulated wealth through taxes, tithes, inheritances, and money donated through *cofradías*—groups of lay persons affiliated with a particular church for a particular purpose, such as building and maintaining a hospital. Over the centuries, the Church in Latin America became one of the wealthiest in the world. For instance, by the middle of the 1800s, the Church owned nearly half of the land in Mexico, and in Peru the Church had a bigger budget than the national government.

> **Hablas Español**
>
> *Cofradías* were organizations, or clubs, created to collect money for the support of an activity carried on by a church.

## Three Changes of Heart

Through colonial times, from about the 1490s to the early 1800s, the clergy sided with the Spanish king. But by the late 1700s, there was a change of heart. The Jesuits demonstrated actual concerns for the Native Americans, protecting them from ambitious Spanish colonialists, while other priests identified themselves with the criollos, those born in the New World, and their wish for autonomy. In 1810, two Mexican padres—Father Hidalgo and Father Morelos—armed themselves with swords and guns and started the war of independence from Spain. Twenty years later, a Cuban priest—Father Varela—conspired against the Spanish Crown.

After independence, however, the Church again aligned itself with those in power: the aristocrats and the military. It was a relationship that lasted well until the twentieth century, fostering a stereotypical image of the Church as an institution interested only in maintaining the status quo.

In 1960s, there was again a change of heart, and the clergy sided with the poor and the disenfranchised. Two priests are representative of this change. One was Father Romero, from El Salvador, who was murdered by the paramilitary for criticizing the government and supporting the leftist student movement. The other was Father Ernesto Cardenal, who fought against the Somoza dictatorship and served in the communist regime that ruled Nicaragua in the 1980s. Cardenal was an advocate of liberation theology, which maintained poverty was against the will of God and that capitalist governments oppressed the poor.

> **Para Tu Información**
>
> *Romero,* starring Raul Julia, is a powerful movie about Father Romero's support of the disenfranchised in El Salvador and his deadly struggles with the government.

## Northern Ways

The Catholic Church came to the United States in the sixteenth century. From St. Augustine, Florida, where a chapel was erected in the 1560s, padres set out to introduce Christianity to Native Americans as far north as the Carolinas. On the West, priests traveled with Juan de Oñate as he explored the territory. Upon settling in New Mexico in 1595, one of the very first acts undertaken by Oñate was to ask the priests to celebrate mass. For the next hundred years, missions were built throughout California and Texas, where the good padres taught catechism to Native Americans while introducing new ways to plant and harvest crops.

In 1848, after the Mexican-American war, the Mexican padres were forced out of the United States and were replaced by Anglo priests who didn't practice Mexican religious celebrations. Parishes were run by clergy of Italian and Irish descent, who discouraged the preservation of Mexican and Spanish customs as well as the use of the Spanish language. This practice was prevalent through most of the twentieth century.

In the 1960s, just as was happening south of the border, priests on the West coast began to identify with the struggle of Mexican immigrant farm workers, supporting labor leader César Chavez's attempts at obtaining better wages and medical care for Mexican grape pickers. In Florida, the Church worked closely with the exiles fleeing Castro's regime in Cuba. One priest, Father Walsh, helped a prominent anti-Castro leader—Polita Grau, sister of a former Cuban president—devise ways to get out of the island the children of parents who were imprisoned or suffered persecution. Today, the Catholic Church sponsors political refugees from Latin America, provides sanctuary for illegal immigrants, manages soup kitchens, and finds employment for new arrivals.

**Living La Vida Literaria**

In the memoir *A Hunger of Memory: The Education of Richard Rodriguez*, the author recalls the day he was told not to speak Spanish again: "... one Saturday morning three nuns arrived at the house to talk to [my] parents. Stiffly, they sat on the blue living room sofa. I overheard one voice gently wondering, 'Do your children speak only Spanish at home, Mrs. Rodriguez?...Is it possible for you and your husband to encourage your children to practice their English when they are home?' Of course, my parents complied ... In an instant, they agreed to give up the language ..."

*Polita Grau.*

*(Courtesy of Cuban Heritage Collection, Miami University)*

# The Presence of the Church

Until recently, the Catholic Church permeated the daily ins and outs of the average person in Latin America: the morning began with a mass; workers left for work and students for school after the priest offered his blessings; prayers were said with each meal; the day ended with the church bells tolling.

The Church built the schools, hospitals, and cemeteries. The Church told the parishioners what movies to see and what books to read. It told the faithful what holidays to celebrate and how to celebrate them. It officiated local and national activities, from a day of national mourning to a soccer game.

The priest visited parishioners regularly. He welcomed babies to the world, taught children how to behave in this world, and sent the deceased to the next world. The padre settled quarrels, advised sweethearts, and reconciled spouses. The padre drank wine with celebrants during festivities and comforted families during tragedies. He was a friend and a brother. Through him, God was in his glory and all was fine with the world.

No wonder the instant Latinos arrive in the United States, many of them set out for the nearest Catholic church.

# The Protestant Way

The vast majority of Latinos, about 80 percent, describe themselves as Catholics. But in the last few decades, a growing number—anywhere from 5 to 15 percent—have migrated toward Protestantism. This is a testament to the persistence and dedication of Protestant missionaries, evangelists, and *creyentes*.

Protestants weren't allowed in Latin America during colonial times, and even after independence, they still weren't welcomed. But during the mid and late 1800s, a few countries proved receptive to the ways of the Protestants. In Chile, for example, English businessmen established churches and even had their own cemetery. In 1898, at the end of the Spanish-American war, missionaries headed for Cuba and Puerto Rico. In Puerto Rico, missionaries divided the island into sectors to avoid competing with each other. Thus, the Presbyterians had their territory, as did the Baptists, and so on.

The democratic and participatory structure of Protestant churches, and the emergence of Latin American ministers, coupled with their commitment to working with the poor, attracted over four million converts in Latin America during the 1950s, especially in Central America. The growth was so dramatic that in 1959 Catholic scholars and theologians met at Georgetown University to devise ways to reverse the trend. However, the growth has continued, and it's estimated that today there are about 50 million Protestants south of the border.

**Para Tu Información**

During the 1960s liberal Catholics and Protestants in Latin America joined forces to develop a political-religious ideology called Liberation Theology. The ideology emphasized the social role and responsibility of churches while promoting the study of Christianity through the perspective of the poor and disposed. Rejecting capitalism, liberal theologians advocated social and political change through peaceful means.

# Protestantism in El Norte

Mexican-Americans had their first major encounter with Protestants around 1848. During that time, Anglo Protestants—along with the rest of the United States—were venturing into the West and the Southwest. The major denominations represented by the missionaries were the Baptists, the Methodists, and the Presbyterians. By the 1890s, many protestant churches were founded in California and Texas with newly converted Mexican-Americans administering them. In 1897, the California Spanish Missionary Society was established to organize ministries among Spanish-speaking creyentes.

In the Southeast, Cuban parishioners established protestant churches in Key West during the nineteenth century. In the Northeast, according to theologian Eldin Villafañe, a Spanish-speaking congregation was formally organized in New York City in 1912. The name of the church was *La Primera Iglesia Evangélica Española* and it served parishioners from Puerto Rico. Growth continued, and 20 years later, there were 55 protestant Spanish-speaking churches in the Big Apple. By 1960, that number had increased to 430. These congregations were affiliated with the Baptists, the Christian and Missionary Alliance, Lutherans, Methodists, and Presbyterians. Most of these churches were based in poor urban areas.

There were some problems, though. Latino parishioners felt that their Anglo brothers and sisters didn't see them as equals and that Anglo administrators displayed paternalistic attitudes towards their Latino counterparts. Also, the Latino churches were regarded as appendages to major churches and were treated as such. In other words, Latino Protestant churches were often relegated to a basement or a storefront and not allowed to occupy space within the main church. To protest these conditions, in 1981 Latino pastors and creyentes drafted a document, listing their complaints. Titled, *El Grito de Riverside*—for it was penned at the Riverside Church in Manhattan—the manifesto identified five grievances:

**Hablas Español**

*El Grito de Riverside* means The Shout of Riverside. During the nineteenth century, a grito referred to a call to arms in the wars against Spain.

♦ Social issues relevant to Latinos were not being addressed.

♦ Latino contributions to the church and the ministry were regularly ignored.

♦ Anglo churches were deserting poor areas where Latinos lived.

♦ Latino religious music, theology, and literature were rejected.

♦ Seminaries didn't hire Latino scholars and theologians.

# Pentecostal Paths

Latinos who felt neglected by the Anglo churches, or perceived traditional Protestant services as too cold and detached, gravitated towards the Pentecostal Church. Called "The Third Force" by some theologians, Pentecostalism emerged out of Catholic and Protestant traditions.

### Hablas Español

**Pentecostal** refers to the day of Pentecost, in the New Testament, when the Holy Spirit entered the disciples' bodies and gave them the gift of tongues. It is believed that Pentecostalism emerged from a revival meeting that took place in Los Angeles in 1906.

Often described as the church where people speak in tongues, Pentecostalism emphasizes highly personal participation in religious services, divine healing, and the gift of prophecy as evidence of a spiritual presence in someone's life. According to theologian Villafañe, the Pentecostal Church attracts believers from lower socio-economic levels. In *The Liberating Spirit*, he describes some of the components of Pentecostalism:

♦ **Classical Pentecostals** believe in divine healing, prophecy, and the speaking in tongues.

♦ **Neo-Pentecostals** don't see speaking in tongues as evidence of a spiritual gift.

♦ **Catholic Charismatics** accept Catholic doctrine and the leadership of priests but believe in the active manifestation of the Holy Spirit in the lives of believers.

♦ **Independent Pentecostals** follow a particular leader and might not be associated or connected with a church.

The Pentecostal movement is growing in popularity in Latin America. It is estimated that there are 7 million Pentecostals in Central America and the Caribbean.

# Jewish Traditions

Jews were "personas non grata" in Latin America during colonial times. In Mexico in 1528 the Inquisition, which arrived in America shortly after Columbus had sighted the

New World, sentenced to death two Jewish colonizers accused of practicing their religion. In Peru, during the seventeenth century, several Jewish families were placed on trial for straying away from the Catholic faith.

After Latin America gained independence, the Inquisition was abolished. However, Jews were still ambivalent about the region, so there was no large migration. Towards the end of the nineteenth century, however, Jews were attracted to countries that boasted thriving cities and a growing economy. Argentina was a favorite destination, and by 1900 over 25,000 Jews made that country their home.

Jewish immigration waxed and waned throughout the twentieth century. At the end of World War I, there were about 125,000 Jews in Latin America. During World War II, thousands of displaced Jews entered South America through Paraguay and Bolivia. By the 1950s, there were Jewish communities in some of the more cosmopolitan centers of Latin America.

## Jewish Population in the 1950s

| Country | City | Jewish Population |
| --- | --- | --- |
| Argentina | Buenos Aires | 450,000 |
| Chile | Santiago | 30,000 |
| Mexico | Mexico City | 40,000 |
| Uruguay | Montevideo | 48,000 |

# The Way of the Saints

*Santería* is the most recently recognized religion in the world. The Cuban government afforded it such status on the island a couple of decades ago. In the United States, the Supreme Court decreed Santeria a religion in 1993.

This religion emerged in Cuba during the nineteenth century, when African slaves were shipped to the island from present-day Nigeria and Benin. Upon reaching their destination, the Cuban and Spanish clergy set out to convert the Africans. "No problem," uttered the slaves. After all, Catholic deities had some similarities with the Yoruban gods the Africans worshipped. Thus, the martyr-virgin St. Barbara, who wore a red cape and a crown and carried a sword, reminded the slaves of Shangó, the Yoruba goddess of fire, thunder, and lightning. And John the Baptist, that wild man of the desert who fed on bugs, brought to mind Ogún, the wild man of the African jungle who controls iron. In public, the Africans knelt before the Catholic saints. In private, they addressed the saints by their Yoruban names.

*A botánica.*

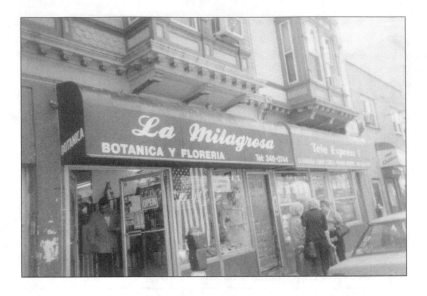

In 1959, Cuban *Santeros*, the believers of Santería, exported the religion to Miami, and from there it made its way to New York and New Jersey and then California. The religion has also spread to the Spanish Caribbean, Mexico, and Venezuela. Santería is practiced in secrecy, so there is no formal tally of its popularity. But one way to measure its growth is to count the number of *botánicas*—the shops that sell Santería ephemera—in a given area. In Union City, NJ, there are at least three botánicas. In Miami, there are over 80. In New York City, you can count over 100.

**Hablas Español** _____

Santería refers to a Saint-like quality or behaving in a saintly manner. In popular usage, it refers to an Afro-Cuban religion. **Santero** is a person who practices Santería. **Botánicas** are shops where you can purchase herbs, folk medicines, and supplies and materials used for Santería. The word alludes to botany, the study of plants, as well as the place in Spain where the infirm could purchase medicinal plants.

## The Ways of Santeros

What do Santeros believe? They believe that each person has a destiny and that each individual must discover and master his or her destiny. The gods, called orishas, help you fulfill your destiny. To do so, you must establish a personal relation with an orisha, and you do so through devotion, sacrifices, divination, and spiritual possession.

If you and your orisha coexist in harmony, all your problems, whether short or long-term, are resolved. To become a Santero, an individual must be sponsored by another Santero and must train in the arts of Santería. After learning how to divine, by reading sea shells tossed on the floor and becoming familiar with the ways and needs of the orishas, a Santero must spend time alone fasting and meditating. Once he or she is ordained, the Santero dresses only in white.

The most dramatic and colorful practice in Santería is the ritual of spiritual possession. This ritual is carried on with a group of believers who dance and sing to the beat of African drums. If the orisha is happy with the ceremony, he or she might join in by possessing a devotee. The incarnated orisha then dances wildly and, upon coming to a pause, delivers messages from departed souls and advises Santeros on personal matters.

**Para Tu Información**

Orishas need food in order to live. At an altar, fruits and vegetables are placed before a statue of the orisha. Sometimes animals are sacrificed. When this occurs, the sacrifice must be performed with speed and minimum pain to the animal. Afterwards, the animal is cooked and eaten by the participants.

## Of the Spirit

Espiritismo, or spiritism, maintains that there is a spiritual world where the spirits of loved ones reside and that, through the use of an espiritista—basically a kind of medium—a person can get in touch with a departed friend or family member. Espiritistas don't necessarily advocate spiritual possession nor do they seek to establish contact with an orisha. While all Santeros can practice espiritismo, not all espiritistas are Santeros; you might want to think of it thus: Santeros are professionals and espiritistas are paraprofessionals.

Variations of spiritism are popular throughout the world. During the nineteenth century, it was quite fashionable in France. In the United States, it was called spiritualism.

Another popular practice with Latinos is that of faith healing. A curandero is a faith healer. A curandero uses herbs, as well as chanting and prayers, to cure the afflicted person. While Santeros and espiritistas call on Christian and African deities, curanderos might turn to pre-Columbian gods and goddesses for divine intervention.

**Living La Vida Literaria**

A pretty good novel that elaborates on the importance of Catholicism for Latinos and also illustrates the ways of a curandera is *Bless Me Ultima,* by Rudolfo Anaya. If you want to learn more about Santería and Santeros, try *The Killing of The Saints,* by Alex Abella. Both novels make great summer reading.

# Personal Contact with the Other World

Latinos often take the supernatural for granted. As they see it, there is a world beyond what people call the "real world." Because of this attitude, Latinos interpret religious experiences in a very personal way, often throwing in their own interpretations. It is not uncommon for a Latino to pray to a departed relative, assigning the deceased magical powers and believing the deceased can bring about changes in this world. Likewise, many Catholic Latinos favor one saint over another and pray exclusively to that saint, even building shrines in their homes—usually in the bedroom—to the saint.

Many Latinos feel that faith and religion are much bigger than individuals. Thus, it is feasible for a Latino to see himself as a good Catholic and still manage to mistrust and dislike priests. In the same vein, a Catholic might visit a santero and a santero might attend masses regularly.

## The Least You Need to Know

+ The vast majority of Latinos are Catholics.
+ From 5 to 15 percent of Latinos attend Protestant churches.
+ Latinos in inner cities are attracted to Pentecostal churches.
+ Santería is a religion that was born out of the marriage of African tradition with the Catholic Church.
+ Latinos tend to be spiritual and very religious.

# Chapter 15

# Where One Eats, Two Share a Meal

## In This Chapter

- ◆ Food of the gods
- ◆ The Columbus cookery exchange
- ◆ A few good recipes
- ◆ The taste of the Caribbean
- ◆ Argentine meat and potatoes

A few years ago, salsa outpaced the sale of the all-American ketchup. Many couldn't believe this development. But all the incredulous had to do was wander into any mall or walk along any main street in America and they would spot Mexican restaurants of all types. The verdict was in: Mexican food is hot.

It's very clear. Gibraltar might tumble, but Mexican food is here to stay—as is Argentine and Cuban, Puerto Rican, and Dominican. It's the Latinzation of American cuisine.

Buen apetito!

### Para Tu Información

Cold sandwiches and the frigid meat of leftover chicken are the legacy of the American culinary experience. Latinos don't usually like cold food. They do like American hot dogs and hamburgers, though, because they're served hot.

### Hablas Español

**Cocina** means cuisine, but it also refers to kitchen. Cocina is the noun; the verb is **cocinar,** meaning to cook. **Latinamericana** means from Latin America.

# Food from South of the Border

For people from the Spanish speaking Caribbean, a sandwich isn't real food, especially a cold sandwich. Just like sneaking down to the kitchen in the middle of the night to grab a cold piece of drumstick is something that is unheard of on the islands. Food is meant to be hot. Anything else is abnormal.

In the last 10 years or so, Mexican cuisine has become extremely fashionable in the United States, rivaling pizza and Chinese food as the most popular Friday night fare. Mexican food is so popular that most Anglos mistakenly think that Mexican cuisine is the whole of Latin American cookery. That's definitely not true, for the *cocina Latinamericana* also embraces Caribbean cooking, Central American cookery, and the cuisine from South America.

But let's begin with the food of the princes, the Aztec princes.

*Mexican Restaurant.*

# Toma Chocolate

A popular song from Latin America encourages a young man at a shop to drink his chocolate: "Toma chocolate, paga lo que debe," croons the crooner, telling his customer to drink his hot chocolate and then pay at the register. Well, the Aztec aristocracy didn't need such prodding to sip chocolate. The drink, which was a bit more bitter than the variation you're accustomed to, was a favorite of kings and princes. Other favorite foods in ancient Mexico included shrimp casseroles, with lots of tomatoes, an unknown item in Europe at the time, and an array of chili peppers used as a preservative.

The Aztec diet was healthy and varied. Aztecs ate a lot of vegetables, beans, and fruits. For poultry, they preferred turkey and varieties of wild birds that included pheasants; for aquatic goodies they fed on the fish and frogs from the lakes and waterways surrounding the capital, Tenochtitlán. They loved fruits, including papaya, and bananas, and enjoyed eating peanuts.

The Aztecs ate their food from bowls and probably used a knife, but most likely they scooped up the food with their hands. The poor farmers in the empire didn't have the luxury of bowls and, if they did have utensils, they didn't take them to the fields where they toiled. Instead, they wrapped their meat in flour tortillas, which were heated on a stone placed above a fire—kicking off a fad, unbeknownst to them, that seeded scores of fast food restaurants five hundred years later. Both rich man and poor man fed on corn, a food so valued and crucial to their existence that it was regularly placed on gods' altars.

### Para Tu Información

Some of the foods the Aztecs and inhabitants of Mexico ate aren't quite so popular today. Such delicacies include dogs, monkeys, snakes, water flies, larvae, and white worms. By the way, the Aztecs also practiced cannibalism, although the scholars dispute the extent of the practice.

## Aztec Recipes

The Aztecs fished by throwing a spear at a fish or reaching under water with their hands to pick up a frog or mosquitoe eggs and other aquatic insects. They either roasted or boiled the insects. Preparation for the fish and the frog was a bit more elaborate. Here is a fish recipe—try it with any edible fish:

> Brush both sides of the fish with oil. Cover it with tomato seeds and finely chopped corn, nuts, and garlic. Sprinkle it with lime. Wrap it up with corn leaves and broil until done.

The Aztecs used maize, or corn, extensively. Here is a recipe, as adapted from *America 1492: Portrait of a Continent Five Hundred Years* Ago by Manuel Lucena Salmoral, for a dish called *atole*:

> Soak corn in water containing slaked lime. After the grains become yellow, boil for a short time. Take off the grains and let them cool. Wash the grains in water until they turn white. Grind the grains, rinse again, and strain them. Put the mixture back on fire to thicken. Season it with chili or honey. Enjoy it hot or cold.

# The Exchange

Spanish conquistadores overcame the Aztec warriors, but Spanish cuisine and the cocina Azteca hit it off in the kitchen. An exchange occurred. The Spanish took from the New World chocolate and vanilla, chilies and potatoes, sweet peppers and tomatoes, and lots of corn. The New World took from the Old pork and beef, chicken and dairy products, rice and olives, and a large variety of grapes.

### Living La Vida Literaria

In *La Capital*, Jonathan Kandell writes about cannibalism:

It set the warriors, priests, and aristocrats apart from lowlier groups. They deserved human flesh because they were closer to the gods than the commoners were. It was through sacrifice and cannibalism that the gods … remained vital and content. And the upper castes communed with the deities by sharing their holy food.

Three centuries after the conquest, Mexican cookery was influenced by still another generation of would-be conquerors. This time, the invaders came from France and, during the 1860s (see Chapter 9), attempted to rule the country. Although the Mexicans kicked the French out, they welcomed some of their cooking practices, such as the use of cheese and chicken, and meatballs cooked in white wine sauce.

The French influence was restricted to Mexico City, where it is most visible today. In Veracruz, an area untouched by the French, the emphasis was and is on marine life. In the Yucatan region, where the Toltecs reigned and the Mayas still live, there is a preference for fruits. North American influences—you know, hamburgers and Coke—are evident throughout all of Mexico.

# Central America

Although in the United States, Mexican food is the best-known cuisine from south of the border, lately Central American dishes are becoming popular in some of the larger urban centers, such as Chicago, Los Angeles, New York City, northern New Jersey, and in some neighborhoods in Dade County, Florida.

Maize is big in Central America. In fact, to tell the story of the conflict between Native Americans and the colonialists and their supporters, novelist Miguel Angel Asturias chose for his protagonist a farmer who planted corn, and he titled the book, *Men of Maize*. In El Salvador, the national dish is called *pupusa*, which consists of ground corn dough covered with meat and beans onto which a thin layer of dough is applied before grilling.

Other favorite foods from the region include:

- **Carne deshilachada:** beef hash with tomatoes, eggs, onions, and peppers fried together.
- **Frijol blanco:** white beans flavored with pork.
- **Pipian:** a spiced stew thickened with tortilla chips.
- **Vigarón:** Fried and chopped pork, shredded cabbage, and yucca with orange or lemon dressing.

# Try This

Here's a version of an ancient recipe, adopted from Eve Zibart's *The Ethnic Food Lovers Companion:*

1. Gather the following ingredients: One cup of quinoa—a type of grain—a bit of olive oil, two green onions, six to eight sun-dried tomatoes, one jalapeño or serrano chili, a clove of garlic, cup of stock water, and three tablespoons of chopped cilantro.

2. Heat oil on pan over medium fire. Sauté onions, tomatoes, chili, and garlic until soft. Pour in the stock and bring to a boil. Stir in quinoa, return the mix to a boil, and then let it simmer covered until liquid is absorbed. Let it sit for five minutes, fluff with fork, and top with cilantro.

**Para Tu Información**

Tortillas are flat, oval, or round, and soft. Tacos are the rolled tortillas you eat as if it were a sandwich. Enchiladas are also rolled but prepared with chili peppers.

**Cuidado!**

Mexican food can be very spicy and hot. When applying chilies to your recipe, taste a very tiny part of the pepper before applying it. A big chunk of Jalapeño or Serrano chile could give you a lifetime of heartburn.

Cuban food isn't hot at all This is also true of the cuisine of the Dominican Republic and Puerto Rico.

# Cuban Taste

Cuban food is the happy mixture of Spanish cuisine, touches of Chinese and African cookery, and remembrances of a Native American past.

Cubans love rice: steamy and white. How did the rice get to Cuba? There are two sides to the story. On one side, experts claim that the Spanish conquistadores brought the rice to the island, as evidenced in the tasty paella, which has lots of chicken and sea food but a lot more rice—yellow rice. On the other side, there are those who claim rice came to the island with the Chinese immigration of the nineteenth century. Either way, rice became key in the diet of the slaves.

## Frijoles Negros

The most typical dish you will find in any Cuban eatery is black beans with rice, no matter how classy or modest the joint. Here is the recipe:

1. Gather the following ingredients: One half pound of black beans; one third cup of olive oil; medium-sized onion chopped in half; a couple of green bell peppers cut in chunks; a clove of garlic, minced; a bay leaf; a pinch of sugar, oregano, and cumin; 1 teaspoon of vinegar.

**Hablas Español**

Throughout Latin America, beans are called **frijoles**.

2. Soak beans overnight. Drain, replace water, and cook until soft, which could take a couple of hours. Sauté garlic, onion, and peppers with the spices. Add to the cooked beans and bring to a boil. Add vinegar. Reduce heat and cover partially. Let it simmer for about 20 minutes. Serve with white rice and *picadillo*, or chopped meat.

## Frijoles Criollos

Beans are big throughout many Latin America nations. Here is another version of a bean dish. Frijoles Criollos, Creole beans, is a Colombian recipe:

1. Gather the following ingredients: One pound of pinto or red kidney beans; half a can of beer; two large peeled carrots; one pound of butternut squash; two cubes of beef bouillon; half a spoon of honey; a dash of salt, cumin, and pepper.

2. Soak the beans in water and retain the water. Cook the beans, the carrots, and bouillon in the water and add more if needed. Remove the beans and the carrots from the water and mix with salt, pepper, cumin, and honey. Return to the pot and simmer for half an hour.

3. While waiting, you can work on the sauce. Here are the ingredients: four very ripe tomatoes; four green onions; two shallots; fresh coriander; a dash of salt, cumin, and pepper; two cloves garlic, minced; two spoons of olive oil. Chop all these finely and sauté in hot oil. Add spices and let simmer covered for 15 minutes, stirring occasionally.

4. When the beans are ready, you can add the sauce or eat it as a side dish.

## Plato Nacional

Though black beans and rice are big in Cuba, the island's national dish, or *plato nacional*, is a concoction called *ajiaco*. This dish exists in one form or another in Chile, Colombia, Mexico, and Peru.

Ajiaco is left-over food. Slaves in Cuba rummaged through everything that was edible in their quarters and pitched it into a large pot of boiling water. The result was a steaming clear liquid soup that contained aji—green pepper—potatoes, yucca, yams, pepper, onion, chicken meat, rice, or thin noodles. The difference between the ajiaco made by the slaves and the version prepared by those with money was the amount of meat. The aristocrats added beef and pork.

**Hablas Español**

Ajiaco is a soup; the word is also used to mean many things mixed in; in some countries in Latin America ajiaco means in bad humor.

Ajiaco might also be called sopón, meaning big soup.

## Puerco, Pica-Pollo, and Puerto Rico

Come Christmas time in the El Caribe, the meal to have is roasted puerco, or pork. In Puerto Rico, the pig is roasted ever so slowly over an open pit. It is brushed with sour orange juice and pimiento, and the combination of the heat and the liquid turns the pig's skin golden and very crisp. Puerto Ricans serve the pork with a sauce that contains garlic, sweet chili, vinegar, lime juice, salt, and olive oil.

They eat the roasted pork with rice and beans, in a variation of the Cuban version. Side dishes include *tostones*, which are slices of *platanos*, plantains, that are punched flat and fried in lots of oil. Tostones are crispy and quite juicy inside. You eat them with lots of salt.

Just as salty is the Pica-pollo of the Dominican Republic. This is fried—usually in lard—chicken; like the tostones, it is crispy but very juicy. An advantage of this meal is that it can be eaten on the go, which is how most Dominicans who live in Santo Domingo, the island's capital, prefer to have it. Another favorite dish is the Dominican Republic's answer to mashed potato: Mangu, which is mashed green plantains with bits of bacon.

# Argentina

Cattle ranching has been one of the main dominant industries in Argentina for at least a couple of centuries. Cows were introduced to the nation by the Spanish sometime in the 1600s and pretty soon herds were running wild in the countryside. Argentina produces some of the world's finest beef. It makes sense, therefore, that Argentines are big beef eaters. When you walk into an Argentine restaurant—they're in style in New York City and Miami—there is no need to ask, "where's the beef?" for you'll see it grilling right before your very own eyes.

> **Para Tu Información**
>
> In the Caribbean, the main meal of the day tends to be lunch. It might consist of rice and beans and meat followed by a dessert that's usually fruit-based, such as guava marmalade, or dairy based, such as a type of custard pudding. In the evening, the meal might be the leftovers from lunch or another serving of rice with different beans and different meat.

Argentine steaks are thick, long, and red-juicy. You can grill rib eye and coat it with roasted peppers, caramelized onions, and chopped garlic. Or you could go for a long strip of flat beef that is pounded thin and crispy. You might want to add a helping of mashed potatoes.

# Steak and Potatoes

If you like potatoes, you'll love Peruvian cooking. Ancient Peruvians raised over 80 varieties of potatoes. Today, at least 30 of the types are still being cultivated. Potatoes are spiced with chili, chicken, and cheese.

Peruvians use quinoa, a grain often described as Peruvian rice, and amaranth. A favorite is stuffed green peppers, called Peruvian *Albondigas*. Here's the recipe:

> Boil mutton or beef until tender. Remove the center of the pepper and stuff it with the meat, ripe olives, and hard-boiled eggs minced fine. Put the pepper in a pot that has been prepared with tomato sauce, raisins, red chili peppers, onion, and broth (could be chicken or meat) and heat slowly for 20 minutes.

| Living La Vida Literaria |
| --- |

Food and love go side by side. In the novel *Like Water For Chocolate*, Laura Esquivel describes how a meal ignites passion:

… the food seemed to act as an aphrodisiac; she began to feel an intense heat pulsing through her limbs. An itch in the center of her body kept her from sitting properly in the chair. She began to sweat, imagining herself on horseback with her arms clasped around one of Pancho Villa's men …

## A Few Adapted Dishes

There are few dishes that, like ajiaco and rice and beans, are favored by people from all over Latin America. The following dishes are popular in many Latin American countries, although each country and region has a slightly different take on the recipe:

- **Arroz con pollo** is rice with chicken. The rice and the chicken are boiled together. The dish might include red peppers, onions, and green peas. In the Puerto Rican version, you might throw in raisins.
- **Ceviche** is a marine delicacy. It consists of different pieces of fish and crustaceans fermented in lime or lemon juice.
- **Flan** is a custard dessert made with sweet condensed milk, evaporated milk, and eggs. It's baked in the oven and, once it's ready, you can top it off with shredded coconut.

# Latin American Spirits

The wine industry in South America is centered in Argentina and Chile. Argentina is the fifth-largest wine producer in the world, and Argentines are the fourth-greatest per capita consumers of wine in the world. Mendoza is the most important and famous grape-growing region. It produces Merlots with plenty of raspberry. Over all, there is a lot of emphasis in blending the grapes with other dark fruits to achieve rich and strong flavors.

The Chilean wine industry began in the 1500s. Seventy-five major wineries produce high quality but economical wines. These wines sell well in the United States and, in fact, many Spanish restaurants are replacing the traditional Spanish product with Chilean imports for the house wine. The Cabernet Sauvignons are well known for their brilliant color and fruity-mineral taste.

The Caribbean region is known for its rum, which makes sense because rum is made from molasses and from the juice of the sugar cane, and sugar is still king in Cuba, the Dominican Republic, and Puerto Rico. Usually white, though it could be amber, the beverage is 80 proof. It's usually mixed with Coke and a touch of lime. The best-known rum brand is Bacardi, which originated in Cuba but is now based in Puerto Rico.

## The Least You Need to Know

- Not all food from Latin America is spicy.
- Mexican food is by far the most popular south of the border cuisine in the United States.
- You could think of Latin American cookery as coming from three regions: Mexico and Central America, the Caribbean, and South America.
- Each Latin American nation has a national dish and is very proud of its particular plato nacional.

# Part 4

# From Mambo to Tango, Songs to Sonnets, Soccer to Baseball

Latino performers are becoming stars—from Music, Sports, and Movies. Baseball players from the Caribbean are household names, and children no longer dream of growing up to be like Babe Ruth; they want to be like Sammy Sosa instead. The perennial Latin lover from Hollywood is getting a new look. No longer is he created and fashioned by producers responding to the American public. Now, the Latin lover chooses the look and the role he wants. How about the ladies? Well, Jennifer López is certainly no fragile señorita waiting for her man to come to her rescue. She comes to her own rescue!

So, welcome to the world of entertainment, Latino style.

# Chapter 16

# The Rhythm Is Gonna Get You

## In This Chapter

- Past and present of Latino music
- With a song from Iberia
- Africa dances
- Tingling tango and nimble mambo
- Caribbean beat

A Puerto Rican pastor was visiting a Miskito Indian village in a far away spot in Nicaragua. The villagers were honoring him with a meal. Near the end of the gathering, three young men with guitars approached the pastor's table and played a tune. When the musicians were finished, an emotional pastor embraced them. He had tears in his eyes. For the musicians had played a Puerto Rican song, "En mi viejo San Juan."

It was not surprising that the youths were familiar with the piece, even though they were miles away from the Caribbean island. That's because the music of Latin America is known and is played the world over. It is a music of variety, from melodic rhapsodies to dreamy laments to heart-thumping beats. Filled with love and passion, it is a music destined to please. No doubt, you have some favorite Latino sounds. Let's now sound out a few more.

# All the Sounds of the Earth

During his stay in Spain in the 1870s, the Cuban poet José Martí was enraptured by the beauty, the fervor, and the feverish dancing of a *Flamenco* ballerina, a Spanish dancer. Watching her every move, he fastened her likeness onto his heart, as if he were an amateur photographer gluing a snap shot in a scrapbook. In a poem, he described her thus: "Her head high, as if to challenge/a shawl over her shoulders/arms forming an arc/she ardently taps her feet." Then he continued, rendering tribute to her looks and motions, and concluding with a line that is well known throughout Latin America:

Baila muy bien la española;
Es blanco y rojo el mantón:
Vuelve, fosca, a su rincón
El alma trémula y solan

Which means: Finishing her performance, the Spanish dancer picks up her red and white cape, and she and her soul retreat into the loneliness of her dressing room.

A little over a hundred years later, another writer, this time the Mexican Carlos Fuentes, was equally enthralled by the Flamenco dancers of Iberia. He described them in *The Buried Mirror:* "… beautiful, dark, tall, and full-figured … their bodies are swathed in frills, satins, silks, lace, complicated girdles, unimaginable underwear, stockings, shawls, knots, carnations, combs … they raise their arms … half bronze, half dream." What transfixed these two writers was not only the art and anatomy of the dancers, but the recognition that in the dance and the music there were echoes of other worlds: Africa, Spain, and Latin America.

# Dance, Ballerina, Dance

Think of Spanish music. What comes to the mind? The *bailarina espan[tl]ola*, the flamenco dancer. Yet this quintessential Spanish art form dates back to Imperial Rome and to the Moorish Empire. Observes Fuentes, "The dancing woman comes from afar. She can be found on the floors of Pompeii." It's believed that the singing that accompanies the flamenco dancer arrived in Spain with the Moors during the eighth century. The singing is similar to the chanting of the Moors, who were Muslims, with a repetitive, melodic, and soul-searching pattern. The use of the tambourine was also a Moorish invention.

So was the guitar. Maybe. For there are two theories regarding its introduction in Spain. One proposes that the *guitarra* española was a Moorish creation known as la *guitarra morisca*. Another school of thought maintains that it was the Romans who transported the instrument to Spain, long before the Moorish invasion. This type of guitarra is called latina. By the middle ages, both instruments were in use in Iberia. How were they different? The shape of the morisca was oval while the *guitarra latina* had curved sides.

One guitarra or another, flamenco dancing and music progressed in southern Spain and during the sixteenth century, *gitanos*, Spanish gypsies, took the form to heart and to the dancing floor. Over the next few centuries, flamenco was molded into the art form that we know today. By the nineteenth century, flamenco dancing and music was well known and well liked in Latin America.

## The Flames of Flamenco

The style of singing that accompanied Flamenco dancing influenced the style of singing preferred by Native-Americans from Mesoamerica and the Caribbean. Through songs, Native-Americans celebrated religion and sought to establish a connection with their ancestral spirits. Scholars describe this singing, which is still around today, as something of a maintained pitch alternating with spoken recitations and repetitive patterns. It is a controlled singing, using two or three principal notes.

Flamenco singing, on the other hand, uses different pitches and it allows for improvisation. It is not meant to be controlled but to show passion.

The indigenous pattern of singing and the Flamenco style combined in Latin America after the conquest, evolving into a new version, which allowed for a more personalized, and freer, performance as well as the introduction of secular themes. The singing also shaped the folk songs that were sung later on in Latin America. The folk songs, which were popular with the Spanish and their descendants, were of two types, *romances* and *coplas*. The latter were tunes written in couplets, two rhyming lines. The romances were tunes sung by the conquistadores around the campfires.

In Spain, the romances told stories of great deeds. In many ways, the romances were a musical version of a news broadcast as the *romancero*, the singer, sang about battles during the reconquest of Spain. In Latin America, the romances

**Hablas Español**

Flamenco is Flemish. One theory is that when a Spanish soldier heard for the first time other soldiers singing Flamenco, he thought they were singing in Flemish.

**Hablas Español**

Songs that tell stories, employing a rhyming scheme, are **romances.** The romance in Spain was influenced by the Moors and the Romans before it was transported to the Americas. The original romances sung in Spain told of the adventures of great knights. A **romancero** is a singer of romances.

repeated some of those stories but later on, they incorporated events that took place in the New World. By the 1700s, the romances had shifted to local affairs, and even affairs of the heart.

# From Africa, with Music

African rhythms arrived in the Americas in the mid 1500s, and when the slaves took up their instruments, what the Spanish settlers heard was music to their ears, delightful music that made them want to dance. This was a novelty. For Flamenco dancing was a performance to be watched. But when the African slaves in the Caribbean, and in some South American countries, played their music, the audience didn't want to watch, they wanted full participation. Singer Gloria Estefan expresses it best when, invoking the persuasive powers of Afro-Caribbean music, she sings: "The rhythm is gonna get you."

African music was sacred. It was meant to attract the gods to this world. And it was a ritual of participation. Everyone present was beguiled into a musical trance. The music consisted of vocal calls and responses. There was a lot of emphasis on rhythm, and the dancing movements were quick-paced, with the rhythmic thrusting of the hips and the pelvis. The prominent instruments were drums of all types and sizes. One of the objectives of the singing and dancing was spiritual possession.

*Afro-Cuban Dancers.*

*(Courtesy of William Luis)*

The songs were originally rendered in an African language, Yoruba, for example. But as time went on and generations of slaves were raised in the New World, the songs were sung in Spanish, though maintaining some African expressions. Here is the first line of a popular Afro-Caribbean tune, where the singer wishes a good day to an African deity: "Ñeñeren cumaran, buenas noches/ Buenas noches, Como esta Usted?", meaning, "Good evening, good evening, how are you?"

## Bang the Drum *Not* Slowly

African music remained relatively intact in the Spanish Caribbean. Spanish masters allowed slaves to perform their songs and rituals. There were a large number of freed Africans who formed societies called *cabildos*, where they practiced their ancient dances and organized *comparsas*, dancing groups, to perform in the streets during carnivals.

African music merged with Spanish music, particularly in a dance movement that consisted of foot tapping to create a beat. Usually performed by a man, the dance was called a *zapateo*. Picture a Spanish gypsy dancing flamenco. Picture an African dancer lacing his hand behind his back. Combine the two dancers into one and what you get is the zapateo. This particular dance became popular in Cuba and Peru.

---

### Living La Vida Literaria

In *I Wonder As I Wander: An Autobiographical Journey*, Langston Hughes describes the rumba and the sone: "Rumbas and sones are essentially hip-shaking music of Afro-Cuban derivation, which means a bit of Spain, therefore Arab-Moorish, mixed in. The tap of claves, the rattle of gourds, the dong of iron bells, the deep steady roll of drums speak of the earth, life bursting warm from the earth, and earth and sun moving in the steady rhythms of procreation and joy."

---

Other dances that emerged were the *conga*, the *rumba*, and the *sone*. The conga was a procession of dancers, forming two lines and facing each other, that swayed to the thump thump of a drum, taking three steps forward and then happily shaking their bodies. The rumba was similar to the conga. The sone, on the other hand, was a slow, romantic melody. It used a *clave*, two pieces of wood tapping against each other, while musicians gently played the drums. Guitars were sometimes used, and the song told a story of love and heartbreak.

# City Sounds

The music that most people associate with Latin America evolved in the nineteenth and twentieth centuries. Created in cosmopolitan centers, it was popular in nature. That is to say, it was meant to be neither sacred nor political, but pure entertainment.

In the nineteenth and early twentieth centuries, the music deemed proper by the upper classes—operas and classic works by European composers—was performed in concert halls, theaters, and at aristocratic functions. Popular music was played in salons, cafés, and *cantinas*—neighborhood bars—at vaudeville or burlesque theaters, known in some Latin American countries as *teatro bufo*. One such teatro, *The Alhambra* in Havana, became legendary for its introduction to Latin America of such popular tunes as "Quiereme mucho" and "El negrito del batey."

Later in the twentieth century, popular music reached a large audience through radio, movies, and television. Unlike folk songs, romances, and flamenco music that changed slowly in style and format, popular music was constantly evolving. Influenced by tunes from France, Spain, and the United States, popular music in Latin America would go in and out of fashion and, in the process, it would make stars out of its performers, usually singers and orchestra leaders. A few countries achieved international recognition for their brand of popular music, including Argentina, Cuba, Dominican Republic, Mexico, and Puerto Rico. These countries popularized and perfected a certain sound or dance, or type of singing, that is perennially associated with them.

### Hablas Español

**El negrito del batey** means the little black fellow from the batey, a small village. **Negrito** is a term of endearment applied to both whites and blacks.

A popular love tune, **Quiereme mucho** can be translated as love me with all you have.

### Para Tu Información

The two most famous tango singers ever were Carlos Gardel and Hugo del Carril.

### Living La Vida Literaria

In *The Buried Mirror*, Fuentes sums up the tango: "[It] tells a tale of frustrations, nostalgia, fragilities, insecurities. But it is above all a potent sexual event. It takes two to tango: a man and woman, embracing. And in it they realize both an individual and a shared destiny, and the impossibility of controlling it ..."

## It Takes Two to Tango

From Argentina comes the *tango*. To be precise, from the brothels of Buenos Aires comes the tango, first as a dance and then as a type of song. Evolving in the 1880s, there are many theories regarding its origins. It was influenced by a Cuban dance called the habanera, as well as the sensuous movements of Africans performing a sacred ritual, and probably the fancy footwork of Flamenco dancers.

The first dance where dancers embraced, the tango consisted of an abrupt halt, a quick turn, and a promenade with lots and lots of legs twisting around the partner's legs. As a song, the tango is melodious but with sudden endings of phrasing, creating a choppy quality.

The tango was an international, and scandalous, sensation. The Pope banned it and European army officers were not allowed to dance it. Yet, in London, Paris, and New York, thousands packed clubs where the tango was played and sung in the 1930s.

## Cuba Does Mambo

Cuban musicians claim that their island has had the most influence in the making of Latin American music. We'll let the musicians argue about that, but it is the case that in the twentieth century, Cuba produced popular genres that reached Europe and the United

States. These genres included the cha-cha-chá, the mambo, and the already mentioned conga and rumba. Says poet Ricardo Pau-Llosa in an essay published in *ReMembering Cuba*, "The sounds of Cuba of the first half of the twentieth century constitute the most recognizable yet varied, the most alluring yet complex popular music of the world."

The *cha-cha-chá*, or chachacha, was invented by a violinist, named Enrique Jorrín, in the late 1940s. It was an adaptation of a slower-moving waltz, called a *danzón*, that forced the dancers to pick up their pace and movement, thus shuffling their feet on the dance floor and producing a chachacha sound. The instruments used were bass, strings, guitars, timbales and conga drums, a piano, and a lead flute. The chachacha singer had to have a light and happily sonorous voice. The chachacha became a fad in New York City, where people were joyfully shuffling to the tune of "Cherry Pink and Apple Blossom White."

### Hablas Español

The shuffling sound made by feet on the dance floor might be described as a **cha-cha-chá**. It's a made up word that has no meaning in Spanish.

### Para Tu Información

There are a few feature films revolving around Latino and Latin American music.

- *La Bella del Alhambra* (1989), is a Cuban film that captures the era of vaudeville on the island. The star is Beatriz Valdés (in Spanish with English subtitles).
- *The Mambo Kings* (1992), starring Armand Assante and Antonio Banderas, tells the story of two Cuban musicians who perform in the *I Love Lucy* show and become celebrities in the New York City club scene of the 1950s.
- *Selena* (1997), the film that made Jennifer Lopez a top star, is the biography of the Mexican-American singer of Tex-Mex songs.

The *mambo* had touches of jazz and a faster beat than the chachacha. It employed saxophones and lots of brass to a rhythmic beat backed up by drums and claves. Perez Prado became the epitome of the mambo player. In the early 1950s, Cuban musicians toured New York City and the East coast, playing the mambo. Many of their stories were collected by novelist Oscar Hijuelos, who fashioned their anecdotes into his novel, *The Mambo Kings Play Songs of Love*.

# Dancing with a Broken Leg

The *merengue* is the national dance of the Dominican Republic. However, it's such an inviting dance that the merengue is popular throughout Latin America, and it's now a common sight at *bailes* in New York City nightclubs. How do you dance it? Well, you hold your partner as if you were ready to perform a waltz. Then, you step sideways, with one leg leading and the other lagging behind, as if you had a broken hip or broken leg. You may also go forward, or backward, and you may do a little bit of dancing by yourself. But you never let go of your partner's hand.

The tempo is fast, with a main theme that is played over and over again. The merengue has a vocal component but there are also versions with just music. The merengue uses brass and drums and a piano. It could have a big band sound but it's also performed by groups of three or four musicians who might have an accordion.

Legend has it that the merenque was invented by a *Taino* chief who had a new bride and wanted to impress her with his dancing capabilities. The problem was, though, that he had broken his leg. So, because he couldn't jump around, he came up with the dance. A good story, right? Another possibility is that African slaves adapted the merenque from the type of ballroom dances their masters enjoyed during colonial times. Anyhow, the dance originated in the nineteenth century but no one seems to know who was its creator.

# Salón Mexico

For many people, music from Latin America means Mexican music. You can accept this statement or you can debate it, but you'd agree that anyone outside Latin America knows what a *mariachi* looks like and can recognize a Mexican tune. What they have in mind is a musical form called by musicologists *la canción mexicana*—the Mexican song.

## Hablas Español

Bands or orchestras that perform Mexican tunes are called **mariachis.**

La canción mexicana was influenced by the European romance and coplas of the nineteenth century. It consists of a poem that is introduced by a long musical arrangement in which guitars and brass are the featured instruments. In the twentieth century, the Mexican song took on the components of *boleros*, which are sentimental ballads similar to the kind of tunes Frank Sinatra sang, becoming more lyrical and danceable.

A variation, *la cancion ranchera*—also called rancheras—brought to the urban scene folksongs from the countryside. In the 1940s, composers and performers paid attention to the *corrido* (see also Chapter 17), which was popular during the Mexican revolution, but has been neglected by trained Mexican musicians. Two singers of boleros and rancheras became household names in Latin America and in Europe. Good looking and muscular, they were regarded as the ideal Mexican males: Pedro Infante and Jorge Negrete. Even though both died in their youths in the early 1950s, their records still sell today.

Like these two tenors, the genre known as the Mexican waltz has proven long-lasting. One waltz, "Sobre las olas," meaning over the waves, was influenced by European waltzes. Melodic and jubilant, it is commonly played by foreign orchestras in foreign capitals. In

Mexico, it is considered the second national anthem. Cielito Lindo, a fast-paced waltz written by Quirino F. Mendoza during the Mexican Revolution, can still be heard on radio stations and was recently performed by the three tenors—Carrera, Domingo, and Pavarotti.

# Lovely Lament

The lament is a genre where a composer laments the human condition. It is song of sadness and tears. There are religious laments and laments of lost love. But the most famous musical laments come from Puerto Rico: "Lamento borincano" and "En mi Viejo San Juan." Both epitomize the beauty of the form with poetic lyrics, rich imagery of the Caribbean, a rhyming scheme easy to memorize, and a sweet longing for the past and the old ways.

"Lamento borincano" was written in 1929 by Rafael Hernández, one of Latin America's most beloved composers. It tells the story of a young farmer who leaves for the market, hoping to sell all his products and return home with money and the promise of better life. Instead, the farmer earns no money, not even a penny, and finishes the day heart-broken. In his sadness, he realizes that his plight is also the plight of the poor farmers on his island. But he will not give up and will sing for his heart and Puerto Rico: "dejame que te cante yo"—allow me to sing to you, he implores.

The song was an instant hit. It is popular throughout Latin America, where the universality of the theme allows people from different nations to take ownership of it.

"En mi viejo San Juan," by Noel Estrada, has become the hymn for many Latinos:

> En mi viejo San Juan
> Cuantos sueños forjé
> En mis años de infancia
> Una tarde partí
> Hacia extraña nación
> Y no pude volver
> Al San Juan que yo amé
> Pedacito de patria

**Hablas Español**

**Lamento** is Spanish for regretting a particular condition, be it of the heart or social.

The stanzas in the song tell the story of a young man who must leave his homeland. Year after year, he plans his return to his childhood town but he's never able to fulfill his dream. He grows old and tired, longing for his country.

# The Musical North

When Latin American immigrants headed north, they may not have had much in their suitcases, but their hearts were packed with music. In the United States, the music took on new forms, blending together different musical traditions from different countries in

Latin America as well as North American jazz and rock. At least two forms emerged from this mingling: *música tejana*, meaning music from Texas, and *salsa*.

Música tejana is the marriage of Mexican folk traditions and Texas music. Using an accordion, a 12-string guitar, and a ranch drum, the tejana was influenced by French and German music. Its sound is reminiscent of the polka and the mazurka. It is a fast-paced dance that combines a two-step movement with the sideways swinging of the bodies while holding hands. One version is known as *música norteña*, meaning from the north, and it's usually played by small bands called *conjuntos*. Another version is closer to swing and even rock; it's played by a full orchestra, called an *orquesta tejana*.

The most famous performer of música tejana was the legendary Selena, who added touches of American pop and rock. Beautiful and a crowd-pleaser, Selena was about to cross over to American audiences when she was gunned down at the age of 24.

**CAUTION**

## Cuidado!

In late 1960s and early '70s, an orchestra dominated the air waves with the sounds and beat of Mexican music. Called, the Tijuana Brass, the orchestra won 11 gold records as well as securing the top charts for many months. The orchestra was the brainchild of Herb Albert, a talented musician, and the sound he cultivated relied on the use of brass and marimbas. It was a lovely sound, most pleasing to the ear. However, neither Albert nor his musicians were Mexicans. You might want to enjoy the old albums, but don't think of Herb Albert and the Tijuana Brass as exemplifying Mexican music.

## Hablas Español

**Salsa** means sauce. According to one story, about 60 years ago a Cuban orchestra leader wanted his musicians to put a little more life into the mambo number they were playing. The maestro said, "echale salsita"—throw in some sauce. The expression became popular in the musical world.

*Salsa* is by far the most popular and well-known blend of Latin American music in the United States. It is primarily a Cuban sound—conga, mambo, rumba—combined with the Dominican merengue and Puerto Rican rhythms, as well as Big Band and jazz touches. It's fast and furious and it uses everything a big band can throw in: drums, trumpets, saxophones, guitars, pianos. In some versions, there's singing. In this category, the brightest star is Cuban-American Celia Cruz with her powerful and yet sweet-tuned voice. When the emphasis is music, without vocal arrangements, the king is Tito Puente, who held court with his virtuoso playing of timbales until his recent death.

*Salsa king Tito Puente, receiving an honorary degree.*

*(Courtesy of Bloomfield College, NJ)*

# Back to the Classics

Like anywhere else, there is also a classical tradition in Latin America. The first pieces composed during colonial times were of a religious nature. In the nineteenth century, Latin American composers modeled their works on their European counterparts, though sounds from South America and the Caribbean were noticeable in their composition. The Cuban José White composed concertos and pieces that proved popular in Paris while the Argentine Zenón Rolón wrote symphonies, military marches, and operas.

Of particular interest in the twentieth century are Astor Piazzola, whose symphonic works reinterpret the tango in a classical format; the Mexican Carlos Chávez, who incorporates Indian motifs in his experimental symphonies; and the melodic Ernesto Lecuona, from Cuba, whose concerts and rhapsodies are underscored with the beat of drums and claves.

# For Your Listening Pleasure

You can't just read about music and musicians. When you're describing a sound, "words"—as Gloria Estefan says—"get in the way." So, the thing to do is spin some of the following CDs:

- ◆ For Cuban sounds and salsa: *Celia Cruz, La Negra Tiene Tumbao*. Label: Sony Discos. Released in 2001.
- ◆ For lamentos and Puerto Rican music: *Añoranzas-Homenaje a Rafael Hernández*. Label: Sony Discos. 1998.

- For Mexican tunes, try: *Jorge Negrete y Pedro Infante*. Label: Orfeon. Released in 1994.
- For tejana: *Selena, Dreaming of You*. Label: EMI Latin. 1995.
- For merengue, listen to: *Clasicos de Oro del Merengue Dominicano*. Label: Max Music. 1998.
- For pure salsa, grab: *Tito Puente Swings Lupe Sings*. Label: Farria. 2000.
- For the tango, go for: *Tango, Exitos de Carlos Gardel*. Label: Orfeon. Released in 2000.

One of these recordings will become a favorite. Whether it's the sensuous tango or the heart wrenching lamento, one thing is for sure: The Latin rhythm is bound to get you.

## The Least You Need to Know

- Latin American music is the product of African, Native American, and Spanish musical traditions.
- Latin American music was also influenced by French and American music.
- Argentina, Cuba, and Mexico have produced the most recognizable Latin American sounds.
- Puerto Rican music is known for its beautifully and melodic sad lamentos.
- The merengue is a Dominican creation and probably the easiest dance people with two left feet can master.

# Writing with a Spanish Accent

## In This Chapter

- ◆ The first Latino writers
- ◆ Literally speaking
- ◆ The ballad and the bandit
- ◆ The look and feel of Latino literature

While a cable station was broadcasting a film adaptation of the novel *In The Time of the Butterflies,* by Julia Álvarez, at a mall a bookstore was setting up an intricate display of books written by several Latinos, including Rudolfo Anaya and Junot Díaz. In the meantime, a guest speaker at a public library was leading a book discussion on the latest novel written by Cristina García.

Clearly, the word is out: Latino writers are in, and they're hot. How hot? Read on to find out.

## Latino Literature

"It helps if you're a Latina."

The comment was made at an American Library Association conference in Atlanta, Georgia, a few years ago. It expressed the frustrations of an Anglo author whose manuscript had been rejected by Algonquin Press, the publisher of the Dominican-American novelist Julia Álvarez. Cynicism aside, the observation carried a bit of truth. For in the last decade or so, Latina writers have flourished and many, like the aforementioned Julia Álvarez—along with Sandra Cisneros and Judith Ortiz Cofer—have become familiar names to avid readers.

But it's not just the female of the species who are taking the book world by storm; Latino authors also share the spotlight. For example, Cuban-American Oscar Hijuelos is a Pulitzer Prize winner and his novel, *The Mambo Kings Play Songs of Love*, was made into a major motion picture; Puerto Rican Edwin Torres' two novels, *Q & A*, and *Carlitos' Way*, were movie vehicles for stars Nick Nolte and Al Pacino; and the essays and memoirs of Mexican-American Richard Rodriguez are part of the literary canon—the books students study in colleges—and always draw attention from the national media.

The flurry of activities prompted a publicist at a major publishing house to claim the end of the twentieth century as the era of Latino writers, in the same vein that the 1960s was the decade when the general reading public discovered Afro-American writers. Valid as it might be, the pronouncement suggests that Latino literature is a rather recent development. But this is not so. For just like the Latino presence in United States, Latino literature has been around for quite a while; indeed, a very long while.

# In the Beginning

If we think of Latino literature as that body of works that describes life in the good ole USA and is written by a writer who is either Spanish, or of Spanish descent and who feels a certain emotional attachment to Latin America, then we must include the *cronistas* in the genre. Remember Cabeza de Vaca (see Chapter 3)? His account of his wanderings throughout the Southwest was published in 1542 under the title of *La relación*. Latino expert Nicolás Kanellos observes in *Herencia: The Anthology of Hispanic Literature in the United States:* "*La relación* may be considered the first anthropological and ethnographic book in what became the United States [and] the first book of 'American' literature written in a European language."

Just as other *exploradores* followed on the heels of Cabeza de Vaca, so did other writers. Some of the cronistas were inspired by hearing stories about Cabeza de Vaca's adventures and some by reading his famous account. Either way, these writers chronicled their experiences, with some of them publishing their *crónicas* as books while others stored their manuscripts in church archives, not to be published until many years later. The bottom line is that way before there were accounts written in English about life in America, there were Spanish-language crónicas and *relaciones* describing the lands that would become California, Florida, New Mexico, and Texas. Some of these documents include the following, in order of appearance:

> **Hablas Español**
>
> The literary genre that told of the conquest and colonization of the New World is known as a **crónica**. A writer of crónicas is a **cronista**. A **relación** is an account of the discovery and colonization of a territory.

◆ In the 1540s Fray Marcos de Niza wrote *Discovery of the Seven Cities of Cibola*.

◆ In 1542 Cabeza de Vaca wrote *La relación* (The Account).

◆ In the 1590s Alonso Gregorio de Escobedo wrote *La Florida*.

◆ In 1610 Gaspar Pérez de Villagra penned *The History of New Mexico*.

◆ In the 1670s Fray Juan Crespí recorded many journals and diaries.

◆ In the 1710s Fray Matías Saénz de San Antonio wrote many letters to Mexico.

---

### Living La Vida Literaria

Cabeza de Vaca's crónica is certainly one of the best-known works of the genre. However, the most popular crónica, which many scholars see as emblematic of the type, is the tale of the conquest of Mexico told by Bernal Díaz de Castillo, a participant in the event. Titled *The True History of the Conquest of New Spain*, the volume reads as if it were an action novel, containing all the elements of a bestseller: sex and violence, intrigue and murder. It was the basis for the popular novel and 1940s film, *Captain from Castile*.

---

After the colonization of the West coast and Florida by the Spanish and the Mexicans, there was a pause in literary activities. Historians believe that colonizers kept diaries about their lives in the New World, and it is also known that in New Amsterdam, Sephardic Jews, who arrived in the 1620s, maintained records in Spanish of religious activities and other events. Unfortunately, the bulk of these manuscripts have yet to be uncovered, if they still exist at all. Historians have had better luck with the nineteenth century.

# Nineteenth Century Nueva York

In the nineteenth century, novels and poetry were the genres of choice. This was the era when patriots from Latin America trekked to the Northeast to seek political asylum, settling first in Philadelphia and later on in New York City. Educated, from an affluent background, and intensely nationalistic, the patriots took up the pen to combat the Spanish crown. They wrote *independentistas*, pro-independence pamphlets, speeches, and novels.

In 1826, *Jicontécal*, possibly the first historic romance written in Spanish in the New World, was published in Philadelphia. Written by Father Félix Varela, in a throwback to the writing friars of the colonization, it told the story of the conquest of Mexico by Hernán Cortés. The novel condemned the abuses committed by the Spanish colonizers and criticized Spain's oppressive regime in Latin America.

**Hablas Español**

**Independentistas** were the advocates of independence from Spain or any colonial power.

**Para Tu Información**

*Cecilia Valdés* was made into two operas during the twentieth century. One version, under the title of *Mariía La O*, was a loose adaptation composed by Ernesto Lecuona; the second, titled *Cecilia Valdes*, by Gonzalo Roig, was a faithful musical re-telling of the story. The opera is regularly performed throughout Latin America and Europe.

It was a theme picked up by the half-dozen novels published during the period. Of these works, *Cecilia Valdés*, written by the Cuban Cirilo Villaverde and published in 1882 in New York, is the most salient. Set in colonial Havana, *Cecilia Valdés* is about the doomed love affair between a white aristocratic playboy and a beautiful light-skin mulata. It is a story of passion told passionately. At times melodramatic, the novel seeded the terrain for the passionate soap operas that would dominate Spanish television in the United States and Latin America a hundred years later.

# Of Poets and Pain

During the nineteenth century, poetry was big in the Big Apple. The legendary poet José Martí wrote some of his most beautiful poems while in New York City. As did the Mexican poet, Anastasio Ochoa y Acuña. Perhaps, the most noticeable volume of poetry to emerge was the anthology *El laúd de los desterrados*, the exile's lute, copyrighted in 1858. This book, considered as the first collection of exile literature published in the United States, sings of the pang of exile. Laments one poet, "In my country dwells my thoughts/Lies my heart/ What a horrible torture/This exile is."

Poetry was just as popular on the West coast, but the intent was different. The poets in California, New Mexico, and Texas weren't nostalgic about the old country—after all, they were still in the old country—instead, they wanted to reaffirm *lo mejicano*, the Mexicaness, in their lives.

Why? Because up to 1846, these poets were Mexicans living in Mexican territory, but after the end of Mexican-American war, these Mexicans became American citizens living in American territory. The change of government, and nationality, alarmed the poets, as well as the rest of the Mexican population in the United States, who feared the now dominant Anglo culture would swallow up Mexican traditions. Not only that, but they knew that Anglos in general felt superior to Mexicans, belittling Mexican history, culture, and social values. So, to combat the Anglos, the poets celebrated their Mexican heritage, re-telling stories about the Aztecs, the colonization of the West by Mexican *caballeros*, and the adventures of brave *charros* and outlaws who rebelled against the Anglos, becoming instant folk heroes.

## The Ballad of Gregorio Cortez

The type of poem that celebrated folk heroes was known as the *corrido*, the ballad. Performed to music, the corrido consisted of 20 to 24 stanzas, with each stanza carrying four lines. Here's an example:

> In the county of Karnes,
> Look what has happened;
> The Major Sheriff died,
> Leaving Román badly wounded.
>
> They went around asking questions,
> About half an hour afterward,
> They found that the wrongdoer
> Had been Gregorio Cortez.
>
> Now they have outlawed Cortez,
> Throughout the whole state;
> Let him be taken, dead or alive;
> He has killed several men.

**Hablas Español**

**Corridos** come from the Spanish verb correr, which means to run. As such, a corrido is a ballad on the run, that is, constantly changing its story line and being performed over and over again by different performers.

These lines come from one of the most popular *corridos* of all time, "El Corrido de Gregorio Cortez." The ballad tells of a Mexican *vaquero*, a cowboy, who was unjustly accused of a crime, shot a sheriff in self-defense, was unsuccessfully pursed by the Texas Rangers, and finally turned himself in to the authorities to protect his family. Representative of the genre, the Cortez ballad proclaimed that the United States, with all its might, as represented by the Texas Rangers, could neither outwit nor defeat the spirit of lo mejicano, as symbolized by Gregorio Cortez. Kanellos points out that the corridos were expressions of resistance, a celebration of the victories of the underdogs over Anglo invaders.

# Latino Literature Learns a New Language

Corridos are still popular in border towns and northern Mexico, where corrido singers sing of the exploits of the underdogs. And true to the genre, the corridos are still written in the Spanish language. But that's the exception in the Latino literature of the twentieth century. For in leaving the 1800s behind and crossing over to the 1900s, Latino writers forsook their mother tongue and began to write in English.

It didn't happen all at once. In 1917, Mexican physician Mariano Azuela wrote in Texas *Los de abajos*, the first novel about the Mexican revolution and a classic of Latin American letters. In 1928, the journalist and satirist Daniel Venegas came out with *Las aventuras de Don Chipote*, about a Mexican immigrant traveling throughout the United States. But the trajectory towards the choice of English over Spanish was on its way. It had to do with numbers. For writing and publishing in English attracted a larger audience.

That is why Puerto Rican author Jesús Colín, from New York City, gave up his mother tongue and in the 1920s opted to write in English for *The Daily Worker*, a communist paper with a circulation of 10,000. Likewise, in 1945 Josephine Niggli wrote the novel *A Mexican Village*, about a Mexican-American—with the emphasis on American—who visits Mexico to discover his roots. The novel was the first to introduce Mexican culture and folklore to a large, national and non–Spanish-speaking audience.

### Para Tu Información

Much of Latino literature of the nineteenth and early twentieth centuries was published in newspapers. On the East coast, Anglo publishers owned the Spanish dailies and published the works of Latin American patriots whose eyes were focused on Latin America. On the West coast, Mexican-Americans owned the newspapers and published stories and poems written by contributors whose interest lay in the United States.

In the 1960s, Mexican-American writers drafted novels—*Bless Me Ultima* by Rudolfo Anaya, for example—that initially came out in literary journals of limited circulation, were picked up by small presses, and were eventually published by mainstream houses, like Warner Books, which assured greater distribution. These writers initiated a movement that four decades later would set a new trend in American literature: the appearance of Chicano writings, Nuyorican poetry, and Cuban-American literature in mainstream publications.

# Chicanos, Nuyoricans, and Cubanos

Chicano (for the meaning of the term, revisit Chapter 4) literature is driven by the author's awareness of what makes him or her Mexican, and the struggles to maintain his or her ethnicity while fighting discrimination. The protagonists are usually Chicanos and the setting is often pastoral. The best-known Chicano novel is Anaya's *Bless Me Ultima*, a lyrical coming-of-age tale about a young boy, his fascination with a faith healer, and the comings and goings of the small town where he lives during World War II. Gary Soto has emerged as a popular poet and writer of children's literature with a keen sense of humor and loving appreciation of Mexican traditions. Sandra Cisneros has charmed millions of readers with her poetic memoir, *House on Mango Street*, about a would-be writer eager to leave her Chicago neighborhood and see the world. But by far the most controversial writer is Richard Rodriguez, who doesn't use the term Chicano, preferring to describe himself as an American. His two autobiographies, *A Hunger of Memory* and *Conversations With My Mexican Father*, are literary feats that reveal a writer masterfully using language to describe his philosophy of education and social and political views.

Nuyorican literature flows out of New York. Though there are novels, such as *Down These Mean Streets*, by Piri Thomas, and *In Nueva York*, by Nicholasa Mohr, which belong within this group, Nuyorican literature is the province of poetry, a poetry that is lively, savvy, and that raises the uses of Spanglish, the marriage of English and Spanish, to an art form. A poetry that is meant to be performed, its authors often read their works at the Nuyorican Café, a popular hangout in Manhattan for artists and academes. An extraordinary presence in this universe is the gifted Tato Laviera.

Nuyorican literature describes life in the city, throbbing with the beat of a subway train. Nuyorican writers bask in the glory of New York and differentiate themselves from their compatriots in Puerto Rico. They affirm that they come from the island of Puerto Rico but are shaped by the island of Manhattan.

From the island of Cuba comes Cuban-American literature. The first generation of Cuban-American writers saw themselves as more Cuban than American. They wrote in Spanish with the objective of reporting to the world the atrocities committed by Fidel Castro. A typical novel, *Territorio Libre* by Luis Ricardo Alonso, details Castro's transition from idealist liberator to reactionary dictator.

But by the mid-1980s, younger Cuban-American writers began to forget the correct use of Spanish and started to feel more at home with English. During that decade, Oscar Hijuelos' *Our House in the Last Country* became a bestseller. Writing in an English that echoes the descriptive prose of Charles Dickens, the novel captures the New York of the 1950s as the young protagonist comes to terms with his dysfunctional family.

A decade later, the most popular Cuban-American novel thus far was published. Titled *Dreaming in Cuban* and written by Cristina García, a former journalist, it told how the Cuban revolution affected the lives of several women: a grandmother, her two daughters, and her Cuban-American grandchild. Though a lot of the action takes place in Cuba, the novel is as well a chronicle of the Cuban community in Miami and New York.

> ### Living La Vida Literaria
>
> Cuban-American writing tends to be poetic, descriptive, and leisurely paced. The one exception is Virgil Suarez, whose MTV fast-paced style depicts very Americanized Cubans trying to grab the proverbial piece of the pie.

# Don't Forget About the Dominicans!

Dominican-American literature is the new kid on the block, appearing as recent as 1992 with the publication of the novel *How the García Girls Lost Their Accent*, by college professor Julia Álvarez. The professor-turned-novelist narrates the lives and times of several sisters from the Dominican Republic who are trying to adjust to life in the United States. For the García girls, the old country is Eden while the new country is chaotic. Yet, the chaos allows the opportunity for freedom from the male-dominated society of the Dominican Republic.

Recently, two other Dominican authors surfaced: Junot Díaz and Angie Cruz. Díaz assumes the pose of a journalist, but has the touch of a poet. His collection of short stories, titled *Drown*, sketches a family trying to stay together while eking out a living in the United States. Angie Cruz, who was discovered by Bill Cosby, renders a photographic view of Dominicans who live in Washington Heights in the novel *Soledad*. Both Díaz and Cruz use the language of the street but with the rhythm and softness of Caribbean sounds.

# All the World Is a Stage

The Latino literary expression extends beyond prose; it also embraces drama. Aside from providing entertainment, the theater has served as a safety valve for the release of political, social, and religious tension. One of the first acts undertaken by Juan de Oñate, after settling New Mexico, was to stage a rendering of the Spanish war against the Moors, during the Reconquest, to inspire his soldiers and settlers to further glories.

> **Living La Vida Literaria**
>
> Angie Cruz draws a vivid picture of Washington Heights, a neighborhood in New York City that is home to thousands of Dominicans: "Hydrants erupt, splashing cold water over the pavement … Merengue [music] blares out of car speakers, the Dominican flag drapes in place of curtains on apartment windows … and old issues of *El Diario* burst out of the trash cans on the corner …"

Here is the basic progression of Latino drama:

- During colonial times, religious plays were performed in churches and outdoors.
- In the nineteenth century, theaters in Los Angeles, New York City, and Tampa produced classic works by Spanish playwrights.
- Early in the twentieth century, a preference evolved in the West coast for dramas that told stories about Mexicans in the United States, both from a historical and contemporary perspective, written by Mexican-Americans. During the same period, in Tampa comedy was big, though many productions dealt with such social issues as racial discrimination and labor.
- Late in the 1960s, Mexican-American Luis Valdez wrote pro-labor dramas that were staged atop flat bed trucks in the middle of a field, attracting Mexican migrant workers.
- A few years later, he wrote the classic *Zoot Suit*, about the killings of Mexicans by American soldiers during the 1940s, which was performed on Broadway.
- In New York City, Cuban-American Ivan Acosta penned *El Super*. This bittersweet drama about a Cuban exile sick of living in Manhattan and yearning for the tropics won several awards and was made into a successful film.
- Equally successful was the play *Short Eyes*, about prison life, written by the Puerto Rican Miguel Piñeiro and staged at Lincoln Center in 1974.
- Today, women playwrights like Dolores Prida, with *Beautiful Señoritas*, and Carmen Rivera, with *La Lupe: Mi Vida, Mi Destino*, draw critical attention and recognition.

# Why Oscar Hijuelos Isn't Like Ernest Hemingway

Say, do Latino writers write differently from Anglo writers? Yes. Latino literature addresses topics and conflicts that overall Anglo writers don't approach.

Let's check out a few:

- Latino writers toy with the simultaneous use of two languages, English and Spanish. This practice is dubbed code switching, meaning the insertion of a foreign word or phrase into a conversation conducted in another language.

- Latino writers place their characters on the hyphen, that is, they live between two worlds. In the novel *Bloody Secrets*, by Carolina García-Aguilera, the protagonist, a Cuban-American woman who thrives on her independence and rejection of *machismo*—very American attitudes—still lives at home with her parents and prefers *café con leche* over coffee—very Cuban choices.

- Characters in Latino stories confront discrimination on a daily basis. In the novel *Q & A*, by Edwin Torres, a beautiful femme fatale is rejected by her lover when he learns that her father is a black Puerto Rican. In *Zoot-Suit Murders*, Mexican youths are beaten by American soldiers simply because they don't like how they look.

- The spiritual and supernatural are regularly featured in Latino literature. In *Zía Summer*, by Rudolfo Anaya, an old man blesses the sun every day at dawn and, in return, the sun replenishes him with life. In the works of Oscar Hijuelos, ghosts often spirit their way into the narrative, and the protagonists can sense a tragedy before it occurs.

> **Living La Vida Literaria**
>
> Latino writers are influenced by North American writers. Some of their favorite writers are F.S. Fitzgerald, Ernest Hemingway, and Toni Morrison. But Latino writers are also influenced by Latin America authors. Two of the most influential are the Mexican Carlos Fuentes and the Colombian Gabriel García Márquez.

- Where a Latino character comes from dictates how that character relates to an individual. For instance, In *The Brotherhood of the Dolphins*, by Ricardo Means Ybarra, a Dominican would lend a hand first to another Dominican before helping out a Latino.

- The old country is ever present in Latino stories. In the novels of Anaya, his characters idealize the Mexico of long ago when Native Americans roamed the land. And in Garcia's *Dreaming in Cuba*, one of the protagonists must travel to Cuba in order to achieve inner peace.

*Novelist and poet Virgil
Suárez.*

*(Courtesy of V. Suárez)*

# Books for All Season

With so many books to choose from and so little time to read, what book should you take to bed or the beach? Any one of the authors in this chapter will provide you joyful hours of reading, but here are a few of my favorites:

- *How the García Girls Lost Their Accent*, by Julia Álvarez (New York: Plume, 1992)
- *Bless Me, Ultima*, by Rudolfo Anaya (New York: Warner Books, 1994)
- *House on Mango Street*, by Sandra Cisneros (New York: Vintage Books, 1995)
- *Soledad*, by Angie Cruz (New York: Simon & Schuster, 2001)
- *Drown*, by Junot Díaz (New York: Riverhead Books, 1996)
- *Dreaming in Cuban*, by Cristinia García (New York: Ballantine Books, 1992)
- *Our House in the Last World*, by Oscar Hijuelos (New York: Persea Books, 1983)
- *In Nueva York*, by Nicholasa Mohr (Houston, Texas: Arte Público, 1988)
- *Hunger of Memory: The Education of Richard Rodriguez*, by Richard Rodriguez (New York; Bantam Books, 1988)

◆ *Going Under*, by Virgil Suárez (Houston, Texas: Arte Público, 1996)

◆ *Down These Mean Streets*, by Thomas Piri (New York: Vintage Books, 1997)

◆ *Q & A*, by Edwin Torres (New York: Dial, 1977)

Probably more than any academic treatise or sociological study, Latino literature will flesh out for you the Latino experience, making it more human and more real for you and your friends.

## The Least You Need to Know

◆ Latino literature is not a new phenomenon: it's been around since colonial times.

◆ During the nineteenth century, hundreds of Spanish newspapers published novels and poems by Latino writers.

◆ Until the 1960s, most of Latino literature was written in Spanish.

◆ The three major producers of Latino literature are Chicanos, Cuban-Americans, and Puerto Ricans from the New York area.

◆ Latino literature deals with social issues not generally addressed by American literature: discrimination, economic struggle, and nostalgia for the old country.

# Chapter 18

# Lights, Camera, *Acción*

## In This Chapter

- Hooray for Hollywood
- Latin lovers
- Hollywood, Mexican style
- Tingling tango movie musicals
- What's on *la Televisión?*

Despite the many years of the embargo and the anti-American rhetoric, a crowd of Cubans in Havana waited in line outside a movie house to watch a showing of the film *The Sun Also Rises*. The film was old, the print was in poor condition, and the stars had been dead for years; yet the audience loved it. That's because in Cuba, as throughout Latin America, American movies are popular.

It's a fact: Latinos love movies. Thus, in this chapter we'll take a look at the Latino movie experience from the perspective of Hollywood and south of the border.

So, quiet on the set, please.

# Made in Hollywood

Latinos love American films. In Mexico, pretty ladies mourned the death of matinee idol Rudolph Valentino during the silent era. In Argentina, macho guys combed their hair in the same style as Clark Gable in *Gone with the Wind*. In Cuba, cubanos who behaved in an arrogant and self-assured manner often heard comments such as, "Who do you think you are, Rock Hudson?"

It was a mutual fascination, a love affair between Latin America and Hollywood. But it wasn't always a relationship of equals. Hollywood producers often portrayed Latinos in a negative light; actually, the portrayals were often outright insulting.

Early on in the film industry, studio heads knew their money would come primarily from middle class Americans. That audience wanted good-looking guys—say, Errol Flynn— and sexy dames—say, Marilyn Monroe. And they wanted good to win over evil. On many occasions, evil was personified by a Latino; and if not always evil, at the very least Latinos embodied that which was dark and sinister.

## Bandidos, Lovers, and Beauties

The *bandido* first appeared in the 1910s in such forgettable films as *Across the Mexican Line* and *Along the Border*. The image of the bandido was conjured up in the popular dime novels of the time, westerns written by writers from the East coast. The writers based their characterizations of the bandido on Mexican outlaws and revolutionaries.

### Hablas Español

A **bandido** is a bandit. The Spanish word refers to a person who is a wanted by the authorities and whose name has been published on **bando**— something akin to a Wanted Dead or Alive notice. A courtly gentleman is a **caballero**. The word alludes to a person who is good at riding on horses; it connotes nobility and ancestral linking to Spain.

The outlaws were *vaqueros* who, after the Mexican-American War, rebelled against Anglo rule. The outlaw was the subject of movies like *The Bad Man*, filmed in 1930. It tells the story of an outlaw, his crimes, and his death at the hands of the Texas Rangers. Other movies representative of the outlaws were *The Treasure of Sierra Madre* and *The Magnificent Seven*.

Revolutionaries—soldiers who fought in the Mexican Revolution—were also the subject of Hollywood films. Picture Emiliano Zapata and Pancho Villa, and you'll get the image: daring, brave, wearing a wide-brimmed sombrero with revolver and rifle in hand. The rebel was the inspiration for flicks like *Viva Villa*, made in 1934, and *Viva Zapata*, filmed in 1952, both sympathetic portrayals of these two Mexican patriots.

*Mexican vaqueros.*

# Bandidos from Spain

Another incarnation of the bandido was the outlaw as a gentleman who was courtly, handsome, and gallant; in other words, a *caballero*. But unlike the Mexican bandidos, who were Mexican, the courtly caballeros were of Spanish ancestry. That is to say, the caballero was more acceptable to the average American moviegoer because he was a transplanted European.

The concept of the outlaw caballero might be traced back to writers O. Henry and Johnston McCulley. O. Henry wrote a short story titled "The Caballero's Way," about a Spanish vaquero thwarting the crooked schemes of Mexican hoodlums, and McCulley penned "The Curse of Capistrano," a short story about a Spanish-Mexican Robin Hood. "The Caballero's Way" introduced the Cisco Kid, one of the most popular film characters ever created. Author Gary D. Keller describes Cisco as "a charming brigand who prized a beautiful woman as a gourmet savors a vintage wine ... his method was to ride in, destroy evil, and ride out, leaving a broken heart or two." Nearly 30 Cisco Kid films were made, including a television series.

**Cuidado!**

It has recently been suggested that Zorro was based on the real life character, Joaquín Murieta; in fact, in the film *The Mask of Zorro*, actor Antonio Banderas plays a character named Joaquín Murieta. But the actual Murieta was an outlaw who, according to legend, was avenging the killing of his wife by Anglo cowboys. Murieta didn't dress in black and didn't wear a mask.

The hero of "The Curse of Capistrano" dressed in black, rode a white horse, and with the point of his sword sketched his initial on his foe's forehead: Z for Zorro.

### Hablas Español

**Zorro** is Spanish for fox. As in the English word, zorro suggests conniving and the use of cunning to get a prey.

Zorro first appeared in 1920 in the film *The Mark of Zorro*, starring Douglas Fairbanks. The feature was an instant hit and was followed by a sequel, *Don Q, Son of Zorro*, also with Fairbanks portraying Zorro. Since then, about 20 American film versions have been made, as well as a half dozen European variations. There have been two television series about Zorro filmed in Hollywood, and one in Cuba.

# Latin Lovers

Cisco Kid and Zorro loved the ladies. Dark and handsome, suave and smart, they helped to foster another image: the Latin lover. It was an image of glamour and fantasy that the wife of the regular Joe could fantasize about at the theater as a way to escape the monotony of her day. It was a safe fantasy, since Latin lovers didn't live on Main Street.

The first Latin lover was a Mediterranean type: Rudolph Valentino. The handsome actor became a super star in the 1920s, playing a Spanish matador, or bullfighter, in *Blood and Sand* and a tango dancer in *The Four Horsemen of the Apocalypse*. As his fame grew, so did his artistic and monetary demands. Thus, his producers turned to another actor, the Mexican Ramón Navarro. Navarro starred in the original film version of *Ben Hur*, made in 1926. His dark good looks and acting ability made him a major movie star.

Gilbert Roland, a contemporary of Navarro, was the son of a bullfighter and was raised to be in the bullring, but chose Hollywood instead. He worked in silent films and talkies, and in the early 1950s embodied the Latin lover in the movie, *The Bad and the Beautiful*, where he seduces a college professor's wife and runs away with her, only to die in plane crash.

Closer to our times, and perhaps better remembered, were three actors who typified the Latin lover: César Romero, Fernando Lamas, and Ricardo Montalbán.

# Music Lovers

Like Navarro, the trio of Romero, Lamas, and Montalbán were sex symbols, but with a difference, a musical difference, that is: they sang and danced their way into the heroine's heart. Romero was a romantic from birth—even before birth. For he was the grandson of the romantic poet and patriot José Martí (remember him from Chapter 12?). Very tall and very handsome—even when he was in his '80s Romero robbed ladies' hearts—he was an agile dancer and had a good sense of comedy. He wooed Betty Grable and Sonja Henie, among others. And he played Hernán Cortes—the ultimate Latin lover and ladykiller, among other things—in *Captain From Castille*.

Romero was a home product, that is, he was born and raised in New York City. The Argentine Lamas and the Mexican Montalbán were "discovered" by Hollywood in their native countries. During the golden age of the Metro Goldwin Mayer musicals, producers heard about these two actors, both of whom had worked in films back home. A scout paid them a visit, signed a contract with them, and gave them a ticket to Hollywood. They each made dozens of colorful musicals with such leading ladies as Esther Williams (Lamas married her in real life) and Shirley Winters (Montalbán didn't marry her; he married actress Loretta Young's sister instead). The musicals were light stuff, something closer to MTV, and whenever possible Lamas and Montalbán had to remove their shirts and walk about in shorts or in a bathing suit.

> **Para Tu Información**
>
> The first actor to portray the caballero was Warner Baxter, definitely not a Latino. The second actor was Spaniard Duncan Renaldo. Renaldo was followed by César Romero, a Cuban-American. The latest incarnation of the caballero is Puerto Rican Jimmy Smits.

They were Latin lovers, all right, but as defined by Hollywood. Those who didn't fit the job description were encouraged to go elsewhere. A case in point was the Mexican actor Arturo de Córdova. Immensely popular in Latin America and Europe, de Córdova was a *galán*, a leading man, who was comfortable in comedies, custom epics—he starred in the Mexican version of *The Count of Monte Cristo*—and art films made by Luis Buñuel. But he was too short and looked a little too Mexican for Anglo producers to think of him as a leading man. Had de Córdova wished to play the bad guy, that would have been okay, but that wasn't what he wanted. Thus, de Córdova headed back home, where he made lots of money and won lots critical kudos.

# Mysterious Ways

There was a bit of the sinister to the Latin lover, suggestive of something darker and mysterious. As sexually desirable as the Latin lover was, he was still the other, the outsider, as far as Americans knew. It was no accident that in Latin America the type didn't exist.

Montalbán himself used this "otherness" to expand and extend the roles he accepted. In the late 1970s and '80s, he played the enigmatic Mr. Roarke in the popular television series *Fantasy Island*. Something of a devil, and sometimes a saint, it was Mr. Roarke, dressed in white and with the manners of a prince, who made fantasies come true to those who visited his island, though you didn't always know if Roarke meant it for good or for evil.

Dressed in black, and capable of turning a bad guy's fantasy into his worst nightmare, was Roarke's counterpart: police liutenant Castillo, from Miami Vice. Castillo knew Spanish. Castillo spoke Vietnamese. He was skilled in the martial arts. He practiced *Santería*. No one knew where he came from and where he went at the end of the day. But everyone knew he could be trusted. Edward James Olmos played Castillo, and the role took him from bit player to superstardom.

# Spitfire

There was something else that was odd about Latino lovers: they seldom lusted after a Latina. And this was true about the Latinas, too: they seldom fell in love with a Latino. In the epic *The Alamo*, Argentine actress Linda Cristal was attracted to John Wayne. And in the famous, and controversial, "Spitfire" series, the leading Latina was married to an Anglo.

The "Spitfire" movies were tailored on the explosive personality of Mexican actress Lupe Velez. Beautiful and sexy, when Velez threw a tantrum, the whole world listened, and when she caressed her lover, the whole world watched in silent awe. The Spitfire type was introduced by Velez in *The Girl from Mexico*, filmed in 1939. It was a B production that proved a big draw, prompting RKO studio to shoot seven more films.

Lupe Velez committed suicide in 1944, and another actress took up the role and turned into the supreme Spitfire type: her name was Carmen Miranda. But this was a curious development because Miranda was actually Portuguese and the Spitfire girl was billed as being from Mexico.

With a hat packed with fruits and wearing shoes with very high heels, Miranda incarnated a caricature of the Latin woman. She spoke a mile a minute and her accent was thick. Yet there was artistry behind her façade, and had she not died of a heart attack before reaching middle age, it's possible that she would have graduated to more true comedic roles and less stereotypical performances.

**Para Tu Información**

What were the Spitfire films about? Think of *I Love Lucy* and all the situations she gets in and you get the picture. But there was a down side. Lucy usually won. The Spitfire girl seldom did.

Velez and Miranda passed away, but the Spitfire type lingered. Twenty years later, another beauty, Rita Moreno, had to portray her share of temperamental Latinas before winning an Oscar in 1961 for her role as Anita in *West Side Story*. And even after walking home with the trophy, the Puerto Rican actress had to walk away from Hollywood, all the way to Europe, to avoid being typecast into the Spitfire role one more time.

# The Dark Lady

When Latinas weren't being portrayed as impulsive and explosive, they were rendered in dark hues and situated worlds away. The Mexican Dolores del Río, for example, portrayed South Seas beauties; and María Montez, born in the Dominican Republic, portrayed Arab seductresses.

These actresses created a look. They were dark, their faces were long, and their features were chiseled. There was clear sexuality in their motions. The leading men—Gary Cooper and Tyrone Power, among others—who wanted them didn't want them for company but for sex. And given the choice of whom to marry, they would propose marriage only to a fair-haired beauty.

The bottom line was that the Spitfire and the Dark Lady were female representation of the other, exotic all right but nonetheless an outsider. The average Joe at the theater, tired of his humdrum job and the daily routines at home, could lust after these ladies. And it was all in fun and safe. For his wife knew these tempting Latinas didn't live in the neighborhood.

**Cuidado!**

The negative disposition towards the dark lady wasn't restricted only to Latinas. In movies, the temptress and the villains traditionally were either dark or wore dark clothes. For example, in the early Westerns, the good guy always wore white and the bad guy dressed in black.

# Greener Pastures

The Latin lovers and the dark ladies of the screen did manage to unburden themselves of the types bestowed on them by Hollywood. Here's how:

- **Fernando Lamas** became a successful television director. After the 1950s, he chose to play the villain in numerous films. Comedian Billy Crystal introduced the actor to a new generation of viewers when he caricatured Lamas in Saturday Night Live with a character who would greet people with "You look maaahvelous."

- **Ricardo Montalbán** portrayed one of the most memorable characters to emerge out of *Star Trek*: the evil Khan, featured in television, a feature film, and a series of books. Montalbán also played a boxer, a World War II hero, and a priest, among many other roles. He dedicated his life to improve the lot of Latinos in Hollywood, contributed to dozens of charities, and worked extensively within the Catholic Church. A few years ago, the Pope invited him to the Vatican and honored him with a humanitarian award.

**Para Tu Información**

During the day, Zorro was Don Diego, an effeminate wealthy dandy with a loyal servant who was mute. At night—or during a crisis—Don Diego would dash to a cave within his mansion, where he kept his horse and Zorro paraphernalia. If it sounds familiar, it should. For the popular series Batman and Robin aped the concept of Zorro and updated it to the twentieth century.

◆ **César Romero,** the original Joker in the Batman television show, became an icon of the 1960s. Though to the very end of his long life he remained tall, dark, and handsome—which was the title of one his movies—he played a gangster, performed in comedies, and even acted in an anti-Castro movie, always trying to shed away his Latin lover persona.

◆ **Dolores del Río,** tired of being typecast as an exotic beauty, eventually moved to Mexico City where she starred in dozens of films. She won four Mexican "Oscars" and was widely admired in Europe. In her later years, she returned to the American screen to play Elvis Presley's mother in a western.

# Positive Portrayals

In the late 1940s and 50s, there were some attempts at depicting Latino characters as heroic. In the western *The Ox-Bow Incident*, Mexican-American Anthony Quinn is falsely accused of a crime and lynched by Anglo cowboys. Quinn faces his death bravely, and the audience mourns for him. The Anglos, on the other hand, are depicted as bigoted and cowardly. In *Border Incident*, Ricardo Montalbán is an undercover American agent investigating the killing of several illegal aliens. The film places Montalbán on equal footing with his partner, agent George Murphy.

---

**CAUTION**

### Cuidado!

Here is brief list of Latino stars who kept their ethnicity and nationality a quiet affair:

◆ Mel Ferrer: Cuban-American

◆ Raquel Welch: Peruvian-American

◆ John Gavin: Mexican-American

◆ Dick Himes: Argentine-American

◆ Rita Hayworth: Mexican-American

◆ Yvette Mimeux: French-Mexican.

---

Exploitation of Mexican workers is the theme of the 1954 production *The Salt of the Earth*, about miners fighting for better working conditions. Shot in a documentary style and employing amateur actors, the film was successful throughout Latin America. Initially censored in the United States for its negative portrayals of Anglos, the film became a cult phenomenon on campuses across the states.

True breakthrough, however, didn't happen in movies but on the small screen in the early 1950s. It was a production that perfected the newly created situation comedy genre, featured the first American-Latino married couple on television, and set the standards by which all network comedies would be measured from then on. Can you guess the show? That's right: *I Love Lucy*.

---

### Living La Vida Literaria

In the novel *The Mambo Kings Play Songs of Love*, Oscar Hijuelos describes Desi Arnaz thus: "He was a pleasant looking man with large friendly eyes and a thick head of black hair, shiny as sealskin. Dressed in cuffed trousers, wide-lapeled sports jacket, short-collared shirt, and a slick-looking black tie decorated with piano keys and a crocodile-shaped tie clip, he definitely seemed prosperous and self-confident."

---

# We All Love Lucy

*I Love Lucy* is legendary. There are numerous books, films, and documentaries about the show and its stars. Five decades since its creation, this t.v. comedy has never been off the air. Right now, as you hold this book in your hand, someone, somewhere, is watching *I Love Lucy*.

It was the first show in which an American and a Latino were married to each other and treated each other with equity, respect, and love. It was probably the first multicultural show ever. For although Desi Arnaz plays a character with very middle class values, he remains forever Cuban. It's this Cubaness actually that serves as the catalysts for a lot of the action. In one episode, for instance, Lucy conjures up her own rendition of Cuba in an attempt at making her husband, who seems a little depressed, happy. That the Cuba she imagines looks more like Mexico doesn't disturb Arnaz for he knows that his wife's love extends beyond national and cultural boundary. On the other hand, the very red-headed and very American Lucille, so different from the Cuban women of Arnaz's childhood, is quite exotic for Arnaz.

Handsome Arnaz converts the Latin lover into your regular José. He worries about losing his hair. He worries about money and having a job and buying a house in the suburbs. Women find him attractive—and he is—but they can also find him at the supermarket arguing with the cashier for charging him too much money.

### Para Tu Información

When Lucille Ball and Desi Arnaz were proposing the concept of their situation comedy to a television producer, it is rumored that one network tycoon turned down the concept, saying, "The American public won't buy the idea of a Cuban man and an American woman married to each other." To which, Lucille Ball, pointing at Desi, replied, "But, sir, we're married to each other."

*Lucy and Desi, 1956.*

*(Photo used with permission of Desilu, too, LLC)*

## Desi's and Lucy's Legacy

Throughout Latin America, Arnaz became an icon of the American Dream. In pre-Castro Cuba, the government awarded Arnaz the Carlos Manuel de Céspedes honor award. Over the years, Arnaz served as a role model for actors, writers, and even scholars who carved a name for themselves studying the Cuban's accomplishments. And there were many accomplishments. For Arnaz, along with Lucy Ball, changed the landscape of American t.v. The couple …

- Became first television performers to own the show they were starring in.
- Introduced live filming of a t.v. show.
- Developed the concept of the 25 minute half hour show, to have space for five minutes of commercials.
- Perfected the three camera filming technique for sit-coms.
- Pioneered the idea of reruns.
- Made it evident that Lucy and Desi loved each other and had conjugal relations.
- Presented for the first time on national television the theme of pregnancy.

Though Arnaz had tremendous influence on television, it didn't carry over to the big screen. Few Latino actors achieved a reputation similar to Arnaz's. And the stereotypes continued to flourish with some minor changes. For instance, in the 1960s, the bandido metamorphed into a narco-trafficker—in such movies as *Scarface* and the television series *Miami Vice*—and the spitfire into a prostitute or a maid in films like *Down and Out in Beverly Hills*.

For a change of pace, Latinos had to turn their gaze south of the border.

# Down Mexican Ways

No sooner had the Lumiere brothers premiered silent films in Paris in 1896, than Mexican producers adapted theaters to showcase the new invention. For the next 10 years or so, Mexican film-makers toyed with cameras and projectors, capturing images of trains pulling into a station, filming dictator Porfirio Díaz going for a horse ride in a Mexican forest, and recording battles during the Mexican revolution in 1910. But the entertainment industry didn't really get going until the 1930s.

## Cuidado!

> Mexican films produced their own stereotypes. American women were often portrayed as sexually starved and eager to find release, and sexual liberation, through an encounter with a Mexican. In the film, *A Toda Maquina* (Full Speed Ahead), shot in the 1940s, an American beauty lusts after leading man Pedro Infante. More recently, Jane Fonda, portraying a spinster, discovers the meaning of life after macho man Jimmy Smits makes love to her in the production *Old Gringo*, written by Carlos Fuentes.

In 1936, the first popular Mexican movie was released. A musical, it was titled *Allá En El Rancho Grande* (In The Big Ranch). It was a Mexican western with Mexican vaqueros and the leading man was a singing cowboy. The setting was a wealthy hacienda. The plot was simple: the singing cowboy falls in love with a beautiful señorita; as he romances her, he fights off bad guys. There were gunfights and fistfights and lots of singing.

The formula worked. The movie was a hit throughout Latin America, establishing Mexico as the leading maker of Spanish-language films and exporting leading men and women who rivaled, in Spain and Latin America, American actors and actresses. Two of the most popular males were the cowboy tenors Jorge Negrete and Pedro Infante. Negrete was an anachronistic dead ringer for Robert Goulet. Infante was a Burt Reynolds type. Both men died young: Negrete of a terminal illness, Infante in a plane accident.

# The Beauty and the Comico

A ravishing beauty named Maria Felix emerged as a major star south of the border. An elegant brunette with a reserve that hinted of untamed passion, Maria Felix would have been cast as a Spitfire role in the United States. However, in Mexico, she played a femme fatale as well as a revolutionary, a Native American as well as an aristocrat, often starring in movies where the men served as her stooges. From Mexico, Felix traveled to Spain and Italy and back to Mexico, reigning supreme in all of these countries. Upon her death in April 2002, all of Latin America mourned her. Mexican President Vicente Fox said, "She gave everything to Mexico … we have suffered a great loss."

### Para Tu Información

Often, Argentine and Mexican films were made in the United States. Most of tango singer Carlos Gardel movies were shot in New York City and then shipped to Buenos Aires. The Mexican version of *Dracula* was filmed in the same set with the American crew working during the day and the Mexicans shooting at night. The film, *The Bad Man*, had two leading men. For the American version, Walter Huston was the bad man. For the Mexican version, matinee idol Antonio Moreno played the title role.

Probably the most famous actor of all was Mario Moreno, known as Cantinflas, a comedian with the agility of an acrobat and the linguistic acrobatics of Abbot and Costello rolled into one. Trim and small, Cantinflas' facial features echoed of Aztec influences. He embodied the best aspects of the macho culture: He was honest, humble, courtly, loyal, and a protector of ladies and the weak. No wonder he played D'Artagnan in the Mexican version of *The Three Musketeers!*

Latinos in the United States went to see the Mexican stars at Spanish movie houses in the barrios of Los Angeles, New York, Tampa, and Union City, in New Jersey. On weekends, these local theaters were packed, and there was always a new feature.

Most of Mexican productions didn't—and still don't—appeal to Americans, who found the movies too long and melodramatic. But now and then, a Mexican vehicle sparks the interest of such dailies as *The New York Times* and *Washington Post*. Here are but three: *El* (He), about a sexually obsessed man, and *Los olvidados* (The Forgotten Ones), about urban poverty, both made by Luis Buñuel; and *Like Water for Chocolate*, a feminist love story.

*Cantinflas.*

# Argentine Ways

The accompanying feature at the Latino movie house was usually a flick from Argentina. After Mexico, this southern cone country produced the most popular Spanish language films in the Spanish-speaking world. The industry dates back to the 1930s.

Argentine productions included thrillers, lots of comedies, a few swashbucklers, and historical and biographical epics similar to Hollywood. But what characterized the film industry was the creation of a unique product: the tango musical. The popularity of the tango in Argentina made it a natural choice. In the early 1930s, singer Carlos Gardel became an idol in a series of heart-wrenching love stories. *El Dí[as]a Que Me Quieras* (The Day You Love Me), one of his most beloved films, is the love story of a man who worships his wife and then loses her to a disease. *Mi Buenos Aires Querido* (My Beloved Buenos Aires) is the moving story of an immigrant who longs to return home. Like Infante and Negrete, Gardel died young—in a plane crash in Colombia—and the death increased his fame and cult following. Even today, 70 years after his death, fans still bring flowers to his tomb in Buenos Aires.

Tango lovers were eager for a Gardel substitute and they found it in Hugo del Carril. Resembling Robert Taylor and immaculately dressed, often wearing black with a white scarf wrapped around his collar, del Carril had a powerful voice and a winning personality. He played in dozens of love stories, but was also able to perform in comedies. As his good looks wore away, del Carril turned to film directing and producing. In the 1970s, he toured New York City, packing Madison Square Garden where he relived the old days of the Tango musical by singing dozens of tangos.

### Para Tu Información

Evita Duarte was another Argentine luminary. Her acting skills were limited, but her charm was endless. So endless, in fact, that she charmed an army general, who eventually married her and made her a powerful first lady. By that time, however, she had changed her name to Evita Perón.

During the era of Perón, the Argentian government censored films, even dictating what movies to make. In the 1960s, censorship eased and a former leading man, Armando Bo, teamed up with his voluptuous wife to produce erotic films the likes of which had never before been seen in mainstream movies in Latin America. The star, Isabel Sarli, became as popular as Marilyn Monroe and inspired Latin American writers to pen poems and essays about her.

A handful of Argentine films drew critical attention in the United States. *Camila* was a popular flick about a doomed love affair. *The Official Story*, about the military dictatorship of the '70s, earned its star, Norma Aleandri, an Oscar.

# Made in Cuba

Cuban cinema was born in 1959, right after the triumph of Castro's revolution. Prior to the political change, the film industry was rather lame. Movies were usually co-produced with Mexican companies and were shot in both countries. From this period, the most memorable was *The White Rose*, a biography of poet and patriot José Martí.

As soon as Castro secured his power, his government took over the film industry. Films were effective vehicles for persuasion. Through movies, the Cuban government could show Cubans how to create a revolutionary society. Through movies, Castro could export to Latin America his message of revolutionary change and the need to overthrow capitalist regimes.

Inspired by Castro, Cuban cinematographers went to work enthusiastically. They made the right decision from the very start: They rejected socialist realism—which depicted the daily struggles of dedicated socialists with the intent of converting the audience to socialism or communism—and emphasized stories of universal appeal with likeable characters. The first successful film was *Historia de la revolución*, three sketches depicting the struggle against

Batista's dictatorship. There was an American-like epic quality to the film—for instance, the recreation of a major battle between rebels and tanks in the middle of the streets—but hand-held cameras were used to emphasize an individual's perspective.

Several more hits followed:

- *Memorias del subdesarollo,* about a well-to-do landlord adjusting to life in Castro's Cuba.

- *Lucia,* three different stories about three different women dealing with political change.

- *Fresa y chocolate,* about the friendship between a gay man and a militant.

- *Guantanamera,* a comedy about the transporting of a corpse from one end of the island to the other.

**Cuidado!**

Unlike Argentina, Mexico, and the United States, Cuban filmmakers didn't cultivate their stars; rather the movie itself was the star. Thus, people who watch a film from Cuba do so for the sake of the film and not the actors. Although several performers—the leading lady Mirtha Ibarra, to name one—achieved international fame, no fan clubs emerged the way they did with Gardel, Infante, and Negrete.

# Legendary Latinos

While some Latino actors achieved fame and recognition in the United States and Latin America, a few became international superstars, working in European productions. Some even evolved into contemporary symbols of beauty and high fashion. Here are but a few:

- **Anthony Quinn** was born in Mexico and married Cecil B. De Mille's daughter. He always managed to keep his ethnicity vague, using it as a tool to portray a multiplicity of ethnic roles. You name the nationality, and he played it: he was a Greek and an Arab, a Mexican and a Spaniard, an Italian and a Cuban. He was featured in hundreds of films but he is best remembered as Zorba, the Greek.

- **Raúl Juliá** came from Puerto Rico. He was one of the biggest attractions in the Puerto Rican Traveling Theater, from which he jumped to Broadway, grabbing the spotlight in such productions as *Two Gentlemen from Verona* and *Betrayal.* Audiences will never forget his portrayal of the revolutionary in the movie *Kiss of the Spider Woman.* It is said that his two favorite roles were Father Romero, in the biography of Romero, and Gomez in the *Addams Family.* Stomach cancer stole him from a world of promise.

- **Jennifer López** is a big name and a big star. She makes more money than any other Latino star—actually, she makes more money than most people in Hollywood. A singer and a dancer, fame came to her as a result of her portrayal of the Tex-Mex singer Selena.

◆ **Andy García** gained recognition as an FBI agent in *The Untouchables* and as Al Pacino's nephew in *The Godfather III*. Conscious of his good looks, he never disrobes on screen, lest he be typecast as a Latin lover. He even shied away from the role of a Cuban musician in *The Mambo Kings*, lest he be typecast as a Latino forever and a day.

◆ **Rita Moreno** has won an Oscar, an Emmy, and a Tony. She can dance, she can sing, she can act. She rebelled against stereotypes after *West Side Story* and has chosen her films carefully, working on a thriller with Marlon Brando and spoofing the Spitfire stereotype in *The Ritz*.

Talent, training, and persistence helped to make all these performers into legends. But the root of their success came from something else, not always measurable: In one way or another, they touched the hearts of hundreds of movie-goers, making them laugh or cry. That's Hollywood, with a Latino touch.

## The Least You Need to Know

◆ Latinos love American movies.

◆ For nearly 80 years Hollywood stereotyped Latinos.

◆ Desi Arnaz and Lucille Ball revolutionized the t.v. industry as well as portraying the first multicultural couple on television.

◆ Mexico produces the most films in Latin America: about 100 a year.

◆ Argentine films cultivated the genre of the Tango musical.

# Chapter 19

# Let's Play Ball

## In This Chapter

◆ Sports Latinos watch and play

◆ The beautiful game of soccer

◆ Caribbean beisbol

◆ Boxing Hoya

"Let's play ball."

The invitation, happily and excitedly shouted over a crowd of picnickers, was a call to action. Within minutes, players had been selected, teams formed, and a ball was soaring in the summer air. It was a typical Sunday afternoon ball game, with a difference. For the ball was a *balón*, and the ballgame was not baseball but soccer.

Today, soccer is big in the United States, big because of the growing Latino presence. However, the rise of soccer doesn't mean the death of baseball, as some fear: for there are as many Latinos who love baseball as love soccer.

So, let's go to bat and find out about sports and Latinos.

# A Lot of BS ...

When in comes to sports, Latinos are full of BS. That is, BBS: boxing, baseball, and soccer.

These are the three sports that Latinos like to watch the most. And of these three, baseball and soccer are the two sports they practice they most. There is no place in Latin America where one of these games isn't played. Some countries prefer baseball. Some countries go only for soccer. And some are partial to both.

Of the three sports, soccer is the oldest. The Romans and the Chinese played it, not against each other, though. As did the Mayas and Toltecs. The version played in ancient Latin America was a combination of soccer and basketball. It was played inside a courtyard where two tall walls flanked the players. There were two rings protruding out of the walls, and the team that managed to pass the ball through one ring was the winner. It sounds easy, but it wasn't. For the players could only propel the ball by using their heads, shoulders, and legs. Hands and feet weren't allowed to touch the ball.

## USA Soccer

In Florida, Native Americans played a version much closer to contemporary soccer. There was a goal and a defender and the teams moved the ball forward and backward by kicking it. The British played a more violent version of the game, where the goals were miles away from each other and the teams had to run through valleys and cross lakes, often punching and pushing and kicking opponents. It was so much like a mini-war that rules were established early in the 1800s to curb the violence.

---

### Living La Vida Literaria

Spanish chronicler Gregorio de Escobedo described a game he watched in North America during the late 1500s in his book, *La Florida:* "They arrange themselves twenty on a side and play the game in a brisk, athletic manner. The ball carrier handles it smartly and he plays ... with sure shots that ... he scores on each shot. They erect goal posts made from pine trees about seven feet tall and on top of this goal they place a figure ... It is a rough game which many times prove costly to ... an unfortunate player who gets seriously injured."

---

The more refined adaptation of the game proved popular in the British Isles and Europe. Historians believe that British sailors brought this version to the Americas in the nineteenth century. In 1904, a governing body, the Federacion Internacional de Futbol Aficionado, dubbed FIFA, was formed to encourage competitions between nations. In 1908, soccer was accepted into the Olympics.

In the United States, however, players adopted the more physical version of the game called rugby or association football, where opponents were allowed to push, knock, and throw each other to the ground. Rutgers and Princeton Universities were the first universities to play this variation of soccer, now called football, in 1869.

For a hundred years soccer lay dormant in the United States. In 1975, soccer superstar Pelé joined the New York Cosmos of the North American Soccer League, NASL, in an effort to attract new fans. But the general public didn't take much notice until nearly a decade later when the growing Latino presence in the United States was seen kicking *el balón*, the ball, in parks and in schoolyards, and Spanish television was broadcasting games from Latin America. Then, something happened: parents realized that soccer was more gentle than football and faster than baseball and that it a was game that encouraged participation of both young girls and young boys in the same team. Soon, towns created leagues that started to compete with each other.

**Para Tu Información**

In 1995, Major League Soccer (MLS) was created. It consisted of 10 teams and had a roster of national and international players from Europe and South America. Seven years later, the MLS boasted 17 million fans attending their games. By now, the league had enough pull to draw a lavish contract to broadcast, through ESPN, ABC, and several Disney cable channels, MLS and World Cup games for four consecutive years.

# A Passionate Game

Soccer games are 90 minutes long. Each half is 45 minutes with a rest period of 10 minutes. During tournaments, games might last only 60 minutes with a 5-minute rest period. Indoor games are played with fewer players and might last 40 minutes with no rest period. The objective of the game, which is played on a field with the opposing teams' goals at opposite ends of the field, is to score more goals than the opponent. The team with the highest score wins.

*Balón-pie*, soccer, is a game of passion. Nations take immense pride in their teams. The pride and the passion have led to violent confrontations, even war. In 1969, El Salvador and Honduras went to war over a soccer game. Well, it's not that simple.

During the 1960s, over 300,000 Salvadorans were living in Honduras. While squatting on lots needed by the local government, the immigrants were also accused of taking jobs away from Hondurans. The Honduras government took over the lands, gave it to local residents, and sent the immigrants home. The Salvadoran government accused the Hondurans of abusing and maltreating the nationals.

Relations were already tense between the two countries when, in June of 1969, the Salvadoran soccer team traveled to Honduras for a match. Upon arriving, Honduran soccer fans hurled insults at the visitors. To make matters even worse, their arrival coincided with a teachers' strike. The strikers situated nails on the main roads leading to the city, and as the buses ferrying the Salvadorans entered the metropolis, the tires blew out. The players interpreted this as a personal affront. Burning with anger, the Salvadorans team took to the field with vengence. It was a violent game with lots of shouldering, kicking, and tripping. The Salvadorans lost the match. For the second game, the Hondurans traveled to San Salvador, where the hotel they had booked was burned down. Transported to another site, a group of Salvadorans serenaded the visitors all night long. The frustrated and tired team lost the match to the Salvadorans.

The rematch took place in Mexico. The winner was Salvador. The fans went ballistic, to say the least: fights broke out in the stadium and the fracas spilled out on to the street. When the Hondurans returned home, they claimed the Salvadoran team had cheated them out of a victory.

The two governments stepped in, not to soothe temper but to ignite passions. Depending on which country you side with, you could blame either one for attacking the other. But it doesn't matter, for Honduras and San Salvador went to war. Lasting four days, the conflict left 3,000 dead and 6,000 wounded and it caused $50 million in damages. Fortunately, most soccer matches don't result in wars; actually, they are usually friendly, if fierce, competitions.

> **Cuidado!**
>
> In 1985, at the end of a match between England and Italy, 39 fans were killed in the ensuing fracas. During the next decade, there were numerous riots involving British fans. In the 1990s, there were tragic incidents in Australia, Brussels, Greece, and Turkey, to name only a few.

> **Hablas Español**
>
> **Balón** is Spanish for ball. **Balón pie** is another term used for soccer; it means, foot on the ball. In Latin America, soccer is referred to as **futbol,** alluding to the early days of the game in Europe when it was association football; a **futbolista** is a soccer player.

## Latinos' Favorite Players

Hundreds of Latino soccer players have achieved fame throughout Latin America. Here are but a handful:

- ◆ **Diego Maradona** was born in Argentina in 1960. Rumors have it that he could play soccer before he could talk. True or not, as a child he was the "pibe de oro," the golden kid, for his ability to dribble the ball and to propel it into the net from any position on the field. He made history in 1986 during the World Cup competitions in Mexico City when he scored one goal with his hand—which the ref didn't see— and then a few minutes later, dribbled past six British defenders and the goalie and scored another goal.

♦ **Pelé** is the most beloved *futbolista*, or soccer player, of all time. The Olympic Committee voted him the top athlete of the twentieth century, an incredible honor considering Pelé didn't play in the Olympics at all. Born in Brazil in 1940, Pelé, whose real name is Edson Arantes do Nascimento, holds every major scoring record in the country: he scored 1,281 goals in 1,363 games. He led Brazil to three World Cup championships in 1958, 1962, and 1970. A forward, Pelé had perfect passing, imaginative dribbling skills, and accurate shooting. Pelé is a Brazilian—and technically not a Latino—but every Latino sports fan loves him.

♦ **Ronaldo** is regarded as the greatest futbolista since Pelé. At the age of 16, Ronaldo starting playing professionally, scoring 54 goals in 54 games. In Europe, he played for the Barcelona team, which, supposedly, dished out nearly $20 million to attract the young Brazilian. In 1996, Ronaldo was elected as The World Footballer of the Year. His full name is Ronaldo Luiz Nazario da Lima.

♦ **Carlos Valderama** is probably the most recognizable soccer player in the world: his big curly blonde hair floats in the breeze as Valderama rushes from one spot to another during a match, giving the impression that his head is on fire. Born in Colombia in 1961, Valderama captained his country's national team in three World Cups: 1990, 1994, and 1998. Elected as Colombia's Player of the Century, he is known for his pinpoint passing. He has played for European teams and joined the MLS in 1996 where he was voted Most Valuable Player. He's nicknamed El pibe, the kid.

# Let's Play *Beisbol*

Cubans don't play soccer. Neither do Dominicans and Puerto Ricans. They play baseball.

They played beisbol from day one. According to Himilce Novas, in *Everything You Need To Know About Latino History*, "… the Taínos and Siboney Indians who lived in the Caribbean … played a game with a wooden stick and ball similar to baseball, which both the Spanish and the African people … adopted." Roberto González Echevarría, a literary critic and baseball expert, disputes the claim, arguing that the natives left no record of the sport.

Historical debates aside, Cubans were definitely playing baseball on the island sometime in the 1860s. One theory is that Cuban sailors, who had visited the States and seen the game, brought it to

**Cuidado!**

Legend has it that Fidel Castro wanted to be a ball player and was a gifted pitcher. Scholar Roberto González Echevarría contests such assertions. He has a photograph of Castro holding the ball in a way that betrays a pitcher of little skill, and also points out that in Castro's high school year book, the future dictator posed as a basketball player and lists many sporting activities … but not baseball.

Cuba. Another possibility is that American smugglers bringing goods to the island taught the Cubans the game. However it happened, the game was popular. And it spread to the rest of the Caribbean and Mexico and Central America.

## Peloteros

Cubans and baseball hit it off from the first inning. For the Cubans, it was a symbolic gesture. As they saw it, embracing a game that hadn't originated in Spain and that came from America, the nemesis of the Spanish crown, was an assertion of their wish for independence.

And the more they played it, and the better they got at the game, the more they identified with baseball. *La pelota*, as they called it in Spanish, became more than a national pastime, it became part of the national character. To be Cuban meant to love la pelota and to be a gifted *pelotero*.

The reputation of Cuban players extended beyond the island. During the first two decades of the twentieth century, American leagues regularly recruited Cuban peloteros. The players were placed in two categories: white Cubans and dark-skinned Cubans. The white players joined such teams as the Boston Braves and the Cincinnati Reds.

The black peloteros played in the Negro Leagues. Martín Dihigo, nicknamed "el maestro," played for the New York Cubans and the Baltimore Black Sox. He played all positions, though as he neared his thirties he concentrated on pitching. He was inducted in the National Hall of Fame in 1977 and is enshrined in Cuba's and Mexico's Baseball Hall of Fame.

> **Para Tu Información**
>
> One player who achieved fame in the major leagues was pitcher Dolf Luque. Luque played in the United States in the spring and fall and in Cuba during the winter. In 1923, Luque had, according to González Echevarría in *The Pride of Havana*, a 27 and 8 record.

> **Hablas Español**
>
> **Pelota** means ball, but Cubans use it to refer to the game of baseball. A **pelotero** is a baseball player.

During the age of the color barrier, Cuban players helped to integrate the teams: for while black peloteros couldn't join the major league, light-skinned players were recruited. Many African-Americans hoped that the inclusion of such players might promote a liberalized attitude. Whether or not this was a factor in bringing African-American baseball great Jackie Robinson to the majors, no one can tell, but it certainly couldn't have hurt.

In the 1950s, American recruiters scouted Cuba for fresh and cheaper talents, and out of this crop came Orestes Minoso, who played for the Cleveland Indians and the White Sox. But the flow was shut off after the Cuban Revolution, and players weren't allowed to transfer to American teams. The only way for a pelotero to play in the United States was to defect, which is what the famous Orland "El Duque" Hernández did by escaping from Cuba on a boat in December 1997 and then signing a contract with the New York Yankees.

## From Santo Domingo

With the talent stream from Cuba dried out, recruiters from the north ventured to the Dominican Republic where the game had been played since the 1900s. In 1907, professional teams were established, and during the next 30 years or so many Dominican players joined teams in Cuba and Puerto Rico. In the meantime, African-American players went to the Dominican Republic to play, and during the 1950s it was common for American and Dominican teams to play against each other.

In the 1960s, the Dodgers and other teams set up camps and ran clinics and baseball academies in the Dominican Republic to identify local talent. Some of the academies not only trained the players but held classes in English and taught survival skills to prepare players to make it in the United States. The first player to join an American team was Osvaldo Virgil, who signed up with the New York Giants.

Right-handed pitcher Juan Marichal, known as the Dominican Dandy, was recruited when he was 19 years old by the Boston Red Sox, and then switched to the Los Angeles Dodgers. Playing over 15 years, his career record is 243 victories and 142 losses. He was inducted into the Baseball Hall of Fame in 1983. In 1984, shortstop Tony Fernández signed on with the Toronto Blue Jays, setting records for fielding and hitting. Fernández has been honored with four Golden Glove Awards, which recognizes superior fielding talent.

**Para Tu Información**

Baseball players from the Caribbean encountered discrimination while playing in the United States. The Cuban Dolf Luque was often greeted with racial slurs when he came onto the diamond, even though he was fair and had blue eyes.

Since the 1950s, the Dominican Republic has sent more than 170 players to the major leagues. About 6 percent of baseball players in the leagues are from the Dominican Republic; half of the foreign nationals in the majors are Dominican. Such statistics have prompted Dominican politicians to say that the island now exports baseball players rather than sugar.

## Puerto Rican Peloteros

The first baseball game in Puerto Rico took place in 1896. Two years later, American soldiers stationed on the island at the end of the Spanish-Cuban-American War were seen playing the game. During the 1920s, Cuban and American teams touring Puerto Rico helped to popularize the sport.

Amateur games were played on beaches, parks, and racetracks. After World War II, baseball stadiums were built to serve the emerging professional teams. Since then, the island has hosted a winter league and has participated in the Caribbean Leagues competitions and in the Olympics. In 1942 pitcher Hiram Bithorn was the first Puerto Rican to play in the major leagues; he was followed by Luis Rodríguez Olmo, who joined the Dodgers. Over all, Puerto Rico has sent over 150 players to the leagues.

**Cuidado!**

When a certain country produces a lot of good athletes, there is a tendency to assume that this is the result of racial and ethnic characteristics. However, not all the people from a given country are good at playing a particular sport.

Puerto Rico produced the most legendary Latino baseball player of all. The son of sugar mill workers, Roberto Clemente played as a teenager for a team that featured Negro League and major league players. In 1954, he signed on with the Brooklyn Dodgers and was then drafted by the Pirates. An all-around right fielder, who excelled in batting, fielding, and base-running, he won 12 consecutive Golden Glove awards. In 1966 he was chosen Most Valuable Player. In 1960, he helped the Pirates win the world championship.

**Para Tu Información**

Clemente spoke out against racism in sports. A humanitarian, he organized relief efforts to help Nicaraguans after an earthquake in 1972. He was riding on the plane, overloaded with food and medicine for the Nicaraguans, when it crashed into the ocean. Clemente was never found. The Hall of Fame waived the five-year waiting period for induction, and Clem-ente was enshrined in Coopers-town in 1973.

## Leyendas, or Legends

Here are few of the peloteros admired by Latinos. It's a very incomplete list and chances are someone you have read about doesn't show up here.

- **Luis Aparicio** was one of the greatest shortstops of all time. Born in Venezuela, Aparicio played from 1956 to 1973. He stole over 500 bases and holds the record for double plays, assists, and put outs—which means to retire a batter or a runner. He received the Gold Glove award 11 times. In 1984, he was inducted into the Hall of Fame.

- Panama yielded **Rod Carew,** who signed his first professional contract while he was still in high school and was later named Rookie of the Year in 1967, while playing for the Minnesota Twins. From 1969 on, Carew had 15 consecutive seasons batting over .300 and won seven American League batting championships. In 1979, Carew grew upset by racist comments uttered by the Twins owner and forced a trade to the California Angels.

◆ Dominican-American **Sammy Sosa** is one of the most powerful home run hitters of all time. In 1998, he hit 66 home runs. In 1999, he hit 60. A year later, he hit 50 home runs. Born into a poor family, Sosa played ball for the first time when he was 14 years old. Two years later, the Texas Rangers scouted him and signed him on. After several years in the minor leagues, Sosa joined the Cubs in 1993. In 1997, he signed a $42 million four-year contract. Sosa admired Roberto Clemente and wears number 21 on his jersey to honor his compatriot.

**Para Tu Información**

Latinos have played and are playing other sports beyond baseball, boxing, and soccer. According to Novas, about 12 percent of Latinos play tennis, and 26 percent watch tennis matches on television (which is a higher percentage than among Anglos). There is also growing interest and participation in racquetball, running, skiing, swimming, and weight training.

*Sammy Sosa.*

*(Courtesy of Latino Legends in Sports)*

◆ The Mexican **Fernando Valenzuela** was one of the most celebrated pitchers in recent history. In 1981, he was named Rookie of the Year and Player of the Year. He won his first ten major league games. He led the league in strikeouts in 1981. Considered to have the best screwball in baseball, Valenzuela was a memorable figure on the mound. Fans remember how the player used to look up to the heavens, as if praying, before pitching.

# The Latino KO

At least once during the weekend, the Spanish network broadcasts a boxing match from Nevada, San Juan, or Mexico City. The popularity of the sport is such that many times the boxers aren't famous at all. It's just that Latinos want to watch the sport.

Most Latino boxers followed the same route to amateur and professional boxing. Usually, they were poor and lived in rough and tough neighborhoods where you had to survive by using wits and fists. The boxers could box in formal matches set up by a club or a fraternity, where fans paid at the door to get in. Informal matches were set up in garages or open fields, where sometimes there were no entrance tickets and fans came and went as they pleased.

Puerto Rico has had the most worldwide participation in boxing. The island has produced 34 international champions in different weight classes. In 1975 and 1976, Puerto Rico had four simultaneous champions: Wilfredo Benítez, Alfredo Escalera, Ángel Espada, and Esteban de Jesús. The popular Hector Camacho, immortalized in the novel *Macho Camacho Beat*, by Luis Rafael Sánchez, won five championships in 13 years.

Boxing came to Puerto Rico in 1920 but was outlawed until 1927 when an athletic commission was established to oversee the sport. In the 1930s, the first Puerto Rican world champion emerged: Sixto Escobar.

## Boxeadores

In the last 40 years, Latino boxers have dominated the ring, especially in the lightweight categories. In the range between 131 and 135 pounds, there have been over 15 Latino champions since 1926. In featherweights, from 123 to 126 pounds, 14 Latinos have won championships since 1963. In bantamweights, 116 to 118 pounds, there have been 13 champions since 1963.

Here are a but few of the champions:

◆ **Roberto Durán,** from Panama, won the 1972 lightweight championship. An aggressive and forceful boxer, his energy and strength overpowered his opponents. In 1980, he won the World Boxing Council welterweight title.

◆ Mexican **Armando "Mando" Ramos** boxed only for nine years, but during that time he boxed 40 matches and won two world titles as a lightweight. In 1972, he won the World Boxing Congress championship.

◆ Puerto Rican **José Luis Torres** won the medium heavyweight championship in 1965 with a technical knockout. Torres defended his titles on several occasions, losing in 1966 due to an injury to his pancreas. He learned boxing in the army and in 1956 won the U.S. Olympics title.

## The Golden Boy

Every boxing era has conjured up a golden boy: A superstar who charms audiences with his wit and physique. Once, in the nineteenth century, there was the Irish John L. Sullivan, a heavyweight champ who was also an actor and advocate of Irish-American values. In the 1960s, the golden boy with the pretty face was the Muhammad Ali, "the greatest," as he called himself. Today, the charm and the looks and the skills belong to Mexican-American Oscar de la Hoya.

*Oscar de la Hoya.*

*(Courtesy of Latino Legends in Sports)*

At 5'11", de la Hoya has boxed in the welterweight and lightweight categories. An Olympic gold medallist, de la Hoya turned professional in 1992. Basically undefeated, the boxer is agile on his feet, something of a dancer, and intelligent in his moves, always avoiding a punch to his head and face (he does have a good-looking face to protect).

Earning millions of dollars per fight, de la Hoya does commercials in English and holds press conferences in Spanish. He was born in East Los Angeles in 1973 and learned to box, taught by his father who had also been a boxer, to protect himself from bullies. His motto is, "There's always space to improve."

## The Least You Need to Know

◆ The three major sports in Latin America are soccer, baseball, and boxing.

◆ Soccer is big in Mexico and in Central and South America.

◆ People from the Spanish-speaking Caribbean prefer baseball.

◆ Cuba was once the hotbed of baseball.

◆ The Dominican Republic is the major provider of Latinos to the American leagues.

◆ Puerto Rico is the birthplace of some of the world's greatest boxers.

# Part 5

# Living-on-the-Hyphen

Latinos lead lives of compromises. For in becoming Americans, they leave behind some of their past, their histories, and their traditions. Some, not all. That's why many Latinos see themselves as leading an existence of duality, of being as much a Panamanian as an American, for example. It's what scholar Gustavo Pérez Firmat calls living on the hyphen.

The hyphen means that as a politician, a Latino will push a local, American agenda while espousing issues that are important back home—be it Cuba or Mexico. It means that as a businessperson, a Latino will do what it takes to climb the ladder but will not relegate his or her family to the background

What does it mean for the future? Will Latinos give up their heritage as they become more Americanized? Will they forget about the homelands of their ancestors?

# 20

# Mr. Menéndez Goes to Washington

## In This Chapter

- ◆ Early Latino politics
- ◆ Politics and politicians
- ◆ Latinos on the Belt Way
- ◆ Who votes for whom

Over 20 years ago, the governor of New Jersey, Thomas Kean, surprised political observers when he actively courted the Latino vote. A Republican, he wasn't expected to pursue such a political course; after all, Latinos were the province of the Democrats. However, the strategy worked and, when, re-elected to office, the governor thanked the thousands of Puerto Ricans who had crossed over party lines to vote Republican.

The governor was one of the first elected officials to realize the potential of a sleeping giant. Today, politicians actively seek Latino support. President Bush did so in California, Florida, and Texas—as did Bill Clinton before him. Not everyone agrees on how much of an impact the Latino vote has, but politicians believe the vote is important and don't want to risk losing it to their opponents.

That's what we'll read about in this chapter: Latino politics, Latino politicians, and the politics of being a Latino.

# The First Politicians

Mexican-Americans were the first Latinos to actively participate in American politics. After the Mexican War of 1846, Mexicans living in the United States were granted American citizenship. Discriminated against by Anglo settlers, Mexican-Americans tried to obtain legal protection and equity by becoming involved in local and national politics.

One of the first politicians was the priest José Manuel Gallegos, from New Mexico. Highly educated and from a well-to-do family, Gallegos was elected territorial delegate to the U.S. Congress in 1851. A Democrat, in 1860 he was appointed Speaker of the House. When the Civil War broke out, Gallegos, who was known for his support of the Union and his anti-slavery stance, was arrested by Texan Confederate soldiers. Released at the end of the war, Gallegos was elected once more to Congress.

The first Latino to serve in the Senate was also from New Mexico. Dennis Chávez was elected five times, from 1930 to 1962. A supporter of President Roosevelt's New Deal, he sponsored irrigation and flood control projects in New Mexico. Chávez championed civil rights and equality for all Americans.

> **CAUTION**
>
> ### Cuidado! _____
>
> The success of Gallegos and Chávez shouldn't be taken as indicative of acceptance of Mexican-Americans in the political arena during the late 1800s and early 1900s. Most Mexican-Americans had very little contact with politicians and had no political influence at all. The exception was New Mexico, where there were four Mexican-American governors, three Senators, and seven members of congress. Cynics suggested that this was due to the fact that these Mexican-American officials were all light-skinned and came from money.

Chávez's political rise coincided with the formation of the League of United Latin American Citizens—LULAC. Made up of middle and upper class Mexican-Americans, the organization promoted the political and economic rights of Mexican-Americans, with emphasis on "the American," since one had to be a citizen in order to join the group. In 1949, LULAC lobbied successfully for fair employment laws. During the 1950s, the group fought against segregation in schools, swimming pools, and even in theaters. At a time when it was difficult for Mexican-Americans to find mentors and join the "old boys network," LULAC provided an avenue for success and fostered a Mexican-American business network.

# Chicano Voice

In the 1960s, Mexican-American militants referred to compatriots who wanted to succeed in the mainstream as *vendidos*, sell-outs, and formed organizations that challenged LULAC's middle class values and its interest in promoting assimilation. There were two organizations that were quite radical and extreme. The members of Alianza dumped the term Mexican-American and opted for *Chicano*, a word used to describe poor Mexicans. Maintaining that Chicanos were the rightful owners of the territory taken over by the United States in the nineteenth century, the leader of Alianza and some of his followers set out in 1967 to claim the land by force. After taking over a courthouse in New Mexico and shooting down two sheriffs, the rebels took off for the hills, where they were captured a few days later.

Less prone to violence was the Mexican-American Political Association (MAPA). The association believed that only Mexican-Americans could care for and represent the interests of Mexican-Americans. In the 1960s, MAPA tried to incorporate East Los Angeles as a Mexican-American city. The attempt was unsuccessful, but it indicated willingness to use the electoral process to bring about political and social change for Mexican-Americans.

### Hablas Español

**Vendido** is meant as an insult; it describes a Latino who has sold out his ethnicity, choosing to be more American, or Anglo.

This was the strategy employed by the Mexican American Legal Defense and Education Fund (MALDEF). MALDEF helped to change public policy towards Latinos. In 1973, the organization filed a suit in California claiming that the financing of schools through property taxes promoted inequality. The organization won, and later on more than 25 states passed similar laws to reform school financing.

### Para Tu Información

The Mexican-Americans from Alianza and MAPA described themselves as Chicanos, a term used as an expression of solidarity with poor Mexicans.

# Three *Caballeros*

By the 1960s, New Mexico was no longer the sole provider of Latino politicians to the federal government; now there were representatives from California and Texas, too. Working within the political mainstream, several Mexican-Americans made great strides. Savvy and dedicated, they played by the rules. First, they joined a political party—usually the Democrats—then, they worked within the organization, following orders and spouting the party line. After achieving recognition within the party—so they could benefit from the political machine—they were elected to local offices before heading for the nation's capital.

This was the path followed by Edward Roybal, from California, and Henry B. González and Kika de la Garza, from Texas. The three were elected to Congress during the 1960s.

Collectively, they fought for social and economic reforms to benefit immigrants, bilingual education, civil rights, and campaigned for Presidents Kennedy and Johnson.

Individually, Roybal was responsible for showing the political ropes to Mexican-Americans from Los Angeles who wanted to enter the political arena; González was the first Mexican from Texas to be elected to Congress and served as the role model for dozens of young Latino politicians, like the legendary Henry Cisneros; and de la Garza championed better treatment of immigrants and promoted good relations between the United States and Mexico (he was revered in Mexico and decorated with the Aztec Eagle Award).

Roybal's daughter, Lucille, followed in her dad's steps—like father, like daughter—and was elected to Congress.

# New York Lords

In the Big Apple, Puerto Ricans were first involved in politics during the nineteenth century. However, their aim was nationhood: the creation of a Puerto Rican nation, free from Spain. Puerto Rican patriots conspired against Spain and sought funds to support the independence movement and freedom fighters back home. When the Spanish-American War was over and the United States took over Puerto Rico in 1898, Puerto Rican politicians in the United States lobbied for the departure of the Americans from the island and the establishment of a republic—similar to what happened in Cuba in 1902. One of the leaders of this struggle was Eugenio Maria Hostos (see Chapter 12).

Other Puerto Rican leaders and politicians wanted *Borinquen*—the island's original Indian name—to remain a commonwealth. Their side won out, as the United States didn't relinquish the island. This decision fueled the anger of a few radical *independentistas*, who in 1950 unsuccessfully attempted to assassinate President Harry Truman and in 1954 opened fire on the House of Representatives, wounding five members of Congress.

Equally frustrated were the Puerto Rican youth in Manhattan. Tired of discrimination, school neglect, and poverty, they emulated the strategies used by the Black Panthers and in the 1960s formed a group they called The Young Lords. Wearing berets à la Che Guevara, the Argentine rebel who was an idol, they took to the streets of the barrios and demanded better public schools in poor neighborhoods, the cleanup of abandoned lots in Harlem, and enforcement of housing codes so that landlords would maintain the tenements where Puerto Rican families lived. They also demanded bilingual education for the 125,000 Latino children—mostly from Puerto Rico—attending New York City schools, and participation in city politics.

The Young Lords were successful. In 1974, the Board of Education implemented a bilingual education program where Spanish-speaking children were taught in Spanish until they mastered English. Bilingual teachers and Latino administrators were hired. And Puerto Rican politicians were elected to public offices at the city and state levels.

One factor that helped in the political arena was the expansion in 1975 of the Voting Act of 1965. This act was originally created to protect the voting rights of African-Americans in the South. In 1975 it was expanded to forbid literacy tests and knowledge of English as a requirement for voting and mandated bilingual ballots—after all, Puerto Ricans were Americans whose first language was Spanish—and safeguarded against redistricting to dilute Latino vote through gerrymandering.

# Dos Caballeros Plus a Lady

Three Puerto Rican leaders emerged: Herman Badillo, José Serrano, and Nydia M. Velázquez. Badillo was elected to Congress in 1970. A faithful supporter of the Kennedys, the Kennedy political machine helped to send Badillo to Washington, where he became a luminary in the political firmament. Badillo sponsored legislation to provide job training for non–English-speaking immigrants and fought for the end of age and marital discrimination in the workplace. After serving seven terms, Badillo left Congress to accept the post of deputy mayor under Edward Koch. Appointed to the board of New York colleges, recently ran for mayor but lost. Beginning his career as a Democrat, today Badillo is a Republican.

Serrano was born in Puerto Rico in 1943. After paying his dues in the local New York political scene, he was elected to the New York State assembly in 1974, from where he made his way to D.C. in 1990 as a member of the House of Representatives. A Democrat, Serrano sponsored a bill to create educational programs that would reduce the rate of school dropouts and successfully opposed efforts in Congress to make English the official language of the country. He has lobbied for the end of the military use of the island of Vieques in Puerto Rico and has fought against police abuse of minorities.

**Para Tu Información**

Vieques is an island off Puerto Rico. It's used by the U.S. Armed Forces for bombing and target practice as well as military games. Many people in Puerto Rico believe that the flora and fauna of Vieques is being destroyed by the American army's activities.

In 1992, the first Puerto Rican woman—Nydia M. Velázquez—was elected to Congress. Of humble origins, Velázquez was a college professor before going off to Washington. In Congress, she supported unpaid family and medical leave, lobbied for faster procedures to register voters, and advocated for social and economic programs for women and the elderly.

# Cubanos

Cuban-Americans are the newest kids in the political block. From 1959 to the mid 1970s, Cuban Americans focused their energy on devising strategies to remove Castro from office. In 1961, they participated in the Bay of Pigs invasion. For the next decade or so, they lobbied the United States to maintain the embargo and develop any strategy that would help change the government on the island. As the United States demonstrated a lack of interest in the actual ousting of Castro through force and as many congressmen and senators seemed partial to Castro, a few radical exiles took violent steps to change the situation. A Chilean ambassador and former representative of the Salvador Allende regime was murdered by a Cuban. A group named Omega Seven murdered a suspected Castro agent and planned the bombing of New York theaters where pro-Castro events were held.

## Para Tu Información

The Cuban American National Foundation was founded in 1981 to promote a transition in Cuba from a dictatorial regime to a pluralistic society based on free-market economics. It engages in peaceful anti-Castro activities through support of the embargo and the distribution in Cuba of noncensored information. Working out of Washington, D.C., the foundation is modeled on the American Israel Public Affairs Committee, which lobbies for pro-Israel legislations and programs. It is focused solely on Cuban affairs, and it seldom deals with domestic matters affecting Latinos in the United States.

In the 1980s, a prominent Cuban businessman, Jorge Más Canosa, founded the Cuban American National Foundation, a powerful and effective lobbying group that helped Presidents Ronald Reagan and George Bush win the Cuban vote in Florida. During the same decade, Cuban-American politician Bob Menéndez made his way to Congress.

Menéndez's political rise is a textbook case. In high school in New Jersey, Menéndez was president of the student body. While in college, he was elected president of the Union City Board of Education—one of the youngest persons in the country to hold such a position. From the Board of Education, he moved to City Hall as mayor of Union City. In the mid-1980s he was elected state assemblyman and later on, he was elected to Congress. Menéndez, a Democrat, is applauded for the creation of a bill to end hate-crimes and for his liberal positions on welfare reform. Cuban-Americans admire his staunch anti-Castro positions.

Just as anti-Castro are his compatriots from Florida, representatives Ileana Ros-Lehtinen and Lincoln Díaz-Balart. Congresswoman Ros-Lehtinen was the first Latina elected to the Florida State Legislature and the first Latina elected to Congress. A teacher and owner of a private school, Ros-Lehtinen has served in Congress since 1992. She has advocated programs for drug-free workplaces, tuition refunds for college students, and the Cuban embargo. Lincoln Díaz-Balart, who is related to Fidel Castro, was elected to the House of

Representatives in 1992 and has labored for the rights and protection of legal immigrants and has favored the Cuban embargo. Both Ros-Lehtinen and Díaz-Balart are Republicans.

## More Politicians

Since 1822, more than 59 Latinos have been elected to Congress and two to the Senate. Today, there are 21 Latinos in the House of Representatives:

| State | Representative | Affiliation | Elected |
|---|---|---|---|
| Arizona | Edward Pastor | Democrat | 1991 |
| California | Joe Baca | Democrat | 2000 |
| | Xavier Becerra | Democrat | 1992 |
| | Grace Napolitano | Democrat | 1998 |
| | Lucille Royball-Allard | Democrat | 1992 |
| | Loretta Sanchez | Democrat | 1996 |
| | Hilda Solis | Democrat | 2000 |
| Florida | Lincoln Díaz-Balart | Republican | 1992 |
| | Ileana Ros-Lehtinen | Republican | 1989 |
| Illinois | Luis Gutiérrez | Democrat | 1992 |
| New Jersey | Bob Menéndez | Democrat | 1992 |
| New York | José Serrano | Democrat | 1990 |
| | Nydia M. Velázquez | Democrat | 1992 |
| Texas | Henry Bonilla | Republican | 1992 |
| | Charles González | Democrat | 1998 |
| | Rubén Hinojosa | Democrat | 1996 |
| | Salomón Ortiz | Democrat | 1982 |
| | Silvestre Reyes | Democrat | 1996 |
| | Ciro Rodríguez | Democrat | 1997 |

# Caucusing

In 1976, Latino politicians in Congress formed an informal organization dubbed the Hispanic Caucus. The purpose of the group was to voice and promote, through the legislative process, issues affecting Latinos. Heavily Democratic and liberal, at the moment there are no Republican representatives in its membership. One member,

**Cuidado!**

There are no Latino governors and only two Latinos have been elected to the Senate in the last two hundred years.

Bonilla from Texas, felt the group was too liberal and withdrew from it; the two representatives from Florida—Díaz-Balart and Ros-Lehtinen—left the caucus when one of its members visited Fidel Castro in Cuba.

The Hispanic Caucus offers scholarships to Latino college students who have demonstrated political leadership on a campus. It offers a fellowship program for graduate students and an internship program where a Latino spends nine months in D.C., learning about the political process.

The Caucus also functions as an information bank for Latino organizations and institutions working with Latinos. It has collected money for the homeless after September 11 and has assisted Latino survivors of the attack to get in touch with social agencies and charities.

# All Politics Is Local

Though the Latinos in Congress have achieved national prominence, they all had their beginnings in their barrios. For, as politicians often say, all politics is local, and when these politicians were rising local talents, they sought the help of patrones—party bosses—and the local political machine. It's an old formula, used by the Irish in New England and the Italians in New Jersey. There are analysts, however, who maintain that the political machine system doesn't work for Latinos. This might be so, but the ascendancy to power of Badillo in New York and Menéndez in New Jersey suggests otherwise.

Not all Latino politicians go to Congress—in fact, not all politicians make it to Washington—but many achieve national recognition through the work they do at home. Their local accomplishments serve as a trampoline, propelling them to positions of national significance. Henry Cisneros was one such individual. As the mayor of San Antonio, he was credited with the rebirth of that beautiful city. The fame spread to Washington, D.C., where he served in President Clinton's cabinet and was once considered Vice Presidential material. Though at the present he's not in the spot-light due to personal and financial problems, he's sure to rebound.

> **Living La Vida Literaria**
>
> Earl Shorris, in *Latinos: A Biography of a People*, renders Henry Cisneros in poetic canvas: "…a tall man, just entering middle age, attenuated as a statue of Don Quixote, but with Oriental elegance, as if he were a prince of the Mexica … cool, gracious; he spoke in paragraphs, a dark brown Englishman with Indian eyes who stood as straight and thin as a knife …"

Mel Martínez was Chairman of Orange County, Florida, where he managed the county's budget and programs. After campaigning for state politicians and co-chairing the Bush/Cheney campaign in Florida, Martínez went to the capital as Secretary of Housing.

# The Latino Voter

There are two types of Latino voters: 1) The individual who is American by birth, and 2) the naturalized citizen.

It might take a while for naturalized citizens to understand that their vote could shape public policies that in turn will affect their lives. Their experiences in Latin America might have been far different. Maybe they came from a country where public policies were made without input from ordinary citizens and changes in the policy were made only by the mighty and the rich. Therefore, it's not surprising that it might take time for it to dawn on new citizens that their vote counts and that they have power through voting.

Latino power at the polls is growing. As recently as 10 years ago, political commentators were lamenting Latino lethargy, complaining that maybe one out of twenty Latinos voted. But a recent study conducted by The Tomás Rivera Institute indicated a growth of about 40 percent in Latino registration and political participation. Thus, it's not surprising that both Bush and Gore addressed Spanish-speaking audiences in Spanish in the 2000 presidential election and that the Bush camp ran Spanish ads on Spanish stations.

**Para Tu Información**

Power through voting has been visible lately. In the last general elections, 5 percent of all voters were Latinos. Although 5 percent isn't going to elect a candidate, it contributes a great deal to the election. This is why observers now think of the Latino vote as the swing vote that made a difference for presidents Clinton and Bush.

# Who Votes How?

Mexican-Americans, Central Americans, Dominicans, and Puerto Ricans tend to vote for Democrats; probably about 70 percent of these registered voters prefer candidates from the Democratic Party. Cuban Americans, Nicaraguans, and some Chileans—many of whom had opposed the socialist regime of president Allende—identify themselves, for the most part, with the Republicans.

Latinos also take into account a candidate's ethnicity; if the candidate is not a Latino but courts the Latino vote, this politician will likely do well with the community. When two Latino candidates confront each other, the community will generally back the politician who has been in office the longest.

**Cuidado!**

Political affiliation doesn't guarantee a political position. For example, Cuban Republicans shy away from restrictions on immigration and don't favor the legislating of English as the country's official language. Likewise, Democrat Bob Menéndez maintains a very conservative line on Fidel Castro, a posture not shared by Democrats.

*U.S. Representatives Lucile Roybal-Allard (left) and Ileana Ros-Lehtenin (right).*

*(Courtesy of their offices)*

# What Do Latinos Want?

Latinos have three sets of needs: local, national, and international.

Local concerns include:

- Monitoring discriminatory acts by local institutions
- Legislation to curb crime
- Gun control
- School finance
- School programs for immigrants
- Programs to create jobs
- Upkeep of neighborhoods
- Recreational programs for children

National concerns include:

- Immigration
- Amnesty for illegal immigrants
- Redistricting of political districts to reflect growth of Latino population
- Programs to create jobs at national levels
- Bilingual education
- Opposition to English-only legislation

International concerns include:

- Free trade between the United States, Mexico, and Central America
- Easing border restrictions
- Political change in Cuba
- Political change in Puerto Rico
- Financial aid to Latin American countries

The international interests of Latino politicians is reflective of their heritage. But not all voters want their representative to worry so much about events back home. For instance, non-Cuban voters in New Jersey have criticized Congressman Bob Menéndez for his ongoing interest in Cuba and political events there. However, it might be said that the representative's focus on the island is not any different from those colleagues who are interested in what's happening in Ireland or in Israel. If anything, interest in activities outside the United States brings a welcome diversity and universality to American politics.

## The Least You Need to Know

- The majority of Latino voters register as Democrats.
- Cuban-Americans tend to be Republicans.
- The political machine seems to work for Latino politicians.
- The states with the largest Latino representation in Washington, D.C. are California and Texas.

# Your Negocio Is My Business

## In This Chapter

- The Business of Latinos
- Economic enclaves
- Bodega dreams
- Corporate Latinos

Main Street, USA.

As you walk down the street you see a Mom and-Pop shop, a grocery store, a pharmacy, and a beauty parlor. And, yes, at the corner there's a newspaper stand.

Your average Main Street. But there's a difference. The store signs are in Spanish, and the shop owners and the clients are talking in Spanish. This is Main Street, Latino style.

Latino Main Streets have been springing up all over the United States. Like the Chinese during the late 1800s and the Italians during the early 1900s, Latinos are creating self-supporting neighborhoods that conduct businesses in a language other than English. Such neighborhoods are called economic enclaves, and they line the streets leading to the American Dream.

It is the business of Latino businesses. And if you haven't guessed by now, the business of this chapter is business, Latino style.

# Beginning a Business

Juan Manuel Salvat was sailing to Cuba under the cover of darkness, planning to sneak onto the island to conduct an anti-Castro raid. He had done this before. But tonight he wasn't thinking about his mission. He was thinking about his wife and children and the knowledge that he was getting too old for clandestine work. He decided that it was time to rechannel his patriotic fervor into more peaceful and less dangerous ways.

One way to do it was by setting up a business. He mused about importing bananas from Venezuela, where he had a friend. However, he didn't just want to support his family; he also wanted to continue his anti-Castro work. What if he were to go into publishing? He could earn money by publishing the works of Cubans who wanted to tell their side of the Castro story.

> **Para Tu Información**
>
> Two generations before Salvat, another businessman went into the world of publishing, setting up a newspaper legacy that is still thriving today. His name was Ignacio Lozano. A Mexican exile from the Mexican Revolution, he founded two newspapers during the 1910s—*La Prensa* and *La Opinión*—in Texas, established a publishing house, and set up a bookstore to sell the books he was printing.

With a loan from the Small Business Administration and funds that relatives and friends gave him, he opened a bookstore. Two years later, he talked to an uncle who had a printing press. Working out of a garage, Salvat founded Editorial Universal. He distributed review copies of his books to local dailies and such prestigious journals as *World Literature Today*. Thirty years later, Salvat was the major publisher of works by Cuban authors living in the United States, had a well-known bookstore in Miami—a gathering place for *tertulias*, informal symposiums—and had received numerous chamber of commerce and business awards.

> **Hablas Español**
>
> The word for business in Spanish is **negocio**. It refers to the abstract concept of business as well as a particular shop.

# Negocios Latinos

Salvat is not alone. He is one of 1.4 million Latinos who own businesses in the United States, a figure that grew by nearly 250 percent between 1987 and the year 2000. This is the culmination of a development that had been occurring quietly since the 1970s.

*Growth of Latino business since 1977.*

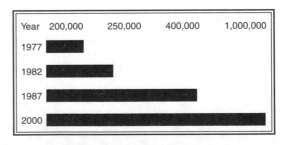

| Year | 200,000 | 250,000 | 400,000 | 1,000,000 |
|------|---------|---------|---------|-----------|
| 1977 | | | | |
| 1982 | | | | |
| 1987 | | | | |
| 2000 | | | | |

## Negocios de Familias

A lot of the Latino businesses are owned by one individual, who then hires family members and friends. Some family members work without pay, so that the profits can be put right back into the business. Often, family members helping out keep a second—or primary—job to supplement the income; on many occasions, the owner has a second job as well.

Over 60 percent of the negocios concentrate on services and retail trade. The most visible and known Latino business is the *bodega*. Any place where Latinos gather, a bodega emerges. A bodega is a grocery store that specializes in selling products from Latin America. There's a lot of emphasis given to the particular nationality that is served. Thus, bodegas in Miami carry a lot of Cuban items, while a bodega in New York City tends to carry products from the Dominican Republic and Puerto Rico. Bodegas on the West coast tailor to the needs of the Mexican-American community.

But a bodega is more than just a grocery store. It serves as a meeting place for *compatriotas*, who catch up on news from the old country, gossip with old friends, and learn about recent political developments—for example, in Washington Heights, in New York City, Dominicans meet at the bodega to campaign for políticos back home. The *bodeguero*, the owner, may also lend money to some of his customers. Usually, though, the bodeguero extends credit to his clients so they can buy what they need during the week. The owner jots down the amount of the transaction on a slip of paper bearing the customer's name; at the end of the week, the customer pays up.

*A bodega.*

## Bodegas and Bolita

There is also a shady side to bodegas. In many bodegas, Latinos can play *la bolita*, an illegal lottery based on the results of horse races or a lottery in another country (one or the other, but not the two combined). Say you play the number 12. If a horse bearing that number comes in first place, then you win half the loot collected at the diverse bodegas participating in la bolita in the region. Or if the number 12 is part of the winning number in a national lottery in a Latin American country—say Colombia—then you win.

A few bodegas in New York City and other areas are fronts for drug dealers. Roberto Sauro in *Strangers Among Us*, reports on the drug trade in bodegas in the Washington Heights area of New York City. Customers don't always know about the illegal activities going on. But, according to Sauro, many of these bodegas have lower prices than the competition, since the earnings come from the drug racket. Understandably, such practices are frustrating to the owners of legitimate businesses.

> **Hablas Español**
>
> **Bolita,** meaning a little ball, is an informal, and illegal, lottery game.

## Profiling Latino Businesses

Latino business owners tend to be new at the game, going into the negocio without much experience. They are young, from their mid-20s to their early 50s, married, and have limited schooling in the United States. As managers, they have no formal training, and they learn administrative techniques as they go along.

Latino business owners are attracted to the following negocios:

- Bodegas
- Restaurants
- Clothing stores
- Specialty shops, such as odds-and-ends shops that sell inexpensive items
- Repair services, such as automotive or air-conditioning

Latinos tend to set up business in the areas where there are large Spanish-speaking communities, usually in or near an urban area. About 80 percent of the negocios are located in California, Texas, Florida, New York, and New Mexico. Some cities that serve as home for hundreds of Latino businesses are: Los Angeles, Miami, New York City, Houston, San Antonio, San Diego, Riverside, Anaheim, El Paso, and Chicago.

## Economic Enclaves

The cities where bodegas and other Latino businesses prosper are called economic enclaves. An economic enclave is a town or a neighborhood where a person can conduct business in her own language without having to use English. Think of Little Italy in New York City and Chinatown in San Francisco, and you get a picture of what an economic enclave looks like.

Walking down the block of an enclave, you'll see: a bodega, a restaurant, clothing stores, a jewelry store, a pharmacy, and maybe a law office for immigration services. In Dade County, Florida, Cubans founded investment firms and clinics as well.

# Painting a Picture of Goya

Many businesses that began as a one-person shop grew into corporations that now hire thousands of workers. That's the story of Goya; no, not the painter, but the food corporation.

Goya was founded in 1936. Its founder, Prudencio Unanue Ortíz was originally from Spain but lived in Puerto Rico. In 1915, Unanue moved to New York City, where he spotted a trend: The Puerto Rican community was growing. Visionary that he was, Unanue realized that the trend was going to continue.

---

### Living La Vida Literaria

The Spanish newspaper media courts the bodegas. It's common to find all the major Spanish publications, such as *El Diario,* and the little newspapers, called *periodiquitos,* at the bodegas. The little newspapers are given out free to customers. They announce events of interest to a particular community and summarize developments back home. The periodiquitos make their money from the advertisements; advertisers know that papers in bodegas circulate. As a matter of fact, knowing how important periodiquitos are, a few years ago librarians from the University of Miami visited bodegas in Dade County to collect the periodiquitos.

---

Unanue loved Puerto Rican food. He missed its color and flavor. Realizing that he probably wasn't alone, he decided that he could supply the flavor of the Caribbean to the Puerto Ricans in Manhattan. And he did. He imported beans and desserts and vegetables, placing them first in bodegas and then in supermarkets, too.

## If It's Goya ...

If there is one food product that has fostered millions of loyal Latino customers, that's Goya. Originally, Unanue targeted the Puerto Rican community. In 1976, his son Joseph took over the company and decided to reach the rest of the Latino community. Goya expanded its inventory to 800 products, including flour, salsa, corn products, and desserts favored by Mexican-Americans and Cuban-Americans.

### Living La Vida Literaria

At the bodegas, or supermarkets, the presence of fruits from the tropics reminds writer Virgil Suárez of his childhood in another land. He writes in the poem "Song to the Sugarcane":

> I spotted the green stalks of sugarcane
> … I grabbed the three
> left and brought them home.
> "Here," I say, "nothing is ever as sweet as this."
> … this was my candy
> when I was a kid growing up …

By 1992, Goya reached nearly $500 million in revenue. Around this time, Unanue, the son, realized that middle class consumers in the United States were concerned about eating too much meat; thus, he started an ad campaign to reach the Anglos, suggesting beans as a substitute for meat. The ads, traditionally seen on the Spanish media, were now seen in mainstream television.

*A display of Goya products.*

Today, all major supermarkets in the country carry Goya products. And there is no bodega, no matter how big or small, without a Goya section.

## Fernando's 500?

Okay, not all of the following businesses would make the Forbes 500 list of top corporations, but they are prominent Latino businesses in the United States:

| Company | Year Founded | Product |
| --- | --- | --- |
| Bacardi Imports | 1944 | Rum manufacturer; sells the product around the world. |
| Condal Distributors | 1968 | Food distributors to supermarkets and bodegas. |
| Eagle Brand | 1984 | Beer distributor to liquor stores. |
| Galeana Dodge | 1968 | Auto dealership in South Carolina |
| Handy Andy | 1983 | Supermarkets based in the west; sells Mexican products. |
| Pizza Management | 1976 | Restaurant and catering business in California. |
| Ruiz Food Products | 1964 | Manufactures and distributes frozen Mexican food to supermarkets and bodegas. |
| Sedano's Supermarket | 1962 | Supermarket chain in Dade County, Florida. |

These companies hire anywhere from 500 to 1,500 workers.

# Soda Pop's *Hombre*

If Goya is the most recognizable brand name in the Latino community, the most famous man in the Latino business community might be the former president of Coca Cola: Robert C. Goizueta.

Goizueta was born in Havana in 1931 and graduated from Yale University in 1953. Back in Cuba, he worked as administrator for several Cuban beverage companies, while representing Coca Cola on the island. When Castro came to power, Goizueta went into exile, and Coca Cola offered him a job as assistant vice president.

In 1981, he became chairman of the board and CEO. Goizueta encouraged research and promoted the idea of a new taste for the beverage. When this experiment wasn't as successful as anticipated, he recommended massive and extensive promotion of the original cola, which he dubbed "classic" Coke. His visionary administrative style kept Coca Cola in the international lead for beverages.

Goizueta died of cancer while still presiding over the corporation. During his lifetime, he received numerous awards, including the Ellis Island Medal of Honor.

# Rich Latinos

*Hispanic* magazine frequently lists prominent Latino business leaders. Some wealthy Latinos leading a pretty good life in the United States include:

◆ John Arrillaga, a real estate developer, lives in California and has more than $320 million in assets.

◆ Arturo G. Torres, the former owner of Pizza Management, Inc., is worth over $105 million.

◆ Robert Alvérez, Sr., who formed the Citrus Coast Corp., has a net worth of over $85 million.

◆ José Milton made his money in real estate in Florida. Worth: over $50 million.

◆ Daniel D. Villarosa was a football player turned investor. He made over $45 million by investing in the media.

# Purchasing Power

Latino businesses exist because Latinos, like everyone else, have needs. Obviously, other businesses are aware of these needs, and they're courting Latinos through advertisements in Spanish. For example, in any given issue of *Hispanic* magazine there are at least 40 ads from giants such as Ford, Verizon, and Continental, to name but a few.

**Para Tu Información**

Here is a breakdown of the Latino purchasing power in selected states:

| | |
|---|---|
| California: | $137,609,480 |
| Florida: | $44,065,520 |
| New Jersey: | $19,674,614 |
| New York: | $42,760,478 |
| Texas: | $74,979,457 |

Latinos are spending money. Sure, there are poor Latinos, but most experts agree that the Latino middle class is growing. For example, in 1998 poverty among Latinos declined by nearly 30 percent, while median income increased by 4 percent.

Economic growth is accompanied by what economists call purchasing power. It's estimated that the Latino purchasing power in the United States is about $452,370,480.

# Corporate World

Latinos are entering the corporate world, grabbing the famous key to the executive's bathrooms. According to Kanellos, writing in *Reference Library of Hispanic America*, of the 1,000 executives administering Fortune 1,000 companies, 3 percent are Latinos. Nevertheless, the number of Latinos in the top echelon of the business world is on the increase. Here are a few facts registered by Kanellos:

◆ **1977:** Carlos José Arboleya became the first Latino CEO and president of a major national bank, Barnet Banks of Miami.

◆ **1979:** Humberto Cabanas was the first Latino CEO of a major company in the hospitality industry, the Benchmark Group in Texas.

◆ **1980:** Frank Lorenzo was appointed president of an international airline, Continental Airlines.

◆ **1989**: Edgar J. Milán served as controller and vice president of one of the largest corporations in the United States, Tenneco, Inc.

# Good News

No matter how you look at it, it is progress and it is good. Today, many companies recruit talented Latinos. *Hispanic* magazine keeps its eye on such developments; once a year it lists the 100 companies that offer Latinos the best deals. According to the journal, as published in its February 2002 issue, these companies "excel in creating business and job opportunities for [Latinos] … they also donate money to educational scholarships and grants." Below are but 10 of these companies:

◆ American Family Insurance

◆ Bank of America

◆ Citigroup

◆ Continental Airlines

◆ Ford Motor Company

◆ General Motors

◆ Nordstrom

◆ Phillip Morris

◆ State Farm Insurance

◆ Verizon

# Dinero

With the entry of Latinos into the corporate world and the rise of a Latino middle class there comes the need for investing. One guru has emerged. Her name is Julia Stav.

Stav has written two bestseller books, is a financial columnist for *Hispanic*, and has hosted a PBS show. Born in Cuba, Stav was a teacher until she and her husband were divorced. Rather than be at the mercy of alimony payments and a teacher's salary, she decided to teach herself everything she could about investment. Reading numerous books on the subject, she first invested with imaginary money and, once she had some experience with her imaginary money, put the concepts into practice with the real dinero. To her delight, dividends began to pour in.

Today, Stav travels the country teaching Latinos how to play the stock market game. She holds investment seminars and gives motivational speeches. Her motto is: "Educate the uninformed from inner city to the suburbs that Wall Street is not just for the rich and privileged."

## The Least You Need to Know

- Most Latino businesses are first-time ventures.
- Most Latino businesses are small and managed by one person, with help from family and friends.
- Economic enclaves are self-sufficient neighborhoods where service is rendered in a language other than English.
- Latino businesses are focused mainly in the service and retail industry.
- During the last 20 years, more and more Latinos have entered the corporate world.
- Latino purchasing power has grown steadily over the last 20 years and it's reaching the half-a-million mark.

# 22

# Going to College

## In This Chapter

- Educational level of Latinos
- Of class and money
- College challenges
- Universities Latinos like

When he was a teen, novelist José Raúl Bernardo worked on a farm in Florida, picking tomatoes. He wanted something more out of life so he made his way to New York City, where he studied architecture at Columbia University. Likewise, at the age of 16, Samuel Betances dropped out of high school, but along the way he befriended an elderly Japanese man who mentored him and encouraged him to read. And read he did, all the way to Harvard University.

These true tales tell you what you already know: education changes lives. Latinos know that, and they're struggling mightily to send their children to college. How well are Latinos doing? Read on to find out.

## La Educación

Esmeralda Santiago's autobiography, *When I was Puerto Rican*, ends when Santiago is accepted to a very exclusive high school in New York City, so exclusive, competitive, and well-known is the high school that attendance there virtually assures entry to any number of prestigious universities and colleges. After a life of poverty on the island of Puerto Rico and a life of poverty on the island of Manhattan, high school and college were the keys to the kingdom for Santiago, the entrance to the Promised Land.

There is nothing new about this development. Millions of immigrants have taken the same path in the last 300 years. Latinos are no exception.

Latino students who stay in college perform as well as any other student. The problem, as some see it, is that not as many Latinos attend college. Not all observers believe this is a problem, however.

Former director of the U.S. Commission on Civil Rights Linda Chavez, for one, believes that Mexican Americans are doing pretty well in education. As she sees it, the problem is that it's hard to separate newly arrived immigrants from long-term residents, and when you lump them all together, you get a more pessimistic outcome. Also, the level of college participation can vary from group to group. For instance, Cuban-Americans in Florida are achieving pretty good rates of college admission and graduation. This has nothing to do with nationality but with economics. According to journalist Earl Shorris, "No matter what else influences the educational lives of Latino children, class is almost always the determining factor. The success of the children of … Cuban exiles proved that an economic and intellectual class reproduces itself …"

### Para Tu Información

Educators believe that for children to do well in school, it is crucial for parents to read to them at home. In Latino households, half the children are not read to. There are many reasons for this reality: parents who don't know the language; parents who have two jobs and are therefore too tired when they're home; reading to children was not a common practice at home; parents who don't have the educational background to realize the importance of this activity.

# Preschool

Preschool could be a tough concept to describe to many Latinos, who see the preschool years as family-time, a period in the life of the child when the parents and the abuelos nurture the children and teach them how to become part of the family. In Cuba, for example, when the idea of preschool programs was activated by the Communist regime, many parents saw it as one more political scheme Castro was using to take children away from the family and bring them closer to the government. For immigrants who go to work and need someone to take care of the children, preschool isn't seen as an academic enterprise but a survival service, a substitute for the parents and the abuelos. Thus, preschool has nothing to do with school, but with babysitting.

To understand preschool as an educational foundation, Latino parents need to be familiar with the notion, know about the American educational system, and have the financial means to pay for it. But even when the government provides assistance in the form of Head Start programs for young children, lack of familiarity with the service often keeps Latinos away. Here are some statistics published by the *Clearinghouse on Urban Education Digest:*

◆ Latinos under age of five are less likely to enroll in early childhood education programs: about 20 percent, compared to over 40 percent for African-Americans and Anglos.

◆ Three out of four Latino youngsters don't participate in Head Start programs.

◆ 70 percent of qualified preschool teachers aren't prepared to help Latino children who might not speak English and are not familiar with the culture.

# Elementary School

Overall, half of Latino children attend schools in urban areas. Due to financial restraints, many of the schools are ill-equipped and overcrowded. It's often difficult to find qualified professionals to work in these schools. Most professionals in elementary schools aren't Latinos. For those who believe role models are important, the four percent or so presence of Latino professionals in public schools is a sign of neglect and disregard for Latino children. However, there are others, like the writer Richard Rodriguez, who assign very little significance to the idea of ethnic role models in education.

---

### Living La Vida Literaria

In *Latinos,* journalist Earl Shorris narrates how difficult American schools can be for a Latino: "On the first day of the first grade Latino children are presented with a wall. It is made of culture and it is very high and thick. To enter the society of school they must get beyond the wall. If they do not overcome it at the beginning, the wall will grow higher and thicker with each succeeding day … The wall is as solid as a word, as enduring as the sting of a slap."

---

Check out the following facts about Latinos in elementary school:

◆ Latino students perform below their non-Latino peers in reading, mathematics, and science by the age of nine.

◆ The majority of students enrolled in Limited English Proficient programs are Latinos.

◆ Many Latino children are placed in lower educational tracks.

◆ Many teachers have lower expectations of young Latino students.

◆ Many teachers assume that a student with a Spanish surname is not proficient in English.

# High School

Secondary schools can be tough for Latino students, who often find their history and culture negatively described or missing altogether from their school books. There have even been cases where liberal teachers have asked Cuban students to write about the good deeds of the Castro regime—without taking into account some Cubans' personal and family losses experienced under the regime.

Generations of Mexican-Americans have had to see themselves as the bad guys in lesson plans about the Alamo. Puerto Ricans, who as Americans are part of the American experience, are taught very little about their island before the twentieth century. Then, there is the paternalistic attitude of some of the teachers who, without intending to, suggest that things American are better than anything south of the border.

*Banner for Latino college fair.*

There are also preconceived notions of underachievement and resentment. In the book, *The Empress of the Splendid Season,* by Oscar Hijuelos, a Latino high school student who gets into a fight with a bully is sent to the counselor to help him deal with his assumed pent-up aggression. Bit by bit, the racism and the insinuations pile up, taking a toll on the youngster.

Here is some information about the Latino high school experience:

- More than ⅓ of Latinos between the ages of 15 and 17 are enrolled below grade level.
- Half of Latino students take general courses rather than specialized courses that help students get into college.

- Only 35 percent of Latinos in high school take college-bound courses.

- A little over 60 percent of Latinos complete high school.

- Half of the Latinos graduating from high school plan to attend four-year colleges.

- About 15 percent of Latinos graduating from high school plan to attend a community college, though, in practice, more Latinos attend community colleges than were planning to.

- The Latino rate of enrollment in college right after high school is similar to the rest of the population.

*High school students at a Latino college fair in New Jersey.*

### Living La Vida Literaria

In *The Empress of the Splendid Season*, Oscar Hijuelos demonstrates how a Latino student can feel out of place in school: "It took him a while to get used to that place ... He sensed that, with some exception, his...colleagues had a kind of class-based narcissism; it wasn't that these kids ... marching with confidence through that world of blue crest embroidered blazers, tennis clubs, European vacations ... and other amenities were not particularly nice, but they seemed ... to act in tandem, like members of the same club, to which he did not belong ..."

The high school graduation rate for Latinos differs from state to state. Ángela Carrasquillo in *Hispanic Children and Youth in the United States* reports the following rates: California, 55 percent; Florida, 75 percent; New York, 58 percent; and Illinois, 48 percent.

# College Life

For Latino familias not familiar with higher education in the United States, the concept of the three types of institutions (four-year research universities, smaller four-year colleges, and two-year community colleges) is confusing, even when the parents attended college back home. In Spanish, a university is the place that you attend upon graduating from high school; there is no such word as college. When college is translated as *colegio*, it generally refers to an elementary and secondary school, not an institution of higher learning. As for community colleges, Latino parents take it to mean a technical or vocational school.

Half of Latino college students are enrolled in a community college. This preference might be the result of Latinos' assumptions that a community college is cheaper than a state college, that it's better to pay for two years of studies rather than four, and that the ability to obtain a degree sooner rather than later allows the student to meet his family responsibilities and job requirements sooner rather than later.

> **CAUTION**
>
> **Cuidado!**
>
> Respect and deference for people in positions of perceived power stop many Latino applicants from questioning a final decision on their financial aid. If a Latino student is told he doesn't qualify for assistance, he will probably accept the answer and not question the decision.

*Latina graduating from college.*

*(Courtesy of Bloomfield College, NJ)*

Check out these facts about college-aged Latinos:

♦ About 45 percent of Latino students attend college as part-timers.

♦ About 35 percent of Latino students graduate in 6 years rather than 4.

- In community colleges, Latino students major in liberal arts studies, business, and health professions.

- In four-year institutions, Latinos concentrate in business, social sciences, and education.

- There are more Latinas—about 60 percent—than Latinos in college.

- Over all, Latinos represent a little less than 10 percent of the 10 million students attending college.

# Failure

For a while, politicians bragged about the fact that there were more Latinos applying to college than decades before, but they were failing to notice that many of these students weren't making it to graduation. In fact, a little more than half were dropping out. It was something of a revolving door policy that let students into college one year and sent them out the next, without a diploma.

Concerned over this issue, studies were conducted to understand the reasons for failure. Some of the conclusions were:

- Not enough Latino professors and administrators to mentor the students.

- Not enough support systems—such as tutorial programs—to assist students with assignments.

- Not providing the students with enough financial aid information to facilitate payment of tuition.

- The campus culture didn't always make the students feel comfortable in the academic setting.

- No "old boys network" system to help the students.

**Cuidado!**

Don't assume that school and college performance is shaped by ethnicity and nationality. The dominant factor has to do with money and educational background. The more money a family has, the more likely a child will perform better in school. The more education the parents have, the more likely a child will perform better in school.

# End Failure

Latino activists made recommendations to address the concerns. Here are some of those strategies as edited from an Educational Resources Information Center document titled *Mexican Americans and Other Latinos in Postsecondary Education: Institutional Influences:*

- Initiate partnerships with schools to find areas of needed improvement in the education needed for and by Latino students.

- Study the academic and social climates of institutions of higher learning.
- Create and support financial aid packages for Latino students.
- Provide information to Latino families about college admissions, financial assistance, preparation for entrance exams, and employment opportunities.

Educator Ángela L. Carrasquillo offers a few more suggestions:

- Latinos need to realize that they can attend and graduate from college.
- Latinos need to stop working while attending school so they can concentrate on schoolwork.
- Latinos need to learn about different funding possibilities to help them to pay for tuition.
- Latino students need better elementary and secondary preparations.

Carrasquillo adds: "University personnel must reach down into the schools to work and motivate the students who will form the college classes a few years later. Mentoring programs ... help students to feel that someone believes in them and thinks that they are capable of doing the work."

## More Help

Latino activists are interested in finding other ways to help Latino children. One suggestion has been the creation of "reading centers," where an adult can read to a young child. The basis for this suggestion is the knowledge that the more a child reads, and is read to, the more he can grasp abstract concepts.

These activists suggest that public libraries can function as reading centers. Another possibility is to keep schools open longer hours so that the school library can function as a reading center.

In Texas and California, some school districts are implementing literacy programs for grammar, and high school teachers are trained to detect slow readers and to work with them directly or through tutors. The emphasis is on action at an early age.

## Resources

Since money is the primary obstacle to a college education, numerous corporations and organizations have established scholarships for Latino students. Here are but three:

- **The Hispanic Scholarship Fund** was created in 1975. Designated specifically to assist Latinos who are already in college, the fund gives anywhere from $1,000 to $3,000 to a student who has taken over 15 credits, which is equal to 4 or 5 courses. Their website is www.hsf.net/scholarship/CollegeRetention.html.

♦ **The Hispanic College Fund** was established in 1993 to encourage students to major in business. The fund is overseen by a board comprised of Latinos who are in business for themselves or hold executive positions in national corporations. Their website is hispanicfund.org.

♦ **The National Association of Hispanic Journalists** offers several scholarships to high school and college students interested in pursuing a career in journalism. The scholarship fund honors the memory of journalist Ruben Salazar, who was killed in 1970 while covering an anti-Vietnam war rally in Los Angeles. The scholarships range from $1,000 to $5,000. The site is www.nahj.org.

# Colleges for Latinos

The Latino students who do get to college tend to study in public institutions. There are about 200 colleges and universities that attract Latino students. Every year, the influential magazine *Hispanic* releases a list of top 25 institutions serving Latino students. The educational journal *Outlook On Hispanic Education* also issues a similar list. Below are the 25 universities chosen by *Hispanic* magazine in March 2002. These institutions have a Latino student population ranging anywhere from 9 to 15 percent. The curriculum offers multiple courses on Latino and Latin American studies. There are Latino organizations and programs that promote Latino and Latin American culture.

The institutions are arranged alphabetically:

Amherst College

Arizona State University

Columbia University

DePaul University

Harvard University

Massachusetts Institute of Technology

New York University

Rice University

Rutgers University

Southern Methodist University

Swarthmore College

Stanford University

Texas A & M University

University of Arizona

University of California-Berkeley

University of California-Davis

**Para Tu Información**

The November 2001 issue of *Hispanic* magazine lists five barriers to success in higher education: 1) Lack of financial resources, 2) Family responsibilities, 3) Feeling different from other students, 4) Lack of academic preparation, 5) Negative attitude about the school.

University of California-Los Angeles

University of California-San Diego

University of California-Santa Barbara

University of Florida

University of Miami

University of New Mexico

University of Notre Dame

University of Southern California

University of Texas-Austin

Although some Latino activists remain skeptics about the role Latinos will play in higher education during this decade, the evidence suggests that progress is being made and that more colleges are recruiting Latino students and helping them to make it through the process. The bottom line is that there is hope, and that academia is a lot more welcoming for Latinos today than it was a generation ago.

## The Least You Need to Know

- ◆ The number one factor affecting educational level of Latinos is lack of money.
- ◆ About half of Latino high school students plan to go to college.
- ◆ About half of Latinos attending college graduate.
- ◆ Problems affecting Latino students in college are based on sociological and financial factors, not ethnicity.
- ◆ The profile of Latinos in education is complicated by the constant arrival of Latinos to the United States, because most studies don't differentiate between new arrivals and long-term residents.

# Chapter 23

# Mañana, Mañana

## In This Chapter

- The reconquest
- Latino population in 2010
- Future issues and challenges
- Language matters
- Politics, Hollywood, and business

It's time to dust off the crystal ball and peer into it. What do you see? Probably nothing.

A better way to figure out the future is to study demographics, check population charts, examine trends in business, politics, and films, and see how cities and towns are changing. And yes, talk to people, find out what they plan to do mañana and how they plan to do it.

In this chapter, we're going to imagine the future of Latinos in the United States.

## The Reconquest of the United States

Over 50 years ago, in the little town of Lansdale, PA (population of 9,762), there was an old church on a quiet street, a church of brick and mortar, where Anglos worshipped. Fifty years later, the town of Lansdale is still small and the church still stands. But the worshipers are now Latino creyentes.

It is a transformation common enough, and one that you can certainly spot throughout the country. Some observers, like the California politician Xavier Hermosillos, call it the Reconquest of America, alluding to the fact that the first explorers of what was to become the good ole USA were Spanish travelers, and that a good chunk of the country was Spanish and Mexican for about 300 years before becoming American. But after John Smith did his stint in the Northeast and the Pilgrims came and the American soldiers defeated the Mexicans during the Mexican War, the history books erased the Spanish and Latino presence from its pages. From then on, the preference was for things British, and that which was of Spanish descent was belittled and tucked away.

> ### Living La Vida Literaria
>
> In *Strangers Among us,* Roberto Suro describes how Latinos change a town: "They are the new people on the scene and so they will serve as catalysts. They fill churches with children. They light up decaying streets with their storefront enterprises."

But no more. Bit by bit the people of Latin America are gaining back the territory and rewriting some history pages. That's why it's called the Reconquest. It's not a planned invasion, however—it's a natural process.

What does it all mean? Basically, it means that Latinos are here to stay, and that there will be more coming. And it is likely that their presence will make changes to some areas of American life, at least in the provinces of education, the arts, and politics.

# The More The Merrier

You already know that there are over 35 million Latinos in the United States, and that the growth began 20 years ago.

*Latino population since 1980.*

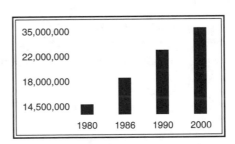

| | |
|---|---|
| 35,000,000 | |
| 22,000,000 | |
| 18,000,000 | |
| 14,500,000 | |
| | 1980  1986  1990  2000 |

The growth will continue. If we wish to be conservative and base our estimate on the growth between 1980 and 1990, which was about 8 million, and we add that figure to the current population, we can say that mañana—that is to say the mañana of the year 2010— the Latino population in the United States will be over 40 million.

# South of the Border

There will be some changes to migratory flow into the United States. Let's see how:

◆ **Argentina:** The economic chaos in the land of the tango is propelling north hundreds of Argentines. There's a catch now, though. Prior to September 11, people from Argentina could come to the United States without a visa. They'd come as visitors and then prolong their stay. That's not so anymore. Today, any Argentine dreaming of the United States must stand outside the American embassy and wait for traveling papers. How about those Argentines who are already here? They'll try to stay, living mostly in Dade County, Florida, and Manhattan.

◆ **Central America:** The possibility of a free trade zone—something like NAFTA—extending to Central America will improve some of the economic conditions in the region. This might reduce the need to cross the border for a better-paying job. On the other hand, working arrangements could be drafted—similar to the Bracero Program of the 1940s and '50s (see Chapter 2)—which could keep the flow from Central America going. Would these workers stay in the United States? Probably.

◆ **Cuba:** The death of Castro and the establishment of a democratic regime will encourage temporary immigration to the United States. Most Cuban experts feel that the Cubans who stayed behind would want to come to the United States, like so many of their relatives, for a taste of the good life they missed under communism. This migration might be in the thousands, and it could be similar to the back and forth jetting that exists currently between Puerto Rico and the United States. In the meantime, Cubans in the United States will visit the island regularly. The Cubans who are already here, though, will follow the path of the Cuban patriots who went to Tampa during the 1890s: after Cuba won its independence from Spain, those patriots remained in Tampa and didn't go back to the island.

> **Para Tu Información**
>
> NAFTA stands for the North American Free Trade Agreement that was signed into law in 1994. The agreement removes most trade tariffs in business transactions among Canada, Mexico, and United States. As a result of the agreement, trade between Mexico and the United States increased over $14 billion in eight years.

◆ **Venezuela:** A hotbed of political conflict. The possibilities for a civil war loom large; in the event of such a tragedy, thousands of Venezuelans will journey to the United States. If President Chávez continues to imitate Castro and establishes a totalitarian regime, thousands of exiles—mostly from the middle class—will flock to Miami. The Venezuelans who are already here—opening clothing and furniture stores in South Florida—will stay.

**Living La Vida Literaria**

In *The Buried Mirror,* Carlos Fuentes describes the border between the United States and Mexico and how Mexicans feel about it:

> ... The United States-Mexico border, some of those who cross it say, it's not really a border but a scar. Will it heal? Will it bleed once more? When a [Latino] worker crosses this border, sometimes he asks: 'Hasn't this always been our land? Am I not coming back to it? Is it not in some way ours?'

What about Mexico? The majority of Latinos in the United States are of Mexican ancestry. The majority of those crossing the border are Mexicans. That will not change.

# Immigration Woes

Mañana, there will be a lot of news items about immigration from Latin America. You will read the articles in the American press, and there will be pieces in the Spanish press as well. For Latinos will be as interested as everyone else in the subject, and the range of opinions will be as diverse as those of non-Latinos. Here are some potential issues:

◆ Most of the Latinos who are long-term residents and those who are newly arrived will support amnesty for illegal Latino residents and will also lobby against quotas and restrictions on immigration.

◆ However, some Latinos will support legislation that denies illegal aliens social benefits such as welfare and Social Security. They will rally against any amnesty programs. They will regard the newcomers as a threat to potential employment as well as drawing attention away from civil rights initiatives, as politicians focus on immigration matters rather than on the fate of Latino-Americans who are legal residents.

◆ Other minority and non-minority groups will voice opposition to immigration from Latin America. In the recent past, African-American politicians have expressed concerns that employers use Latinos as replacement workers, thus displacing African-American workers. Similarly, advocates have indicated displeasure when Latinos claim that they are taking back America. In fact, a confrontation emerged in Los Angeles when a Latino politician was nominated for a commissioner's post and the African-American community opposed his nomination. Although not all Latinos cared for the chap, many of them still rushed to his support. The reason was simple: he was one of their own and he needed their help.

# The Least Likely Place

Latinos will head to other spots not commonly associated with Latino communities. The most recent example of this trend is North Carolina, where the Latino population has grown nearly 400 percent in the last decade. In a *Hispanic* magazine article, published in February 2002, a Peruvian preacher recalls that a few years ago he didn't have a Spanish-speaking congregation in North Carolina. Today, he tends to 300 families, mostly from Mexico.

**Para Tu Información** _____

The Bilingual Education Act was passed in Congress and signed into law in 1968. It set up a series of legal directives mandating instruction in both English and a foreign language for students in public schools. The foreign language chosen was determined by the native language spoken by the majority of the non–English-speaking children in the school. Implementation of the act was supported by the allocation of $626 million in federal funds, distributed during the first ten years of the act.

Why are there Latinos in the heart of Dixie? Because of jobs, especially in construction and landscaping, which require little knowledge of English. The flow will continue, and the Latino population will spread to other states such as Arkansas, Georgia, and Kansas. Pretty soon, the heartland of the United States will pulsate to a Latino beat: *"Oye, como va mi ritmo!"*

**Hablas Español** _____

*"Oye, como va mi ritmo"* is a refrain in a popular Spanish song. It means, "Listen to the beat of my rhythm."

# The Great Education Dilemma

The growth of Latino population will be reflected in schools across the nation. You will see more Latino administrators and teachers—some say about 1,000 more per year. And you will hear a lot more about bilingual education.

Many Latinos support bilingual education. Here's why:

◆ They don't want to slow down the educational process of students who are learning English but who do not yet understand lectures, instructions, and assignments in English. They'd like to teach such basic courses as math in Spanish, while also teaching children how to speak English.

◆ They want children to gradually migrate to English from Spanish.

◆ They maintain that sink-or-swim methods don't work (putting non–English-speaking students into English-only classrooms) and cause tremendous stress for students, prompting failure, and encouraging students to drop out.

◆ They want students to be bilingual.

### Para Tu Información

A Univisión—a Spanish television network—poll conducted in 1998 reveals that the majority of Latinos intend to keep using the Spanish language: 1) 90 percent indicated they will preserve their language; 2) 83 percent affirmed their support of bilingual education programs; and 3) 61 percent believe that a political candidate should communicate in Spanish with Latinos.

## Opponents of Bilingual Education

Many Latinos oppose bilingual education for the following reasons:

◆ They maintain that bilingual education slows down children's progress in schools.

◆ They believe that the program fosters segregation, resulting in any Spanish-speaking child or child with a Spanish surname being placed in a bilingual class without fully assessing the child's actual knowledge of English.

### Cuidado!

Remember that Puerto Ricans are Americans and that they speak Spanish. For Puerto Ricans, the languages of the United States are English and Spanish.

◆ They suggest that many bilingual teachers are in fact not bilingual at all and speak one language better than another.

◆ They complain that in some school districts politicians use bilingual positions to post Latino friends, regardless of academic preparation.

## English Only

The increase in the number of people speaking Spanish will prompt many people to advocate for legislation mandating the use of the English language as the country's official language. Their argument will be:

◆ The use of one language fosters national unity.

◆ The use of one language will assimilate immigrants faster into the mainstream.

◆ The use of many languages could tear the country politically apart, as it happened in Canada, Belgium, and Sri Lanka.

## English Plus

Latinos who oppose the English Only might join supporters of the English Plus movement, which began in Florida in 1985. English Plus acknowledges the importance of English in the United States but also advocates the preservation of other languages and emphasizes the social, cultural, and educational value in speaking more than one language. This is what people might say about English Only:

♦ English Only legislation promotes isolationism and racism, and it will divide the nation.

♦ English Only legislation will separate non-English speakers from English speakers, creating a sense of division of class and inequality.

♦ English Only discourages learning a second language, thus placing the United States at a disadvantage with most developed nations where people tend to speak several languages.

## No Need for English Only

Latinos who oppose legislation of the English language will tell you that it's an unnecessary process because Latinos want to learn and are learning English anyway:

♦ According to journalist Roberto Suro, nearly 95 percent of Mexican-Americans who participated in a national Latino survey indicated that everyone in the United States should speak English.

♦ Studies conducted by Princeton University researcher Alejandro Portes demonstrate that the children of immigrants tend to choose the language of the land they live in as their primary language of communication.

♦ Successful Latinos speak in English and conduct most of their businesses in English, which writer Richard Rodriguez calls "the language of the bankers." Successful performers, like José Feliciano and Edward James Olmos work comfortably with both English and Spanish, but prefer to perform in English.

**Para Tu Información**

There is money in the sounds of the Spanish language. Realizing the potential for 35 million viewers, NBC recently purchased Telemundo, and the Spanish network Univisión created another network, called Telefutura. On cable, there is a fourth Spanish-language television channel called Galavisión.

# Looking at a Latino Hollywood

Talking about performing, Latinos in Hollywood are performing quite well lately, gracias: Benicio del Toro won an Oscar for his performance in the flick *Traffic* and Cameron Díaz earned $15 million for her leading role in *Vanilla Sky*. And, thousands of women are lining up outside the plastic surgeon's office so that they can look like Jennifer López (though it isn't exactly a face lift what they want, but a derriere as *redondo* as López's posterior).

So, mañana there will be more Latino stars showing up in major films and television productions. Their roles will not be defined by their ethnicity alone. López and Díaz will play non-Latinas and actors Hector Elizondo and Marc Anthony will portray non-Latinos. And there will be a sweet revenge for many Latinos, who will take turns at playing Italians, the way a few years ago Italian actors—Al Pacino and Armand Azante, for example— played Latinos.

**Hablas Español**

*Redondo* is Spanish for round and roundness.

But when the likes of Andy García do play a character from south of the border, the stereotype will be avoided, as more Latino writers and film-makers release pictures that move away from stereotypes, such as the movie *In The Time of the Butterflies* and the television series *American Family*.

# Tomorrow's Businesses

A traditional approach to the American Dream for Latinos has been the ownership of a bodega or a market. Although many Latinos will harbor that dream, others will pursue different paths. In New York City, many Dominicans skipped the bodega route and took to the streets, literally, by driving and owning cabs. They set up cooperatives with their own dispatches. The drivers were often professionals, lawyers, for instance, who bought restaurants and gas stations with the profits made from driving all over the Big Apple.

There is good a chance that for many enterprising Latinos, technology will replace bodegas and retail shops as the key to the future. Take Latino Legends in Sports. Ozzie González, a savvy Latino with techie know-how and a love of sports, founded an on-line company in 1999 that specializes in information, articles, and profiles about Latino sport figures. Latinossportslegends.com sells postcards and rare photographs as well as creating web pages for super stars.

Here is a very short list of technology-oriented Latino companies and the profits they made in the year 2001:

- ◆ ABC Computer Services: $1 million in computer and computer-related product sales.
- ◆ Accurate Wire Harness: $9 million in electrical harnesses for automotive industry.

- Batiz.com: $7 million in interactive designs for government agencies.
- Teleoptions, Inc.: $2.8 in sales and distribution of telephone equipment.

# El Señor Presidente

Will a Latino occupy the oval office in the future? Not yet and not likely. But there is a good chance that there will be Latino governors and vice presidents. It almost happened. Once, Henry Cisneros was courted for a vice presidential spot, but due to personal problems his political hopes faded.

Presidents will appoint more Latinos to cabinet posts. Cities of national importance, such as Los Angeles and Miami and New York City, will elect a Latino mayor. It almost happened in New York City and Los Angeles. As for Miami, it has already happened several times and will happen again.

# Mañana Is Only a Day Away

As far as Latinos see it, the theme song from the musical *Annie* tells their story: "The sun will come out tomorrow." And it will be a bright sun.

Latinos are optimistic about their future in the United States. A *Detroit News* headline from October 2000 puts it thus: "[Latinos'] future promising; rise in population, economic clout indicate good times ahead." The sunny disposition was evident in a survey conducted by Spanish television network Univisión in 1998. Here are three key findings:

- 78 percent are satisfied with the economy and their personal financial situations.
- Three out of four parents believe their children will be better off economically than they are.
- Over 90 percent plan to send their children to college.

# Viva Optimism!

Latinos are optimistic about life in the United States. For many life here is a lot better than back home. For those who were wealthy and comfortable back home, political life in the United States is still a lot more peaceful and less restrictive than in the old country. An exile—be it a Cuban or a Chilean—would affirm that freedom is the assurance that no one will knock on your door at three o'clock in the morning and whisk you away in the darkness.

There are some Latino writers who are bit pessimistic, however; but even they still hope for a better future. Intellectuals like Carlos Fuentes, who is often critical of how some Americans in the United States behave towards Latinos and of American foreign policy towards Latin America, feel good about the future of Latinos living north of the border: "I have reason for optimism," Fuentes writes. "We will be able to embrace The Other ... People and their culture perish in isolation, but they are born or reborn in contact with other men and women, with men and women of another culture ... If we do not recognize our humanity in others, we shall not recognize it in ourselves."

## The Least You Need to Know

- In 2010, the Latino population will be at last 40 million.
- Mexicans will still dominate Latino migration to the United States.
- After Castro's demise, Cubans will migrate between the United States and the island.
- The prominent social issues involving Latinos will be education and politics.
- More Latino actors will become Hollywood stars.
- Latinos will set up technological enterprises and other businesses as their way to realize the American Dream.

# Latino Holidays

Latin Americans love a celebration. In one way or another, the holidays listed in this appendix are celebrated by the Latino community in the United States. In some instances, schools might even close or excuse the children from class for a particular holiday, although the event might not be recognized by other American traditions.

## Religious Celebrations

Take a trip through the calendar year to review important holy days and celebrations.

### January 6: El Día de los Reyes Magos/Epiphany Day

Throughout Latin America, Epiphany Day is of more importance than Christmas Day. It's on this day that children receive their gifts, which are usually left under a tree or somewhere in the house by a mago, a wise man. This holiday celebrates the journey of the three wise men who sought baby Jesus and brought him gifts. There are three magi: Baltazar, Gaspar, and Melchor. Traditionally, a child chooses one mago and writes him a letter sometime in December. That mago is responsible for bringing toys to the child. In the United States, some Latino families celebrate Epiphany Day along with Christmas Day. But American influence is big, and Santa Claus is winning over Latino families.

# April: Semana Santa/Holy Week

Holy Week in Latin America is celebrated with lots of religious processions and masses. In some countries, there are re-enactments of the trial and crucifixion of Christ. Until recently, radio and television stations didn't run secular programs during this week. Many movie theaters, however, still suppress films of secular nature, preferring to feature religious epics and films about the life of Christ.

# August 1 to 6: The Feast of El Salvador del Mundo

This feast, in the name of the savior of the world, is a religious holiday for Salvadorans, honoring the role of Christ as savior. Special masses are offered and processions take place throughout the country's towns and cities. Celebrations are also held in some towns in California, Florida, and New Jersey.

# September 8: Día de la Caridad del Cobre

This religious holiday commemorates the appearance of the Virgin Mary in Cuba. According to the story, three shipwrecked sailors—a Spanish, a Cuban white, and a black slave—were rescued from the stormy ocean by the Virgin Mary who, appearing over their boats, calmed the waters and led the sailors to safety. Processions are held in Miami and Elizabeth and Union City, in New Jersey.

# October 18: Señor de los Milagros

This Peruvian holiday recalls the discovery of an intact statue of Jesus Christ amidst the ruins of a church devastated by an earthquake in the 1700s.

# November 2: Día de los Muertos

This is probably the most famous of Latin American holidays. Primarily celebrated in Mexico, it's a day that honors the passing away of friends and family members. According to the tradition, partially based in Aztec mythology, the spirit of the departed joins family and friends over a meal sometimes served at a cemetery, near the burial spot of the deceased. Children might eat pastry in the shape of skulls. Special masses are offered for family members.

# December 12: Día de la Virgen de Guadalupe

This is the Mexican celebration of the appearance of the Virgin Mary to the Mexican Indian Juan Diego in 1531. The event signified the acceptance of the Catholic Church by the Native Americans from Mexico. This is a major holiday as millions of Mexicans attend a mass in honor of the Virgin and Diego and participate in a pilgrimage to the location where the virgin first appeared.

## December 16 to 24: Las Posadas

A Mexican holiday that reenacts Joseph and Mary's search for an inn prior to the birth of Jesus. Children go from house to house asking for accommodations. As the children are turned away, they're given candies and pastry.

## December 24: Noche Buena

The night before Christmas is an occasion for family members to meet and celebrate the holidays. The emphasis is on family, food, and honoring baby Jesus. There's a mass at midnight attended by the whole family.

## December 25: Navidad

Christmas Day is not a big celebration in Latin America. In the United States, Latino families have adopted the holiday and usually exchange gifts, though the Christmas Day dinner is not as popular as it is with other American Christian families.

## December 31: Vispera de Año Nuevo/New Year's Eve

Like most of the world, Latinos party on New Year's Eve. However, there is a lot of emphasis on spending the evening with the family. In some cases, there is a family meal after which the younger members of the gathering leave for a dance or a party. Cubans eat 12 grapes as the clock tolls twelve, a tradition that originated in Spain. In Mexico, thousands attend outdoor concerts featuring prominent stars from Latin America.

# Secular Holidays

Not all holidays in Latin America are religious-based. Many are to celebrate political victories or important individuals in a nation's history.

## January 10: The birth of Eugenio María de Hostos

On this day, Puerto Ricans celebrate the birth of patriot and educator Eugenio María de Hostos. In New York City, schools serving Latinos schedule a day of events celebrating Puerto Rican heritage (see Chapter 12).

## January 28: Birth of José Martí

The birth of Cuban poet and patriot José Martí. This holiday is celebrated by Cubans on the island as well as Cubans living in the United States. In the Miami area, many schools close for the day (check out Chapter 12 for more on Martí).

## February 27: Independence Day

The celebration of the Dominican Republic's Independence from Haiti. In 1844, the Dominicans led a successful rebellion against the Haitians who had taken over the nation 20 years earlier. The last few years, some schools in New York City have held special programs to honor Dominican students.

## March 21: Birth of Benito Júarez.

This is the birthday of Benito Júarez, one of Latin America's greatest, and most clean-cut, heroes (read about him in, you guessed it, Chapter 12).

## May 5: Cinco de Mayo

The May 5 holiday is a commercialized, eating event in the United States where lots of Mexican restaurants advertise discounts and special lunches. The day, however, actually celebrates the victory of the Mexican army against the French forces that had invaded the country in the 1860s.

## May 20: Independence Day

Cuba's Independence was achieved on this date back in 1902. A Cuban president was elected. Even though the United States had convinced the new government to allow for American intervention as needed, Cubans regard this date as the beginning of the Cuban republic.

## Second Sunday of June: The National Puerto Rican Day Parade

One hundred thousand participants march along plush 5th avenue in Manhattan. This celebration attracts over 3 million spectators.

## October 12: El Día de las Razas

In Latin America, there is no celebration of Columbus Day. Instead, the people celebrate the day of all races as a way of acknowledging the encounter between the natives of the Americas and the arrivals of the Europeans and the Africans. In the United States, Mexican-Americans and Puerto Ricans use the occasion to affirm their national heritage.

# Patriotic Holidays

As in the United States, Latin Americans also celebrate a major national legal holiday, which may or may not coincide with their independence days.

| Country | National Holiday |
| --- | --- |
| Argentina | May 25 (known as Revolution Day) |
| Bolivia | August 6 (Independence Day) |
| Costa Rica | September 15 (Independence Day) |
| Ecuador | August 10 (Independence Day) |
| El Salvador | September 15 (Independence Day) |
| Guatemala | September 15 (Independence Day) |
| Honduras | September 15 (Independence Day) |
| Mexico | September 16 (Independence Day) |
| Nicaragua | September 15 (Independence Day) |
| Panama | November 3 (Independence Day) |
| Paraguay | May 14–15 (Independence Day) |
| Peru | July 28 (Independence Day) |
| Uruguay | August 25 (Independence Day) |
| Venezuela | July 5 (Independence Day) |

# Las Palabras: A Glossary

**abuelos**  Grandparents.

**adelantado**  An explorer or conquistador commissioned to explore a territory and claim it for the Spanish Crown.

**ahijado**  Godson; ahijada is Spanish for goddaughter.

**ají**  Green pepper.

**ajiaco**  A soup that uses garlic.

**albóndigas**  Meatballs.

**Anglo**  Someone from North America, usually Caucasian.

**Árabe**  Arab or of Arabic descent.

**baile**  A dance.

**balón**  Ball.

**balsa**  A raft; in Castro's Cuba, it refers to a small homemade raft.

**bandido**  An outlaw.

**barrio**  A neighborhood; community.

**barrio árabe**  An Arabic neighborhood.

**barroco**  A literary style characterized by its intellectual approach to such universal themes as love and mortality.

**beisbol**  Spanish adaptation of baseball.

**bodega**   A Spanish grocery store; bodeguero is the store owner.

**bolero**   A torch song.

**bolita**   Number game, usually illegal.

**Borinquén**   Native American name for the island of Puerto Rico.

**botánicas**   Shops where you can purchase herbs and folk medicine as well as materials used for the practice of Santería; the word alludes to botany, the study of plant.

**boxeadores**   Boxers.

**boxeando**   Spanish for boxing.

**boxear**   To box.

**caballero**   A gentleman; a horse rider; a knight; a person of aristocratic lineage; an individual with courtly manners.

**caballo**   A horse.

**Cabildo**   Society for members of a church; it also refers to a fraternity created by African slaves in the Caribbean.

**cafecito**   Demitasse; small cup of strong coffee favored by Cubans.

**canción mexicana**   A Mexican song.

**canción ranchera**   Tune performed at a Mexican ranch.

**cantina**   A neighborhood bar where drinks and foods are served while listening to music.

**carne deshilachada**   Shredded beef.

**Caudillo**   Local boss.

**ceviche** or **cebiche**   Recipe of raw fish and shrimp; also seviche.

**cha-cha-chá**   A Cuban dance; it refers to the shuffling sound feet make on the dancing floor.

**Chapetón**   A Spaniard or European who has recently arrived in Latin America; used during colonial times.

**Charro**   A Mexican horseman; it alludes to a Mexican man who is manly and brave.

**Chicano**   A Mexican-American.

**El Cid**   The Lord, a historical figure who fought against the Muslims in Spain during the wars of the Reconquest; the word refers to a person who is strong and brave.

**clave**   A music instrument held by hand. It consists of two pieces of thin wood, less than half-a-foot long and which the musician taps gently to produce a repetitive but soothing beat.

**cocina**   Cuisine; kitchen.

**cocinar**   To cook.

**cofradías**   Organizations or clubs created to collect funds for a particular activity usually carried on by the Church.

**colegio**   School; usually it refers to elementary and secondary education. It also refers to a professional association.

**colonizadores**   Colonizers; pioneer settlers.

**compadrazco**   The relation between parents and godparents.

**compadres**   The godparents to your children; co-parents. Compadre means co-father; comadre means co-mother.

**comparsa**   A long line of dancers, one standing behind the other, roaming the streets during Carnival times in Cuba.

**compatriota**   A person who comes from the same country as you.

**confianza**   Trust.

**conga**   An Afro-Cuban dance.

**conjunto**   Small band.

**conquistadores**   Spanish soldiers who came to the New World to conquer it.

**coplas**   Couplets; consists of two phrases or sentences that rhyme. It is a form used in popular songs.

**corridos**   A ballad.

**coyote**   A smuggler of illegal aliens.

**creyente**   A believer, a person who has faith; an individual who attends church.

**criollo**   A person who was born in the New World of Spanish parents or ancestry.

**crónica**   A chronicle is a literary genre that tells of the conquest and colonization of the Americas. A cronista is a writer of crónicas.

**croqueta**   Spanish croquette, usually made of ham.

**Cubano**   A person from Cuba or whose parents come from the island.

**Curandero-a**   A faith healer who uses herbs and natural medicine to treat the infirm.

**danzón**   A nineteenth-century slow, waltz-like dance.

**descamisados**   The shirtless one; expression used by Evita and Juan Perón to refer to the poorest people of Argentina.

**educación** Education.

**emigración** Emigration.

**emigrar** To emigrate.

**encomiendas** The judicial and economic system that allowed a Spanish colonizer to enslave a Native American.

**espiritismo** The practice of spiritualism; it acknowledges that there is a world of spirits that co-exist with the world of the living.

**Europeo** European.

**exploradores** Explorers.

**familia** Family, it usually refers to the extended family—children, parents, and grandparents.

**Federales** Troops belonging to the Mexican government during the Mexican revolution.

**Fidelista** A person who supports Fidel Castro.

**finca** A small farm.

**flamenco** Spanish for Flemish.

**fonda** Casual restaurant or diner.

**frijoles** Beans.

**futbol** Soccer.

**gachupín or cachupín** Spanish immigrant who settles in Latin America.

**galán** Leading man in a film, stage production, or soap opera; the word alludes to galante, gallant, gentlemanly.

**gandules** Pigeon peas.

**gente** People.

**gente decente** Decent people; it alludes to well-to-do families who are known in a particular region.

**golpe de Estado** To overthrow a political regime.

**gringo** An American. It carries a derogatory connotation.

**guitarra** Guitar. It comes from the Arabic kitara and from the Greek citara.

**gusano** A worm. In Castro's Cuba it refers to a person who is anti-Castro.

**hermano** Brother; hermana is sister.

**hermano or hermana de crianza** Adopted siblings, usually informally.

**hijo** Son; hija means daughter.

**hombre**   Man.

**honor**   Honor; it alludes to behaving in a responsible manner and paying respect to others.

**imigración**   Immigration.

**independentista**   An individual who advocates for the independence of his country from a colonial or foreign power.

**inmigrante**   Immigrant.

**inmigrar**   To immigrate.

**judíos**   Jews.

**justicialismo**   The word comes from justicia, justice, and it refers to the practice of a political system based on legal justice and equality for all.

**lamento**   Regret.

**latifundio**   Large holding of lands used for farming or raising cattle.

**latinoamericano**   A person or anything that is from Latin America.

**lealtad**   Loyalty.

**lector**   A reader at a tobacco factory. The reader read to the workers as they rolled tobacco leaves.

**leyenda**   Legend.

**libertador**   Liberator. The term was probably coined to describe the heroic Simón Bolívar who freed from Spanish rule several Latin American nations during colonial times.

**listo**   As a verb, it means ready; as an adjective it means intelligent.

**llano**   Plains.

**lo mejicano**   To maintain Mexican characteristics and values.

**machismo**   The act of behaving in a manly way and protecting your manhood.

**macho**   Male.

**madre**   Mother.

**maestro**   A teacher or a master; followers might call their intellectual or religious leader maestro.

**mambises**   The Cuban soldiers who fought in the jungle against the Spanish army during the wars of independence.

**mambo**   A Cuban dance.

**mañana**   Tomorrow.

**mariachi**   A band or orchestra that plays Mexican music.

**mariposas**   Butterflies.

**matador**   Bullfighter.

**merengue**   A dance from the Dominican Republic; the word also means a pastry made up of beaten egg whites.

**mesoamérica**   Refers to middle America and includes Mexico and Central America.

**mestizo**   The offspring of the union between a white person and a Native American.

**méxico lindo**   Pretty Mexico; an endearing way of referring to Mexico.

**mi casa es tu casa**   A popular saying that means "my house is your house"; a gesture of cordiality and friendship.

**militar**   The military.

**mimar**   To caress.

**modernismo**   Literary style.

**modo de operaciones**   The way a system works.

**mulato**   The child of black and white parents.

**múica norteña**   Mexican music created and played in the United States; música tejana is music created in and played in Texas by Mexican-American composers and musicians.

**negocio**   Business; it could also refer to a shop or a particular business enterprise.

**niño**   Boy; niña is girl. Niño mimado is a Mama's boy.

**El Norte**   The north, meaning the United States.

**novela**   A novel; it refers to the literary genre as well as soap operas on Spanish television.

**ojalá**   The desire for something to occur.

**olé**   An expression of admiration and approval.

**opinión**   Opinion.

**orquesta tejana**   An orchestra that plays música tejana.

**padre**   Father; it also refers to a priest.

**padrinos**   Godparents, in general; padrino is godfather while madrina means godmother.

**palabra**   Word.

**pampa**   South American plain without vegetation.

**parentesco**   Relative-like; said of a person who is treated as a relative or family member.

**pariente**   Relatives.

**patata**   Potato; also called papa.

**patrones**   The plural for patron, the owner of a business or an enterprise; it also refers to a political boss.

**pelota**   Ball, but in Cuban usage it refers to the game of baseball.

**pelotero**   Baseball player.

**peninsular**   Someone who comes from a peninsula.

**periodiquitos**   Newspapers, usually weekly, distributed free of charge through bodegas and Spanish stores.

**pibe**   Argentine expression for young child.

**pica-pollo**   To pick on a piece of chicken.

**plátanos fritos**   Fried plantains.

**político**   A politician.

**pollo**   A hen, it refers to the illegal alien a coyote smuggles across the U.S.-Mexican border.

**prensa**   The press.

**primo**   Masculine for cousin; prima is feminine; the term might be used by friends to indicate closeness.

**primo de crianza**   Adopted cousin.

**quince**   Fifteen; quinceañera is a person, usually a girl, who is celebrating her sweet fifteen birthday.

**la Reconquista**   The Reconquest; it refers to the period when Spain was fighting against the Moors during medieval times.

**redondo**   Round or roundish.

**relación**   An account of the discovery and colonization of a territory.

**respecto**   Respect.

**romancero**   A singer of romances.

**romances**   Songs that tell stories, employing a rhyming scheme; love stories.

**rumba**   Fast and rhythmic dance from Cuba.

**salsa**   Sauce; Latino musical genre.

**santería**   Afro-Cuban religion that combines elements of Catholic faith with African traditions.

**santero**   A person who practices Santería.

**si Dios Quiere**   A popular expression that means if God allows it to happen.

**siboneyes**   Native Americans who lived in the Caribbean at the time of Columbus' arrival.

**simpatía**   A sentiment of spontaneous affection; behaving in a likeable manner.

**sombrero**   Hat.

**son**   Slow moving Cuban dance.

**sopón**   Big soup.

**supremo**   The supreme ruler.

**tabaqueros**   Tobacco workers.

**Taínos**   Native Americans who lived in the Caribbean at the time of Columbus' arrival.

**tampeños**   People from Tampa.

**tango**   An Argentine dance and type of song.

**teatro bufo**   Comic theater.

**telenovela**   Spanish soap opera.

**tertulias**   Informal gathering of writers and professors to discuss intellectual and philo-sophical topics.

**tío**   Uncle; tía is aunt.

**tiro de gracia**   An expression akin to the straw that broke the camel's back; in the mili-tary, it refers to the bullet that is shot through the head of an executed man or woman, to assure the person is dead.

**torero**   Bullfighter.

**toro**   Bull.

**tostones**   Thin layers of fried plantains.

**tupamoros**   Urban guerrillas from Uruguay.

**turcos**   A Turk or a person of Turkish descent.

**vaquero**   Cowboy.

**véndido**   Sold-out, from the verb vender, to sell; it refers to a person who has betrayed a cause or an ideology.

**zapateo**   A foot-tapping dance popular in Cuba, Columbia, Mexico, and Peru.

**zorro**   Fox.

# Libros: For Further Reading

Abalos, David T. *The Latino Family and the Politics of Transformation*. Westport and London: Praeger, 1993.

Abella, Alex. *The Killing of the Saints*. New York: Penguin Books, 1991.

Álvarez, Julia. *How the García Girls Lost Their Accents*. Chapel Hill, North Carolina: Algonquin Press, 1991.

Anaya, Rudolfo. *Bless Me, Ultima*. New York: Warner Books, 1972.

Azuela, Mariano. *The Underdogs*. Pittsburgh and London: University of Pittsburgh Press, 1992.

Bailey, Helen M. and Abraham P. Nasatir. *Latin America: The Development of its Civilization*. Englewood Cliffs, NJ: Prentice-Hall, 1968.

Baker, Daniel B. *Explorers and Discoverers of the World*. Detroit and Washington, D.C.: Gale Research, 1993.

Behar, Ruth. *Bridges to Cuba/Puentes a Cuba*. Ann Arbor, Michigan: The University of Michigan Press, 1995.

Benowitz, June Melby. *Encyclopedia of American Women and Religion*. Santa Barbara: ABC-CLIO, 1998.

Bethell, Leslie. *The Cambridge History of Latin America: Colonial America*. Vol. II. Cambridge and New York: Cambridge University Press, 1989.

Bjarkman, Peter C. *Baseball with a Latin Beat*. Jefferson, North Carolina and London: McFarland & Company, Inc. 1994.

Bonilla, Frank; Edwin Meléndez, and others. ed. *Borderless Borders: U.S. Latinos, Latin Americans, and the Paradox of Interdependence*. Philadelphia: Temple University, 1998.

Burton, Julianne, ed. *Cinema and Social Change in Latin America: Conversations with Filmmakers*. Austin, Texas: University of Texas Press, 1986.

Carrasco, Davíd. ed. *The Oxford Encyclopedia of Mesoamerican Cultures: The Civilizations of Mexico and Central America*. 4 vols. Oxford: Oxford University Press, 2001.

Carrasquillo, Angela L. *Hispanic Children and Youth in the United States*. New York and London: Garland Publishing, Inc., 1991.

Castro, Rafaela G. *Dictionary of Chicano Folklore*. Santa Barbara: ABC-CLIO, 2000.

Chase, Gilbert. *The Music of Spain*. New York: Dover Publications, 1959.

Chavez, Linda. *Out of the Barrio: Toward a New Politics of Hispanic Assimilation*. New York: BasicBooks, 1991.

Cisneros, Sandra. *House on Mango Street*. New York: Vintage Books, 1984.

Conde, Yvonne M. *Operation Peter Pan: The Untold Exodus of 14,048 Cuban Children*. New York and London: Routledge, 1999.

Crowder, Nicholas. *Culture Shock: Ecuador, A Guide to Customs and Etiquette*. Portland, Oregon: Graphic Arts Center Publishing Company, 2001.

Cruz, Angie. *Soledad*. New York: Simon & Schuster, 2001.

Curtin, Philip D. *The Atlantic Slave Trade: A Census*. Madison, Wisconsin: The University of Wisconsin Press, 1969.

De Escobedo, Alonso Gregorio. "La Florida" in *Herencia: The Anthology of Hispanic Literature in the United States* ed. Nicolas Kanellos. New York: Oxford University Press, 2002.

De las Casas, Bartolomé. *The Diario of Christopher Columbus' First Voyage to America, 1492–1493*. Norman and London: The University of Oklahoma Press, 1991.

*Demographics USA County Edition 2000*. Wilton, Connecticut: TradeDimensions, 2000.

Dent, David W. *The Legacy of the Monroe Doctrine: A Reference Guide to U.S. Involvement in Latin America and the Caribbean*. Westport, Connecticut and London: Greenwood Press, 1999.

Dold, Gaylor. *Dominican Republic Handbook*. Chico, California: Moon Travel Handbooks, 1997.

*Encyclopedia of Multiculturalism*. 5 vols. New York: Marshall Cavendish, 1994.

Esquivel, Laura. *Like Water for Chocolate. A Novel in Monthly Installments with Recipes, Romances and Home Remedies*. New York: Doubleday, 1989.

Fuentes, Carlos. *The Buried Mirror: Reflections on Spain and the New World*. New York: Houghton Mifflin, 1992.

Gann, L.H. and Peter J. Duignan. *The Hispanics in the United States: A History*. Boulder and London: Westview Press, 1986.

García Márquez, Gabriel. *Chronicle of a Death Foretold*. New York: Alfred A. Knopf, 1982.

———. *The General in His Labyrinth*. New York: Alfred A. Knopf, 1990.

———. *One Hundred Years of Solitude*. New York: Harper's Row, 1970.

Gónzalez Echevarría, Roberto. *The Pride of Havana: A History of Cuban Baseball*. New York and Oxford: Oxford University, 1999.

Graham, Richard, ed. *The Idea of Race in Latin America, 1870–1940*. Austin, Texas: University of Texas Press, 1990.

Hero, Rodney E. *Latinos and the U.S. Political System: Two-Tiered Pluralism*. Philadelphia: Temple University, 1992.

Herrera, Andrea O. ed. *ReMembering Cuba*. Austin, Texas: University of Texas Press, 2001.

Herring, Hubert. *A History of Latin America from the Beginnings to the Present*. New York: Alfred A. Knopf, 1972.

Heyck, Denis L.D. *Barrios and Borderlands: Cultures of Latinos and Latinas in the United States.* New York and London: Routledge, 1994.

Hijuelos, Oscar. *Empress of the Splendid Season.* New York: Harper Collins, 1999.

———. *The Mambo Kings Play Songs of Love.* New York: Farrar, Strauss, Giroux, 1989.

———. *Our House in the Last World.* New York: Persea Books, 1983.

Isasi-Díaz, Ada María and Fernando S. Segovia. eds. *Hispanic/Latino Theology.* Minneapolis: Fortress Press, 1996.

Jaquette, Jane S. and Sharon L. Wolchik. eds. *Women and Democracy: Latin America and Central and Eastern Europe.* Baltimore and London: The John Hopkins University Press, 1998.

Kandell, Jonathan. *La Capital: The Biography of Mexico City.* New York: Random House, 1988.

Kanellos, Nicolás. ed. *The Hispanic-American Almanac.* Washington, D.C. and London: Gale Research, Inc. 1993.

———. *Reference Library of Hispanic America.* 3 vols. Detroit: Gale Research, 1997.

Kirsch, George B., Othello Harris, and Claire E. Nolte. eds. *Encyclopedia of Ethnicity and Sports in the United States.* Westport, Connecticut: Greenwood Press, 2000.

Levinson, David and Karen Christensen. eds. *Encyclopedia of World Sport.* 3 vols. Santa Barbara: ABC-CLIO, 1996.

Loza, Steven. *Tito Puente and the Making of Latin Music.* Urbana and Chicago: University of Illinois Press, 1999.

Marín, Gerardo and Barbara V. Marín. *Research with Hispanic Populations.* London and New Delhi: Sage Publications, 1991.

Martínez, Rubén. *Crossing Over: A Mexican Family on the Migrant Trail.* New York: Henry Holt and Co., 2001.

Martínez-Fernández, Luis. *Fighting Slavery in the Caribbean: The Life and Times of a British Family in Nineteenth Century Havana.* New York and London: M.E. Sharpe, 1998.

Matibag, Eugenio. *Afro-Cuban Religious Experience: Cultural Reflections in Narrative.* Gainesville, Florida: University Press of Florida, 1996.

McCullough, David. G. *The Path Between The Seas: The Creation of the Panama Canal, 1870–1914*. New York: Simon & Schuster, 1977.

Mörner, Magnus. *Race and Class in Latin America*. New York and London: Columbia University, 1970.

Musacchio, Humberto. *Milenios de México*. 3 vols. México, D.F.: Hoja Casa Editorial, 1999.

Nogales, Ana. *Dr. Ana Nogales' Book of Love, Sex, and Relationships: A Guide for Latino Couples*. New York: Broadway Books, 1998.

Novas, Himilce. *Everything You Need To Know About Latino History*. New York: Plume Books, 1994.

Olson, James S. and Judith E. Olson. *Cuban Americans: From Trauma to Triumph*. New York: Twayne Publishers, 1995.

Padilla, Felix M. *Latino Ethnic Consciousness: The Case of Mexican Americans and Puerto Ricans in Chicago*. Notre Dame, Indiana: The University of Notre Dame, 1985.

Paz, Octavio. *The Labyrinth of Solitude and the Other Mexico*. New York: Grove Weidenfeld, 1985.

Pérez Firmat, Gustavo. *Life on the Hyphen: The Cuban-American Way*. Austin, Texas: University of Texas Press, 1994.

———. *Next Year in Cuba: A Cubano's Coming-of-age in America*. New York: Anchor Books, 1995.

Pessar, Patricia R. *A Visa for a Dream: Dominicans in the United States*. Boston and London: Allyn and Bacon, 1995.

Quiñones, Ernesto. *Bodega Dreams*. New York: Vintage Books, 2000.

Reyes, Luis and Peter Rubic. *Hispanics in Hollywood: An Encyclopedia of Film and Television*. New York and London: Garland Publishing, Inc. 1994.

Rippy, J. Fred. *Latin America: A Modern History*. Ann Arbor: The University of Michigan Press, 1968.

Rodriguez, Richard. *Days of Obligation: An Argument with My Mexican Father*. New York: Viking, 1992.

———. *A Hunger of Memory: The Education of Richard Rodriguez*. New York: Bantam Books, 1982.

Ryan, Alan. ed. *The Reader's Companion to Cuba*. New York and London: Harcourt Brace & Co., 1997.

Salmoral, Manuel L. *America 1492: Portrait of a Continent 500 Years Ago*. New York and Oxford: Facts on File, 1990.

Santiago, Esmeralda. *When I was Puerto Rican*. New York: Vintage Books, 1994.

Schick, Frank L. and Renee Schick. comp. *Statistical Handbook on U.S. Hispanics*. Phoenix, Arizona: Oryx Press, 1991.

Shorris, Earl. *Latinos: A Biography of a People*. New York: Avon Books, 1992.

Skerry, Peter. *Mexican Americans, The Ambivalent Minority*. New York and Oxford: The Free Press, 1993.

Suárez, Virgil. *Palm Crows*. Tucson, Arizona: University of Arizona Press, 2001.

Suro, Roberto. *Strangers Among Us: Latino Lives in a Changing World*. New York: Vintage Books, 1999.

Tardiff, Joseph C. and L. Mpho Mabunda. *Dictionary of Hispanic Biography*. Washington, D.C. and London: Gale Research, 1996.

Thomas, Piri. *Down These Mean Streets*. New York: Vintage Books, 1997.

Tompkins, Cynthia Margarita and David W. Foster. eds. *Notable Twentieth Century Latin American Women: A Biographical Dictionary*. Westport, Connecticut: Greenwood Press, 2001.

Torres, Andrés and José E. Velazquez. eds. *The Puerto Rican Movement*. Philadelphia: Temple University, 1998.

Torres-Saillant, Silvio and Ramona Hernández. *The Dominican Americans*. Westport, Connecticut and London: Greenwood Press, 1998.

Varela, Félix. *Jicoténcal*. Houston, Texas: Arte Public Press, 1994.

Villafañe, Eldin. *The Liberating Spirit: Toward an Hispanic American Pentecostal Social Ethnic*. Grand Rapids, Michigan: William B. Eerdmans Publishing Company, 1993.

Williamson, Edwin. *The Penguin History of Latin America*. New York: Penguin, 1993.

Winn, Peter. *Americas: The Changing Face of Latin America and the Caribbean*. New York: Pantheon Books, 1992.

Zibart, Eve. *The Ethnic Food Lover's Companion: Understanding the Cuisines of the World*. Birmingham, Alabama: Menasha Ridge Press, 2001.

# Index